Urban Schools and English Language Education in Late Modern China

This book explores the meaning of modernization in contemporary Chinese education. It examines the implications of the implementation of reforms in English language education for experimental urban schools in the People's Republic of China.

Pérez-Milans sheds light on how national, linguistic, and cultural ideologies linked to modernization are being institutionally (re)produced, legitimated, and interpersonally negotiated through everyday practice in the current context of Chinese educational reforms. He places special emphasis on those reforms regarding English language education, with respect to the economic processes of globalization that are shaping (and being shaped by) the contemporary Chinese nation-state. In particular, the book analyzes the processes of institutional categorization of the "good experimental school", the "good student", and the "appropriate knowledge" that emerge from the daily discursive organization of those schools, with special attention to the related contradictions, uncertainties, and dilemmas. Thus, he provides an account of the ongoing cultural processes of change faced by contemporary Chinese educational institutions under conditions of late modernity.

Miguel Pérez-Milans is Assistant Professor at the Division of English Language Education in the Faculty of Education, the University of Hong Kong.

Routledge Critical Studies in Multilingualism

Edited by Marilyn Martin-Jones, MOSAIC Centre for Research on Multilingualism, University of Birmingham, UK

Urban Schools and English Language Education in Late Modern China

A Critical Sociolinguistic Ethnography

Miguel Pérez-Milans

Routledge
Taylor & Francis Group

NEW YORK AND LONDON

First published 2013
by Routledge
711 Third Avenue, New York, NY 10017

Simultaneously published in the UK
by Routledge
2 Park Square, Milton Park, Abingdon, Oxon OX14 4RN

*Routledge is an imprint of the Taylor & Francis Group,
an informa business*

Library of Congress Cataloging-in-Publication Data
Perez-Milans, Miguel, 1978–
    Urban Schools and English Language Education in Late Modern China : a Critical Sociolinguistic Ethnography / By Miguel Perez-Milans.
        pages cm. — (Routledge Critical Studies in Multilingualism ; #5)
    Includes bibliographical references and index.
    1. English language—Study and teaching—China.   2. Multilingualism—China.   3. Language and culture—China.   4. Education—China—History.   5. Sociolinguistics—China.   I. Title.
    PE1068.C5P47 2013
    428.0071′051—dc23
    2012046380

ISBN: 978-0-415-50222-1 (hbk)
ISBN: 978-0-203-36618-9 (ebk)

Typeset in Sabon
by Apex CoVantage, LLC

Printed and bound in the United States of America by Publishers Graphics, LLC on sustainably sourced paper.

For Hugo and Gema

Contents

Figures

Acknowledgments

I am deeply grateful to many people whose contributions have been invaluable in the completion of this book.

The administrators, teachers, and students who appear as my participants here allowed me to intrude in their schools and classrooms with immense openness, patience, and warmth.

Some students and researchers from the University of Zhejiang helped me during the data collection process by sharing their social networks and supporting me whenever I had difficulties either in the understanding of specific aspects of the Chinese educational system or in the translation/transcription of instances of Chinese language in my data corpus. They are: Baomeiyi (鲍美怡), Caicai (菜菜), Hefan (何凡), Shirley, Weili (伟力), and Chen Wei (陈伟).

Through an ongoing process of communication and intellectual discussion, the team of colleagues with whom I collaborated on different research projects, while I was conducting the research that I draw on here, provided me with the theoretical and methodological knowledge that backgrounds this piece of work. They are: Luisa Martín-Rojo, Monica Heller, Adriana Patiño Santos, Irina Rasskin Gutman, Esther Alcalá Recuerda, Ana María Relaño, Laura Mijares, Isabel García Parejo, and Rachel Whittacker. Among them, Luisa Martín-Rojo offered me fundamental guidance during my research journey.

The book has also benefited greatly from other colleagues who have offered relevant feedback during the time between the data collection and the writing of the present manuscript. They are: Ben Rampton, Angel Lin, David Barton, Shi-Xu, Taciana Fisac Badell, Joan Pujolar, Melissa Moyer, Alexandre Duchêne, Jan Blommaert, Gabriele Budach, Frances Giampapa, Sylvie Lamoureux, Eva Codó Olsina, Virginia Unamuno, Roxy Harris, Constant Leung, Carlos Soto, Beatriz Macías Gómez-Stern, Cristina Aliagas, Carles Prado, David Martínez, Mario Esteban, and Sai Kin Lee Tsang. Needless to say, the misapprehensions are mine.

I owe my gratitude to Marilyn Martin-Jones, for her trust, support, and guidance throughout the whole process involved in the publication of this book.

This research was supported by the Plan Nacional de I+D+I (2000–2003) of the Spanish Ministry of Science and Technology through the project

"Socio-pragmatic Analysis of Intercultural Communication in Educational Practices: Toward Integration in the Classroom" (BFF 2003–04830), directed by Professor Luisa Martín-Rojo (Autonomous University of Madrid). As part of this project, one of my research fellowships at the Institute of Discourse and Cultural Studies in Zhejiang University, under the supervision of Professor Shi-xu, was key for the undertaking of the fieldwork on which this book draws. In addition, the writing of this book has been fully undertaken under the funding of the *Programa Nacional de Movilidad de Recursos Humanos del Plan Nacional de I + D + I* (2008–2011) of the Spanish Ministry of Education (EX2009–0959), with the invaluable collaboration of Centre for Language, Discourse & Communication (King's College London) and the Faculty of Education in the University of Hong Kong through the supervision of Ben Rampton and Angel Lin. Complementary support has also been received from the *Programa de cooperación con Asia de la Universidad Autónoma de Madrid y el Banco Santander* (2011–2012) through the project "Chinese and English as Languages of the Wider World: a Sociolinguistic Study on Second Language Education and Youth's Interests in London, Madrid, and Hong Kong".

Some sections in this volume draw partially on materials previously published. Section 1.2, Section 4.2.2 and Section 4.3 use some figures and extracts published in "Caught in a 'West/China' Dichotomy: Doing a Critical Sociolinguistic Ethnography in Zhejiang Schools" (*Journal of Language, Identity & Education* 10: 164–185). Section 3.2 contains one figure and translated versions of some extracts appeared in "'Ah! Spain, that's far away from China': reflexividad metodológica y movilidad en la etnografía sociolingüística crítica" (*Spanish in Context* 9:2, 219–243). Section 5.3 draws partially from "Beyond 'safe-talk': institutionalization and agency in China's English language education" (*Linguistics and Education* 23, 62–76). I am grateful to Elsevier, John Benjamins, and Taylor & Francis, for permission to use the related materials for inclusion in the book.

Finally, I am obliged to Glenn Harding, for his language revisions of the English manuscript.

1 Institutions, Modernization, and China's Late Modernity

1.1 EXPERIMENTAL SCHOOLS AND ENGLISH-LANGUAGE EDUCATION IN CHINA: SETTING UP THE STORY

It is 8:20am, on a regular Monday morning in October 2006 in Hangzhou, a six-million-population city located in the north part of Zhejiang province in the People's Republic of China (PRC). I have agreed to meet Ms. Zhu,[1] an English-language teacher who works at a state secondary school close to the city center. We were supposed to meet at 7:40am, as her first class of the day, of eighth-grade students, starts at 7:50am. However, a traffic jam between Zhejiang University, where I am staying, and the school has made me late. Once at the school's main gate, I am impressed by the size of the school installations, which form an array of five-floor buildings distributed around an impeccable athletics track. The entrance contains an electronic panel that seems to be used to announce upcoming special events.

After asking for Ms. Zhu at the reception booth by the entrance, I am shown to her classroom. On the way, I see images and sculptures referring to international scientists (Einstein and Newton, among others) as well as to Chinese philosophers and politicians (such as Confucius and Mao Zedong). We pass groups of students wearing red ribbons on their school uniforms and marching in unison along the corridor. On reaching the door to Ms. Zhu's classroom, I find she is already inside, but she acknowledges my presence through the window and comes out to greet me. She then tries to explain in English (although switching to Mandarin Chinese as soon as she realizes that I understand it) that I can either go in to see the second part of the class in progress or otherwise wait until the next period to observe another eighth-grade group. As I am unsure what to do, she decides to bring me in, and tells the students, in English, to welcome me, which prompts a round of applause.

I am then invited to sit at the back of the classroom. When the English class resumes, I see there are 48 students arranged in rows of desks, all very close to the blackboard and surrounding the teacher's desk in a way that seems a bit claustrophobic to me. Ms. Zhu is using a computer and a projector to display all the text and illustrations on which the classroom interaction is focused. The class activities are progressing at a tempo that is difficult to follow for a newcomer such as myself. The class is working on the "Invitations" unit; after reading and copying the vocabulary for the lesson, the students focus on an illustrative dialogue in their textbooks. As they go through this dialogue, all the participants coordinate their actions in high-speed transitions, as if they have been practicing the same lesson for decades, from choral readings of the text and repetitions of the audio recording played by Ms. Zhu on her computer to role-playing performed by pairs of students.

After the class has finished, Ms. Zhu approaches to ask about my impression of the class. She's worried her English might not be good enough and wants to have feedback from a Westerner, as she refers to me. I am somewhat startled at this representation of myself as an expert in English language because, as someone born and socialized in Spain, all my life I have suffered a deep-felt complex of not being a legitimate English-language speaker. We then engage in a brief conversation about the situation of English-language education in Spain and China, although we both soon realize there isn't much time to do so, as Ms. Zhu is busy, with a great deal to do in the five minutes between the previous class and the next one. Moreover, I have to hurry to my first interview with Mr. Wang, the head of the school, and so we agree to meet again at lunchtime to continue our chat.

It is now 8:45am and Mr. Wang is waiting for me in his office. He asked to meet me at this time because he has to supervise a newly hired teacher during the next period. I express some surprise, not having heard of this duty in a state school before. He then explains that when new teachers are taken on, they must pass a one-year trial period, which in practice means they are regularly observed and evaluated by colleagues and by the school principal before a permanent position is awarded. I can't help feeling confused, and my expression makes Mr. Wang laugh. He seems to understand my reaction perfectly, and says he is well aware of the different educational circumstances in Europe, having observed schools in different European countries during exchange programs he has participated in.

By this point, I am starting to feel a little overwhelmed, as there seem to be many aspects of everyday school life that I don't really understand: is this actually a state school? If so, why do they hire teachers? Why do I have the impression of being in a school which seems overly concerned with "selling" itself to the public (impressive installations, magnificent sports facilities, new technologies in the classrooms, school uniforms, brilliantly routinized classroom dynamics, teachers undergoing continuous evaluation, international exchanges with European schools)? As the conversation unfolds, my problems deepen; in an attempt to get a general description of the school, and thus a better understanding of the type of institution in which I am about to do my fieldwork, I ask Mr. Wang about the characteristics of his school: 对你来说，这个学校有什么特点？ (In your view, what characteristics does this school present?).

This highly imprecise question is then answered by Mr. Wang as follows: 这个学校是叫，它的名字叫 [...] 实验学校, Experimental School 但是他呢又是杭州市的实验学校。什么叫杭州市的实验学校呢？就是说这个学校的办学水平可以起到一种示范作用。有很多项目可以通过我们的改革，我们的示范，去引领其他学校也像我们这样去做。我们中国人非常重要的一个指标 (The name of this school is [...] Experimental School. It is the experimental school of Hangzhou city. What does it mean that it is the experimental school of Hangzhou city? Just that this school plays a model role. There are many reform projects we are implementing, we provide a model for other schools to follow. This is an important indicator for us, the Chinese people.) So, what is an "experimental school"? Things appear to be getting more complicated.

When the interview finishes, I decide to go to Ms. Zhu's office, as another five-minute break is about to begin. She soon appears, carrying a pile of notebooks. Behind her, a group of students come up and stand in line in front of her office. Looking at her, I gesture toward the line of students, suggesting there are too many students waiting for her. She laughs and says they are waiting to receive their individual notebooks with the corrections she has just made, for the last part of the previous class. At this, I feel a little embarrassed to be bothering her again, but nevertheless I stick to my plan, not wanting to leave the school after this first visit without getting a clear understanding of just what is meant by an experimental school: 赵老师，麻烦你！我刚才跟王校长对话。我们说关于这个学校的情况，但是还不太清楚实验学校是什么意思。你有没有关于这个情况说的一本书？ (Sorry to bother you, Ms. Zhu. I've just been talking to Mr. Wang, about this school's situation, but I'm still a little uncertain about exactly what it means for this to be an experimental school. Do you have a book that discusses this situation?).

After asking her students to wait for a minute, Ms. Zhu turns around and speaks to Ms. Peng, a colleague who teaches science and with whom she shares an office. Ms. Peng, at first completely hidden behind a pile of notebooks on her desk, stands up and takes a book from one of the shelves above her and then turns back to her work. Ms. Zhu passes the book to me and explains it is the official book that sets out the educational and philosophical framework around which everyday school life is organized. I take the book and quickly leave the office, so as to let Ms. Zhu get on with her work, and to look for a place in the school where I can sit down, have a look at the book, and find out more about the category of "experimental school". The book does indeed provide some answers to my questions; its first section, titled "The situation that is faced" (面临的形势), explains that the category of "experimental school" is assigned to state schools that implement, before all other state schools in China, the educational and curricular reforms stipulated in national policies, under the Chinese Communist Party's call for a "Chinese modernization" (中国现代化). I then pay special attention to page 2, where a short paragraph illustrates the social implications of this institutional categorization for a school in contemporary China:

Extract 1.1   "The Mission That We Shoulder"

我们原有办学基础不尽如人意，师资队伍整体水平还有得进一步提高，我们的办学设施离现代化标志性实验学校的要求还相差甚远，末来三年更是教育不断创新的发展时期。所有这一些，我们深感任务艰巨。物竞天择，适者生存，教育作为一种市场，无可厚非地进入到这一无私的空间之中。我们在制订这个三年计划的时候，在看到成绩的同时，更应该清醒地认识到我们面临的形势，我们肩负的使命，我们承担的责任。

Our school baseline is not satisfactory; the general level of the teaching staff has still to improve, and school facilities are still far from the requirements of the experimental schools that are the reference for modernization. The next three years are a developmental period aimed at achieving greater innovation. In this respect, our task is a very demanding one. Natural selection, the survival of the fittest, and the adjustment of education to the marketplace must form part of this selfless space. Now is the time to formulate the three-year plan, to consider the results, to acknowledge more clearly the situation that we face, the mission we must shoulder, and the duty that we assume.

(Institutional document, p. 2)

* * *

What I saw and experienced that Monday morning was basically the same for the first visits I made to the three schools in Hangzhou and Wenzhou, the two cities of Zhejiang province where I conducted my fieldwork during 2006 (see Figure 1.1). Although their local conditions varied to a high degree (see Chapter 3), all three schools were institutionally categorized as "experimental", which implied a shared social responsibility in implementing institutional reforms within the Chinese educational system. In particular, these educational reforms were all subject to a national guideline calling for the construction of "quality education" (教育教学质量). One obvious question arises immediately: what are these reforms about? To what extent is observation of these schools relevant for the purposes of a sociolinguistic ethnography? What do they have that will contribute to our understanding of institutions and language-in-education policies in the contemporary world?

Before setting out in detail the focus and the scope of this book, I will comment briefly on the discursive links between the category of "experimental school" that these three institutions share and the wider Chinese national policies on which the guidelines for the construction of a "quality education" are based. These links are twofold. On the one hand, the guidelines are institutionally framed within the modernization principles first established in the late 1970s under Deng Xiaoping's national plan to achieve "Four modernizations" (四个现代化). After the socioeconomic disasters

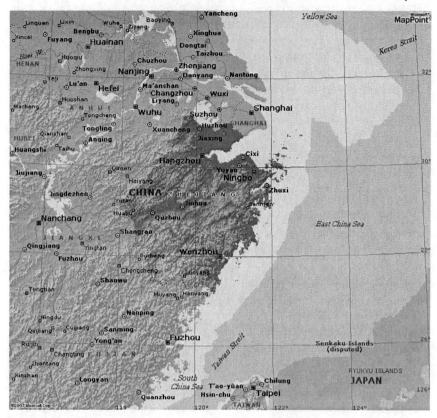

Figure 1.1   Map of Eastern China
Map extracted from MSN Encarta Atlas Site. Retrieved from http://encarta.msn.com.

resulting from implementation of Mao Zedong's policies of the 1970s (i.e., during the Cultural Revolution) this plan was intended to initiate China's economic liberalization and open it up to the international market by reforming agriculture, industry, national defense, science, and technology (Deng, 1978).

In the field of education, this call produced what is considered to be the most important period of educational reforms in Chinese history (Ding, 2001: 172–191; Potts, 2003: 13–19; L. Li, 2004: 1-19; Mok, 2006: 101–117; Mathur, 2007: 135–173). The political representation of scientific and technological modernization as crucial to national economic growth gave rise to a change in the social conceptualization of education, which since then has been considered a key institutional space for both the national modernization of all economic sectors and for the positioning of China as a new international power. As stated by Deng at the National Education Work Conference in 1978, when he advocated a nationwide change in education aimed at achieving the new goal of a "Quality education",

Development superiority resides in knowledge and technology. Social wealth is increasingly flowing to the countries or areas which hold superiority in knowledge and technology. Those who take the advantage in knowledge and technology innovation will occupy the dominant position in development. Education is becoming an increasingly important force for ensuring scientific and technological progress, as well as economic and social growth. (Deng, 1978, quoted in Wu, 2005: 321)

All these ideas crystallized in 1985, with the "Resolution for the reform of the education system" (教育体制改革的决定), which overturned the tenets of the Cultural Revolution (1966–1976) and restructured the entire education system according to two main premises. First, planners sought to regain the academicist orientation that had characterized Chinese reforms in the early 1960s—meritocracy, selectivity, streaming and scientificism (in contrast to the criteria of social class applied in selecting students for higher education, and to the curricular organization oriented toward productive work in farms or factories and to Mao's ideological thoughts, established during the Cultural Revolution).[2] Second, the 1985 Resolution opened the way to the progressive decentralization of school management at all levels (reversing the former control by the communes and the army, established in the early 1970s) (for an overview of the educational policies and structural changes undertaken in China during the 1980s, see particularly Hayhoe, 1984; Cleverley, 1985, 1991; Su, 2002; Potts, 2003; Mathur, 2007; see also Chapter 3, Section 3.3, for a contextualization in the building process of a modern liberal Chinese education system during the 20th century).

To understand the construction of "quality education" in today's China, we must also take into account the modernization steps taken since the 1990s. Although Deng's conversion of China's planned economy into a market-based one produced good results from the start, China was hit by an economic crisis in the second half of the 1980s, which led to civil mobilizations challenging the legitimacy of the Chinese Communist Party (CCP) as the sole political representative of the Chinese nation, and demanding that economic liberalization be extended to the political domain. Accordingly, the political efforts of subsequent Chinese leaders have focused on better integrating Deng's economic reforms into the Chinese political system (Hughes, 2006).

In this political framework, new policies for education during the 1990s were set out in the national campaign for "Patriotic Education" (爱国主义教育), a set of official documents issued since 1991 (and aimed at all institutional spaces, not just schools) with the goal of cultivating loyalty to the regime and rejection of the ideas of liberal democracy, which were officially associated with cultural imperialism (Zhao, 1998).[3]

In view of these links between the local discourses of experimental reform in the three schools studied and the wider context of Chinese official policies—which are also discourses produced in remote space-time locations in relation to national and international socioeconomic/political processes of change, the experimental reforms in education appear to be influenced by economic internationalization as well as by the articulation of new forms of political legitimization. As we see later in this chapter, these two processes of change seem to result from the intersections between the neoliberal and globalizing new economy in the contemporary world—within which the nation-state is not the only economic and political point of reference[4]—and China's specific national conditions, which also need to be taken into account in relation to the political economy of European industrial expansion, colonialism, and postcolonialism.

These processes of (discursive) transformation underlying the guidelines set out regarding quality in education are well illustrated in the curricular reforms that have been undertaken in China in recent decades, which have had a marked impact on the field of language education. As in other non-English speaking countries where it has been institutionalized as the main second language to be taught and learned in schools, English has come to occupy a key position in the Chinese national curriculum, on the basis of its social and institutional representation as a symbolic capital for participating successfully in the new globalized economy. Extract 1.2 is taken from the experimental English-language curriculum followed by the three schools studied, and it shows the extent to which this subject is centrally placed within the framework of the education reforms to be implemented:

Extract 1.2   "Since China's Opening and Reforms"

前言
　　许多国家在基础教育发展战略中，都把英语教育作为公民素质教育的重要组成部分，并将其摆在突出的地位。改革开放以来，我国的英语教育规模不断扩大，教育教学取得了显著的成就。然而，英语教育的现状尚不能适应我国经济建设和社会发展的需要，与时代发展的要求 还存在差距。

Preface

Among the development strategies of basic education in many countries, English language teaching is always an important component of quality education for citizenship and it is placed in a prominent position. Since the opening and the reform, the scope of our English language education has continued expanding and education has made remarkable achievements. However, the status of English language education is not adjusted to the demands of the country's social and economic development and the requirements of our time are not yet met.

(Draft of the experimental English-language curriculum, pp. 1–2)

Under the 1980s reforms, the importance given to scientific and technological modernization aimed at promoting economic growth had a great impact on English-language education, as English was explicitly regarded by Deng Xiaoping as vital to the implementation of China's "open door" economic policies (Deng, 1978). Thus, English was restored to the curriculum of Chinese compulsory education (Ministry of Education, 1978), having been excluded during the Cultural Revolution, when it was associated with imperialism and colonialism (particularly between 1966 and 1970).[5]

In the new socioeconomic context, English was institutionally separated from the humanist subjects in the Chinese curriculum and was officially represented as a technical skill stripped of any association with foreign nations, locations, or traditions (Wu, 2005; Fong, 2009; Gao, 2009), which thus legitimized the recovery and expansion of this language as the main foreign language to be taught at primary and secondary schools in China (Adamson, 2004, 2007; Lam, 2005, 2007). This representation was later reinforced by the education policies issued during the 1990s in the context of the CCP's loss of political legitimacy, which resulted in an ongoing process of curricular reforms officially aimed at adapting English-language education to what were termed "Chinese national conditions" (L. Li, 2004: 346-353).

Recent studies have shown that, although contemporary Chinese textbooks and teaching materials for English-language education have increasingly incorporated the representation of China both as a participant and as a stakeholder with respect to contemporary world problems and successes, they tend to portray cultural identity models in line with the CCP's current official discourses (Orton, 2009). These teaching materials allow young Chinese to imagine themselves playing an engaged role in a global community and interacting in English with a set of native and other speakers (who are more complex people than those in the books of earlier years), in superficial and decontextualized interactions in which "there is no need for knowledge of native speaker belief systems and values, or for details about what they think about how they live their lives" (Orton, 2009: 152).

This book, therefore, tells the story of the three experimental schools observed in Zhejiang province, as they offer an excellent opportunity for what Martin-Jones (2007) argues to be a necessary endeavor in critically oriented research within the field of language and education:

> Critical interpretative work on language-in-education [. . .] gives a window on the contemporary process of change ushered in by globalization and by the emergence of a new world order. In some contexts attempts have been made, since the late 1980s, to forge new educational landscapes through educational reforms, in response to these changing political, economic and cultural conditions. This process has, inevitably, been characterized by tensions, by a shifting politics of identity, and by the emergence of new discourses about language-in-education. The tensions arising out of different dimensions of globalization are only beginning to be explored in critical, interpretative research on education. (p. 176)

The relevance of the experimental schools lies in the fact that, while focusing on the central goal of preparing China's citizens to enter the new international and globalized economic world, they are also part of the mobilization project, to legitimize a particular Chinese national identity in a social space in which other (alternative) identities may be displayed in everyday practice. Accordingly, they are very appropriate as a context in which to study the construction of social categories and subjectivity, providing examples of the ways in which official categories (which are abstract and tend to be fictively homogeneous) encounter the contradictions, ambiguities, and ambivalences of contemporary real life. More specifically, and following Heller's (2011) account of the concerns of a critical, ethnographic, and sociolinguistic approach to language as a situated social practice tied to social organization, the study of these schools is justified because they constitute a key site for the exploration of the links between processes of economic transformation, changes in the organization of a given community, and discursive practices through which that community reconstitutes itself.

These three experimental schools triggered my interest in exploring their social, cultural, and linguistic significance, both within their communities and in wider society. I wanted to understand the implications of these modernization reforms for the discursive organization of daily life in the schools, in general, and for their English-language education, in particular. I wished to examine processes of social categorization linked to modernization discourses in order to understand what counts as a "good school", a "good student", or "appropriate knowledge" in their situated activity, scrutinizing how participants position themselves in relation to these processes of categorization. In this regard, this is not a story about schooling per se; that is to say, the book does not focus on narrow pedagogical concerns. As discussed in Chapter 2, the school is conceived as an institutional site where people display, try out, contest, and negotiate a wide range of identities (official and otherwise) through the use of varied linguistic and communicative repertoires in situated activities.

This is a story of young people and adults at a particular moment in time and space, and of the meanings associated with their linguistic/discursive local practices under the wider socio-institutional conditions briefly sketched out in this first section. These conditions are further discussed in Section 1.3, although I first give a more detailed description of just how I ended up doing this kind of research in this type of school, as the foregoing is only one (deliberately selected) part of the story. The other part will be told from a reflexive standpoint, emphasizing some of the key issues addressed over the course of the book.

1.2 FROM MADRID TO ZHEJIANG: A (REFLEXIVE) RESEARCH JOURNEY

Telling a story in the academic context always implies some degree of risk. All scholars tell stories, even if we do so by leaning on narrative tools that recall positivism. Thus, we have to decide whether we want to hide behind our analysis or not. In the context of social, economic, and political transformations like the ones referred to previously, this decision has important consequences, going beyond aesthetic concerns as to how to portray ourselves in the picture; it also entails an ontological position regarding how we understand issues concerned with language and social change (see Mason, 2002). This is particularly relevant in the case of sociolinguistic research, as the contemporary dynamics of mobility have induced a shift in the theoretical-methodological focus that has serious implications for the interpretation of our own research practices.

In contrast to the former pattern of stable immigration/emigration, the world's trans-local population now moves physically/affectively/ideologically back and forth between here-and-there (Vertovec, 2009), becoming more temporary, changeable, and diversified than ever. Thus, variationist approaches that historically focused on studying the spread (and contact) of autonomous language variables are no longer useful for understanding contemporary societies. Instead, a new "sociolinguistics of mobility" is needed (Blommaert, 2010; Heller, 2011). This type of sociolinguistic enquiry approaches language as situated social practices unfolding over time and across space to account for how people attribute local value/meaning to (and distribute locally) widely circulating material and symbolic resources (including linguistic and cultural resources) under the conditions of specific social spaces/structures and historical moments.

In this regard, contemporary sociolinguistic description cannot disregard epistemological considerations about how researchers and our own fieldwork trajectories intersect with the spaces, social actors, and meaning-making practices on which our analysis is based. In other words, reflexivity is not just a methodological "must" for ethically and politically engaged research, it is theoretically unavoidable. In fact, sociolinguists are social actors who bring their own symbolic and material resources into the social space in which their data are collected. Thus, a reflection on how these resources are mobilized by all participants in the course of the fieldwork sheds more light on processes of interest in contemporary sociolinguistics. This is the case for the fieldwork I carried out in Zhejiang. Data collection in the space of the three experimental schools was discursively and emotionally based upon the constitution of social relationships between myself and my participants that made salient specific trans-local cultural identities institutionally constructed as capitals.

In this sense, a close look at how these cultural capitals are constructed provides a window to a closer view of the specific conditions under which these institutions operate. These cultural identities were built upon my social categorization as a Spanish researcher who had a lot to contribute to the schools because of what the heads of the schools and the teachers considered to be valuable educational experience and a Western linguistic/cultural background. Chapter 3 illustrates how these identities were articulated in each of the schools, but it should be noted here that their discursive salience was locally coconstructed by all participants (including myself), in relation to the specific research journey that had brought me from the educational context of Madrid to the very different one of Zhejiang. As a preliminary, then, I shall flesh out this research journey before going into the discursive construction of the previously mentioned identities.

Observation of everyday practices in the three Chinese schools was not initially conceived as a research project in itself, but rather as a complementary activity to a wider study focusing on education in Spain. This wider project, funded by the Spanish Ministry of Science and Technology and directed by Dr. Luisa Martín-Rojo, was set up to examine how four secondary schools in the Madrid region were responding to the increase in linguistic and cultural diversity resulting from contemporary transnational migration patterns within Europe (see Martín-Rojo, 2010).[6] In particular, this project studied the implementation of the educational programs created to promote full integration into the Spanish compulsory education system of students from a migrant background, and sought to determine what constituted a "good student" or "appropriate knowledge" in the discursive organization of these programs.

In the framework of this wider research, my work was specifically focused on studying a new Spanish language linguistic immersion program known as the Bridging Class (*Aula de enlace*) at a Madrid school (see Pérez-Milans [2006, 2007] for an in-depth account of this study). Over a period of two years, I observed a linguistically and ethnically diverse group of 12 students, from their incorporation into the Bridging Class on arrival in Madrid until their placement in mainstream classes. Among these students, I observed that those coming from China were especially disadvantaged. They tended to be socially constructed as the most culturally and linguistically distant, in an institutional framework in which different language activities and demands were made of the students depending on their national origin, on the basis of a socially constructed cultural hierarchy that assigned different sociocultural stereotypes to each national group. In fact, the Chinese students ended up being institutionally expected to fulfill only the most basic educational tasks, which in turn resulted in a varied range of practices on their part, from resistance to compliance to dropping out of the school (Pérez-Milans, 2011).

Against this backdrop, I was asked by the teachers at the school in question to act as a Spanish-Chinese language interpreter, or cultural mediator, between them and the Chinese students. This situation helped me find my own legitimate space within the Madrid school, but at the same time it contributed to reinforcing the cultural distance that was socially constructed between the teachers and the Chinese students. The meaning-making practices in which these students engaged were not always easy to interpret, and often involved peer-related activities in which previous educational experiences in China were recontextualized for the purposes of mocking institutional discourses in Madrid. Therefore, a full understanding of these meaning-making processes required further ethnographic exploration of the schooling practices in which these young students were socialized before arriving in Spain. Or at least this is what I initially thought. And for this reason I came to Zhejiang, since all the Chinese students in the Bridging Class I was studying had arrived directly from that province.

The decision to extend the Madrid fieldwork with complementary research in Chinese educational institutions brought me to Zhejiang University in Hangzhou city. Under the framework of an interinstitutional collaboration between this university and the university where I was based in Madrid (Universidad Autónoma de Madrid), funded by the Spanish Ministry of Science and Technology,[7] I was appointed as research fellow at the Institute of Discourse and Cultural Studies.[8] Zhejiang University was at that time ranked at the highest level within Zhejiang province, and occupied fourth place among China's best universities. Thus, it was closely linked to discourses of excellence, which indirectly gave me access to social and institutional networks attached to experimental schools, even though this was not my original intention. Among these networks, a group of primary and secondary education teachers, taking a sabbatical year and enrolled in a one-year training program, played a key role in my research.

These teachers came to Zhejiang University from experimental schools all over Zhejiang province and remained on the campus for one year to take part in various full-time specialization courses, in accordance with the institutional pressures for teachers in primary and secondary experimental schools in China to take part in university training programs to meet the demands for the establishment of "quality education". When I first met them, I did not know they were all attached to experimental institutions, but only that they were periodically observing classes in different schools in the city of Hangzhou. Thus, when I approached them to ask for permission to accompany them in these observations, this opened up a new research path, one that I did not recognize as such until this work was under way.

This group of teachers allowed me to accompany them on sporadic classroom observations at different schools in the city. But most importantly, they also helped me to carry out prolonged fieldwork at the three schools that were finally the focus of my study in Zhejiang. They navigated their own personal networks to facilitate my access to these schools and to others across the province, which explains the fact the three schools finally researched were all categorized as experimental, although this was not intentionally planned by me. In particular, these teachers made the first contacts with the heads of the experimental schools and introduced me as someone from a trustworthy network of excellent educational institutions, with people at the front line of the implementation of educational reforms. In other words, they provided me with the social capital necessary to enter the space of experimental education.

It was only once my fieldwork had begun in the three schools that I became aware of their institutional categorization as experimental. At this point, I almost gave up my observations in order to look for new schools, because I sensed that the fact that they were not "ordinary" could hamper the initial aims for my fieldwork in China; none of the Chinese students I had observed in the Bridging Class in Madrid had been socialized in an experimental school. However, my whole research plan was transformed as soon as I became aware of the institutional significance of the category of experimental within the Chinese educational system. From then on, my fieldwork in Zhejiang was no longer oriented toward contextualizing the data previously collected in Madrid; it became a new and independent research study, focusing on the experimental school as a site in itself.

My social construction as a linguistic/cultural capital for the schools, in relation to this research journey between Madrid and Zhejiang, thus provides some initial elements for understanding the particular implications of Chinese official discourses on modernization reforms for the three experimental schools. The importance of this journey for my participants arose from the fact that it could be institutionally framed within discourses of internationalism, West/China interculturalism and institutional excellence, which emerged from how they capitalized on my presence. These ideas surfaced in (a) the negotiation of my entry into the schools; (b) the institutional reports by which the schools exhibited my activities; and (c) the use of my persona to explain the Chinese educational model. Regarding the negotiation of my entry, Extract 1.3 illustrates the extent to which my social categorization as Westerner, Spanish, and English/Spanish speaking became crucial for my access to the field (see the Appendix for transcription conventions).

Extract 1.3   "We Can Also Take Advantage of Your Presence Here"

Miguel: so / in order to get a better understanding of the daily routine of an educational center such as this/ I would need to have access to it and to observe everyday activities / in general / and of the classroom practice / of at least one group / in particular (. . .) this is more or less the research plan that I was thinking of / (if you agree)°

Li: I have no objection // but it might be more interesting if we made it an experience of mutual help and cooperation instead of you just coming here and observing // we could also take advantage of having a Westerner like you here with us / you could help the English teachers and also give our students and teachers some introductory classes on Spanish language / culture / and history / what do you think?

(Translation of field notes taken directly in Spanish, in an interview with a school head)

Ms. Li's explanation shows how my social categorization facilitated access to the school, since this identity was constructed as a linguistic and cultural resource that the whole school community could take advantage of. Taking for granted my legitimacy as a Spaniard and as an English speaker, on the basis of my regional categorization as Spanish and as a Westerner, my presence was represented as an opportunity for the whole school community to learn more about these international languages and their cultures. Thus, the heads of the schools asked me to act either as a teaching

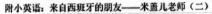

校内信息

附小英语: 来自西班牙的朋友——米盖儿老师（二）

来自西班牙的米盖儿老师在中国的教育学习与考察即将结束，上周他还就中国中小学教育现状及教育体制等方面对 XX 附小的 XX 校长、XX 老师和六年级的两位学生进行了采访，他对教育的探究精神和热中程度令我们钦佩。

在 附小听课期间的四个月内，他认真听课，录音录象，收集学生学习资料，给学生上了一节生动有趣的外语课，还给附小全体老师做了个精彩的讲座，介绍了有关西班 牙文化、教育等方面的知识，教了一些简单的西班牙问候语，老师们收益非浅！在离开中国之前，米盖儿还用中文写了下面一段话，题为: impressions（印象）

我在西班牙研究中国移民学生在马德里的中学校怎么学习西班牙语。这样的学生在西班牙的首都一般都从中国浙江省分来，所以那时候我是感觉的需要来这里研究中国义务的教育，特别这里的教育法。这样的话，我将来在马德里了解中国学生的情况比较好。

我 本来的观点关于中国教育法比现在的不一样。在马德里很多老师认为中国学生在教室里面他们都不要参加因为他们在中国学习的话不用口语。不过，我在这个学校的 英语课想到每天的活动都有根口语关系，老师和学生他们都一起用口语，他们都合作为了达到每课的目标。除了每天的听课，我上个星期给学生教西班牙的文化，所 以那天我们都学习了不一样的东西: 我教了学生学简单的西班牙文化，还有学生也教了我在上课的时候我跟他们怎么合作！最后感谢所有的老师和学生！米盖儿

让我们预祝米盖儿老师此项课题研究取得好成果，也希望西班牙人民对中国教育有进一步的认识和了解，从而宏扬中国教育与文化！

附小英语组 XX 供稿

Figure 1.2   School's official website

assistant in English-language classes on a daily basis or as a lecturer of Spanish language and culture in the course of weekly meetings with their teachers and students. These social categories, thus, set the frame for interpreting the "what", "why", "when", and "where" of my participation in the data collection process.

As regards the institutional exhibition of my presence, the three schools reported on their institutional websites and in other relevant public spaces (local newspapers and signs/posters on their main entrances) all the activities I conducted during the fieldwork. As experimental schools, all were supposed to engage in sustained educational activities related to innovation. Therefore, my supposed linguistic and cultural contribution was exhibited as a symbol of their innovative educational actions. The schools' official webpages were an example of this, being taken into account for their official evaluation. Since these schools were part of a national experimental network in which they were ranked according to the innovative activities that they reported, particularly on their websites, this space was used for exhibition purposes. Figure 1.2, translated in Extract 1.4, is taken from the official website of one of the schools and shows how my coparticipants and myself emphasized my research journey and the activities carried out during the fieldwork in Zhejiang as a contribution to constructing a social image of the school in relation to excellence and internationalism:

Extract 1.4   "A Wonderful Lecture on Spanish Language, Culture, and Education"

Professor Miguel, who comes from Spain, is about to finish his study of education and learning in China. Last week, he conducted interviews with sixth-grade students and their teachers, as well with the school's principal, on the current situation of the educational system. We admire the degree of enthusiasm and spirit of enquiry with which he approaches education. In a four-month period, he has conducted serious class observation, taken audio and video recordings, collected students' learning materials, given a lively and interesting class on foreign language, and has given a wonderful lecture to all the school's teachers introducing the Spanish language, culture, and education and teaching basic greetings in Spanish, from which the teachers greatly benefited! Before he leaves China, Miguel has even written in Chinese the following paragraph titled: "Impressions".

"In Spain, I am doing research on Chinese immigrants learning Spanish in Madrid, within the secondary education system. Most of these students in the Spanish capital come from Zhejiang province in China, so I felt that I needed to come here to do research on Chinese compulsory education, particularly on the educational methods here. In this way, I will better understand the situation of the Chinese students in Madrid.

My initial view of education in China has changed. In Madrid, there are many teachers who think Chinese students do not want to collaborate [orally] in [language] class because in China they do not learn languages by using oral language. But in this school's English classes I have realized that everyday activity has to do with oral language. Apart from everyday class observation, last week I gave a class to the students on Spanish language and culture, and during that class we all learnt different things. While I taught students basic language and cultural knowledge, they taught me how to engage collaboratively in classroom interaction. Lastly, I would like to thank all the teachers and students! Miguel"

Let us wish Miguel good results from his research, and hope the Spanish people get to know more about education in China and promote Chinese education and culture!

(Translation of text in Figure 1.2)

Lastly, the use of my persona to comprehend the Chinese educational model was also possible because of the framing of the social categories of Westerner/Spanish within the discursive polarization between the categories of "China" and the "West" that circulate widely in the public domain and in official discourses in China. Extract 1.5 corresponds to a later moment in the course of the same interview from which Extract 1.3 is taken, and is a representative sample of the kinds of discourse produced in the three schools:

Extract 1.5   "In the West, You Are Now Facing Some Problems"

Miguel: what is your opinion about the current situation of Chinese education?

Li: now we have too much pressure on teachers / students, and school principals in China / and the one-child policy is one of the reasons // parents want the best for their children // the new context of globalization and new technologies such as Internet are making children receive a lot of input even though they are still immature // the West is open but the East was closed before /Spain is a developed country and this is why the birth rate there is low / but here in China not yet because China is still a developing country // this is why we are now facing many challenges in education (. . .) in the West you are now facing some problems concerning student behavior / right? this is why here we are trying to emphasize quality education // that is / not just a proper psychical education but also moral and physical / in order to meet Chinese parents' expectations about education

(Translation of field notes taken directly in Spanish, in an interview with a head of school)

In representing the current international context in terms of change and uncertainty as a challenge to students, Ms. Li argued the need for a specific Chinese model of education that is characterized by the combination of academic and moral content. This representation was strengthened by a discursive contrast between an in group, referred to by the pronoun "we" in relation to the categories of "China"/"East", and an out group, referred to by the pronoun "you" in relation to the categories of "Spain"/"West". The former group was related with the attributes of a developing country while the latter was associated with students' behavioral problems. This led Li to the conclusion that it is necessary to implement a "Chinese" educational model based on the combination of psychological, physical, and moral elements.

In this sense, my identity as a Westerner served to help grasp the educational reforms and practices implemented. In a context of globalization and social change, the positive representation of the cultural in group, in contrast to the negative representation of the out group (which I was assumed to represent), justified the implementation of education reforms aimed at preserving what was considered a specifically Chinese model. In particular, the representation of China as a developing country in the process of opening up, together with the perceived moral problems of the West, justifies a reform in which "moral education", as we see more specifically in Chapter 4, takes a central position. That is to say, this discourse represents Chinese reforms as a specific solution to the challenges posed by globalization, in general, and by the indiscipline of the West, in particular.

Therefore, this reflection about how I was socially constructed by my participants during the fieldwork sets the starting point for delimiting the discursive and organizational changes that the three experimental schools I studied were undergoing, in connection with the institutional discourses of reform outside their individual boundaries and within the Chinese public space. As educational institutions heading the institutional reforms to achieve modernization, they were under great pressure to engage constantly in projects of innovation, although always in line with the official discourse. Thus, the representation of my presence as part of innovation actions related to discourses of internationalism, West/China interculturalism, and institutional excellence involved significant dimensions within the modernization reforms.

Although with some difference in degree as a consequence of the varying local conditions in each of the experimental schools, I was in fact constructed by all three as a form of cultural capital. My presence gave them the opportunity to play the institutional game of modernization and to benefit from it. Thus, they took advantage of my persona (which in turn allowed me access to the schools and to obtain academic products and rewards) and represented themselves as excellent institutions implementing innovative actions aimed at incorporating Western languages and cultures into their educational communities without losing the presumed Chinese educational specificity.

It is now worth focusing more precisely on the links between these discourses emerging from my presence in the three schools in Zhejiang, the institutional discourses of Chinese experimental reforms, as seen in Section 1.1, and the shifting ideas of identity, nation and state in China. These links constitute the framework for understanding where all these discourses come from (and also how and when they emerged) and, in turn, how they constrain (and are constrained by) the institutional organization of everyday practice, both inside and outside the classrooms described in this book.

1.3   IDEOLOGY AND DISCOURSE IN CONTEMPORARY CHINA: PATHS TO LATE MODERNITY

The nation-state is a useful space for discussing the significance of the institutional discourses referred to previously. This space allows us to trace the emergence and the particular configuration of modernization discourses in line with the shifting ideas of identity, nation, and state around which the national construction of modern China has taken place. Thus, it allows us to understand the discourses that emerge from the three experimental schools in Zhejiang as socially, politically, economically, and ideologically constructed over the course of historical events in localized spaces.

The literature on modern nationalism provides us with some basic vocabulary for a better comprehension of the extent to which the nation-state is a relevant space for exploring institutional discourses of modernization as socially, economically, and politically constructed (Anderson, 1983; Hobsbawm, 1990; Billig, 1995). I will highlight three key features. First, this space is a mode of socioeconomic organization tied to the rise of the bourgeoisie in the 19th century and to its interests in expanding economic activities both within and among unified national markets. Second, it involves struggles among the different groups involved in the construction, legitimization, and challenging of this mode of organization. Third, it requires intensive discursive work, both in the institutional arena and in everyday life, for the imagination of the particular configurations of language, nation, and state that contribute to naturalizing this mode of organization and, in turn, to naturalizing the socioeconomic interests of those who have sought to establish it.

These interests, struggles, and discursive configurations have shifted in relation to changing national and international political economies over the centuries, from the early consolidation of the modern nation-state as the main socioeconomic and political reference to its rapid undermining with the late modern constitution of wider transnational and globalizing networks of economic and political organization (Giddens, 1991; Appadurai, 1996; Bauman, 1998; Castells, 2010). In the case of China, its socioeconomic and political organization under the nation-state model can be discursively traced back to the beginning of the 20th century, in the context of European industrial expansion through colonialism. Therefore, the path to the particular configurations of interests, struggles, and discourses on language, nation, and state that make sense of the modernization discourses described in the previous sections cannot be grasped without taking into account this colonial/postcolonial framework.

At this point, I present a very schematic genealogy of these configurations in the course of the transformation of China's national and international political economies. By doing so, I do not seek to condense China's history into a few pages. Nor do I assume that the resulting picture captures all the relevant processes underlying the constitution of contemporary Chinese society. Neither is this an attempt to impose mere "background facts" (Blommaert & Bulcaen, 2000), completely detached from the discursive space of the experimental schools studied in Zhejiang. Rather, I am interested in following the ideological traces connecting local discourses about the experimental reforms and about my persona that emerged during the conducting of my research at the three schools and discourses in other times/spaces.

The story of discourses on modernization in China begins during the second half of the 19th century, in the context of the first colonial contacts with the European powers (particularly with France and England). These powers had initiated their imperial campaigns against China with the aim of integrating its local and regional markets into the global ones. They enforced this process by means of numerous unequal treaties resulting from military interventions, which obliged the Chinese imperial court to establish economic exchanges with Europe. The decisive turning points were the Nanjing Treaty (1842) and the Tianjing Treaty (1861), which put an end to the traditional modes of commercial relationships between China and Europe. Europeans, who had been represented by successive Chinese imperial courts as backward barbarians undeserving of equal commercial treatment, had arrived definitively on the Chinese socioeconomic and political scene (Harrison, 1969; Duara, 1999; Townsend, 1999; Fisac & Tsang, 2000).[9]

The evident technological and military superiority of the European powers, but also of Japan, which had adopted European socioeconomic reforms during the 1860s through the *Meiji* Restoration and defeated the Chinese army a few decades later in the first Sino-Japanese War (1894–1895),[10] provoked debate among Chinese socioeconomic elites about the necessity of embracing modern European political ideas as the only way to ensure their own economic and territorial integrity (Fitzgerald, 1995: 76–77).

Grounded in the philosophical framework of European Enlightenment, these ideas advocated the establishment of a global political and economic order resting upon a network of interdependent and sovereign nation-states all cooperating economically. On the one hand, states were conceived of as institutional embodiments representing the interests of the people living within the geographical territory of a country. On the other, nations were viewed as linguistically/culturally bounded communities resulting from a shared history. The binomial nation-state as a whole was represented as a natural/organic entity which had to compete with others for the accumulation of economic capital and military strength (through technological and scientific knowledge) so as to progress in a supposedly hierarchical and linear scale of evolution (Anderson, 1983; Hobsbawm, 1990).

Thus, from the late 19th century the European Enlightenment conceptualization of the modern nation-state in relation to ideas of sovereignty, progress, technique, science, and social Darwinism provided the ideological framework of reference for social, political, and economic elites in China to mobilize important segments of the population. The quest for China's national regeneration created a market for nationalism which gave "prospective entrepreneurs the opportunity and the incentive to enter the political arena by endorsing a nationalist program and by fashioning their offer in a nationalist shape" (Ferrero, 1995: 208). In other words, these modernization discourses were appropriated by the elites to keep their legitimacy in controlling access to and the distribution of the state's resources in China, on the basis of their anti-imperialist or anticolonialist content.

Nevertheless, these discourses were not adopted unambiguously. They did not replace all other ideological frameworks locally and historically constructed within premodern China; rather, the colonial experience from which the national construction of modern China emerged meant that these modernization discourses were intimately linked, from the very beginning, to a permanent discursive tension between "Western modern ideas" and "Chinese traditions" (Wang & Karl, 1998; Scalapino, 1999). Furthermore, these modernizing discourses were not constructed instantly; nor have they maintained the same form and content throughout the 20th century until the present day.

In the course of the national construction of modern China, these discourses have been built up in different ways, with diverse consequences on the official definition of what constitutes the legitimate national community (and therefore its legitimate members), the appropriate relationship between the State and "the people", and the suitable balance between "modern Western ideas" and "Chinese traditions". In these pages, I will focus on three main ideological junctures that are particularly relevant for tracing how these modernization discourses have been historically, politically, and economically shaped.

The first such ideological juncture concerns the shift from ethno-nationalism to state-led nationalism as the guiding principle for defining the national community. After having attempted to apply modernization reforms only in the economic and military domains, the Qing court found itself unable to halt external aggressions and, therefore, the subsequent erosion of the internal market. This led many Chinese reforming intellectuals and other social elites whose interests were at stake to believe that deeper reforms aimed at traditional political structures were needed to ensure the continuing survival of the domestic market, and these beliefs inspired the revolution that overthrew the Chinese imperial system in 1911. In doing so, European ideas of modern nationalism were re-oriented against the imperial order through the political strategies of ethno-nationalism and its discourses on ethnicity, national cohesion, self-determination, and progress (Dikotter, 1992).[11]

Thus, the notions of "Chinese" and "Han ethnicity" were equated to mobilize the majority Han population against the ethnic Manchu minority that until then had controlled the Qing imperial government (Laitinen, 1990). In this regard, the foundation of the modern Republic of China in 1912, under the provisional political leadership of Sun Yat-sen as the head of the Chinese Nationalist Party (CNP), involved a reshaping of the socioeconomic and political order of the Chinese state away from an imperial organization, which was not ethnically based—as different ethnic groups could (and indeed did) access power as long as they accepted the linguistic and cultural values of the premodern Chinese political community—toward a modern, Han-centered society, in which class stratification overlapped ethno-national categorization (Rhoads, 2000). However, these ethno-nationalistic discourses were soon considered an obstacle to the national construction of modern China.

China was and is ethnically very diverse, with the presence of many ethnolinguistic groups who had been annexed to Chinese political territory during the apogee of Qing imperial expansionism in the 18th century. Thus, the official circulation of ethno-national discourses gave rise to the emergence of non-Han ethnic nationalisms that challenged the project of a unified Chinese nation-state (and market) (Gladney, 1996; Karmel, 2000). These other ethno-nationalisms claimed their own international recognition as separate and sovereign nation-states on the basis of a supposed cultural and linguistic specificity. As a result, the Han political and social elites had to reposition themselves and articulate new modern political discourses in order to legitimize the newly established socioeconomic order under the Republic of China.

From then on, state-led nationalism became the official modern political strategy, redefining the national community away from discourses of ethnicity (Zhao, 2004: 62–70), and official modern political discourses in China began to stress the multiethnic nature of the Chinese nation.[12] These discourses sought to identify the Chinese people with a political community overlapping the frontiers of a threatened state. In other words, self-determination came to be discursively constructed as being related to the freedom of multethnic communities from foreign imperialist interference rather than to the independence of each ethnic group. However, state-led nationalism did not put an end to the privileged position of the Han people in Chinese society; both assimilationist policies from the perspective of the Han majority and peripheral ethnic nationalisms on the part of the minority groups have been an important part of China's modern history (see Harrell, 1996; Newby, 2000; Mackerras, 2006; Chen, 2008; or Postiglione, 2008, for a discussion on the domination relationship historically constructed between the Han majority and the minority groups, in the framework of modern and late modern cultural and economic policies applied in China).

Another ideological juncture I would like to focus on, regarding the configuration of modernization discourses in contemporary China, concerns the shift from liberal democracy to authoritarianism as the guiding principle for defining the appropriate relationship between the state and "the people". When state-led nationalism was installed as the wider ideology for defining the nation, the Chinese government took American liberal democracy as its political model for regulating political participation (Zhao, 2004: 23).[13] Under this model, the notion of "citizenship" became crucial, and thus the political community of the Chinese nation-state was discursively constructed during the first years of the Republic of China as a body of sovereign citizens who were nationals of the state, regardless of ethnicity, religion, or lineage. However, this model was promptly replaced by that of the authoritarian state, as a consequence of the challenges to the consolidation of a unified national market, posed from both external pressures to cede more territories to European states and the internal politicization of provincial consciousness in China (Fitzgerald, 1999: 108).[14]

In the light of these new events, the republican government and the national elites fighting to establish a centralized Chinese nation-state (and market) saw once again that their political and economic interests were challenged and began to seek an alternative political program to that of the Anglo-American variety of liberal democracy. Leaning on the emergence of popular and elite nationalisms that advocated a strong centralized state as the only viable strategy to avoid China's territorial and economic disintegration at the hands of either Western colonizers or Chinese warlords, the CNP turned its attention in 1928 to centrist nationalism, inspired by the potent European fascism of the time (Esteban, 2007: 25–26). In other words, the popular and elite nationalisms ironically contributed to a massive concentration of political and economic resources in the form of a one-party dictatorship, with individuals' rights being limited in the political economy of a modern state-led authoritarian nationalism.

The two political regimes that have since ruled the Chinese state, the CNP (up to 1949) and the CCP (from 1949), placed all state institutions at the service of both the delegitimization of local/regional identities and the mobilization of an official discourse in which the government is identified with the state. In this regard, the party-state authority has been officially represented in China since the late 1920s as the only way to achieve national salvation and economic modernization. In fact, the notion of "patriotism" (爱国主义), understood as love, loyalty, and service to the party-state's reforms, has become a key term in modern Chinese nationalist discourse, which in turn has had consequences for the conceptualization of "citizenship" and therefore for the regulation of the relationship between the state and the nation. In particular, the discursive construction of modernization from the standpoint of an authoritarian party-state has resulted in the representation of the legitimate political community as a body of loyal and trusting citizens with restricted rights, under the tutelage of the government (Hunt, 1993).[15]

A third ideological juncture to be highlighted in the discourses of contemporary Chinese modernization is that of a shift from antitraditional nativism to traditionalist pragmatism, which concerns the definition of the most suitable balance between "Western modern ideas" and "Chinese traditions". Under the political and economic framework of the Chinese state-led authoritarian nationalism, antitraditional nativism was developed by Mao Zedong in his approach to communism during the Cold War (Schwartz, 1951; Schram, 1969; Hunt, 1996), while traditionalist pragmatism was officially and progressively constituted during the post-Mao era, in parallel to China's integration into the new globalized economy (Pye, 1999; Guo, 2004, 2007; Hughes, 2006).

The salience of communism as an ideological drive for China's socioeconomic plans of reform is to be found in the social and intellectual movements that arose following the Treaty of Versailles in 1919.[16] Aware of public discontent with China's weak international position—the country still suffered colonization by Western powers during the 1920s—many Chinese intellectuals and political elites (both inside and outside the CNP) looked around for new, modernizing programs. Although from different ideological positions, all agreed on the need for an antitraditionalist approach to socioeconomic reforms as the only means of overcoming China's economic backwardness and territorial and economic disintegration.[17] However, they did not agree on the necessary position to be taken. Some continued to look toward Great Britain and America as liberal role models for the construction of a bourgeois state led by the CNP,[18] while others were inspired by new ideological sources such as Marxism-Leninism because of its antitraditional, antiliberal, and anti-imperialist contents. These latter thinkers became the founders of the CCP (Zhao, 2004: 59).[19]

In contrast to those of the CNP, the CCP's socioeconomic programs of reform were based on a socialist antitraditionalism aimed at building a workers' state led by the CCP (Hunt, 1996: 55). The key figure in determining this ideological option in the Chinese official political scene was Mao Zedong, who reinterpreted Marxism-Leninism as a form of Chinese "national communism" (Johnson, 1962: 15).[20] He mobilized popular and elite nationalism against the CNP (under the leadership of Chiang Kai-shek, who had succeeded Sun Yat-sen) by representing antitraditional and native modernizing programs as the sole ideological means of achieving the decolonization of China from both the liberal Western world and the old local feudalist socioeconomic order (and associated the latter with the CNP). Thus, communism was constructed as the only way to continue the national salvation project initiated by Sun Yat-sen in 1911 (Friedman, 1994).[21]

This discursive work by Mao Zedong was crucial for the CCP's victory against CNP troops during the Chinese Civil War (1927–1949), and laid the way for the foundation of the PRC in 1949. Mao's reinterpretation of Marxism-Leninism remained as the main ideological reference for Chinese modernization policies until the late 1970s. Although with varying degrees of intensity and emphasis in its implementation, this ideological shift led to the building of a political economy centered on erasing all traces of capitalism, and on the principles of rapid industrialization, the collectivization of the national economy, and the centralization of a communist statist bureaucracy controlled by civil servants, the military, and the CCP's political and administrative cadres.[22] However, attitudes and structures changed progressively following Mao's death in 1976.

The "open door" reforms introduced by Deng Xiaoping in 1978 marked the start of new modernization discourses in China, in which antitraditionalism, antiliberalism, and anti-imperialism were to be increasingly replaced by economic pragmatism, antidemocratic liberalism, and cultural traditionalism. Deng Xiaoping's initial reforms in the economic areas of agriculture, industry, defense, and science and technology were driven by economic pragmatism as their sole guiding principle, with the goal of promoting the indigenization of foreign knowledge to achieve economic growth and national security (Hughes, 2006: 33–34).[23] Nevertheless, the economic crisis experienced in the late 1980s, and the resulting social mobilizations that challenged the CCP's legitimacy as the representative of the Chinese nation, led to a more drastic change in the discursive construction of the country's modernization.

A key moment in this major transition was that of the Tiananmen protests, in which the protesters bypassed the CCP's authoritative position by appealing to a nonofficial patriotism based on the principles of science, liberal democracy, and nationalism (Chu, 1999). The repression of these protests by the CCP provoked the international economic and political isolation of China, and economic liberalization reforms came to a standstill for several years. However, they were again boosted by Deng during his famous "Southern Tour" in 1992 (南巡), although on this occasion within a new ideological framework in which the economic liberalization reforms and the Chinese political system were, discursively, better integrated.

This new official nationalism became institutionalized under the theory of the "Three Represents" (三个代表) during Jiang Zemin's (1993–2003) and Hu Jintao's (2003–2013) governments, and now forms part of the CCP's ideological guidelines, in juxtaposition with Mao Zedong's Thought and Deng Xiaoping's reforms (Guo, 2004: 2).[24] Under this new ideological framework, the CCP's representation as the heir of the modern Chinese revolutionary tradition lost its momentum. In the context of a late modern non–nation-state–centered globalized economy, official discourses began to emphasize the construction of the CCP both as the representative leader of a unified nation (as, for example, in reference to the reunification with Taiwan and Hong Kong, which became an important issue in nationalist discourse), one aiming to be a new international economic power, and as the guardian of a supposedly Chinese/pan-Asian Confucian-based cultural heritage (Davison, 2004: 57–63; Hughes, 2006: 1–9; Guo, 2007: 119–126).

In doing so, the CCP took on two main discursive shifts, which are expressed by the contemporary official slogans of "Socialism with Chinese characteristics" (具有中国特色的社会主义), "Building a Chinese spiritual civilization" (社会主义精神文明建设), and "Socialist market economy" (社会主义市场经济). On the one hand, the party stepped out from Marxism-Leninism as an explicit guiding ideology and accommodated socialism to the interests of Chinese elites and entrepreneurs willing to participate in (and benefit from) the new globalized economy (Hughes, 2006: 42–70).[25] On the other hand, the CCP also discursively appropriated the critiques of the postcolonial and postmodern intellectual movements that had developed in China and in the Asian region against the universal values historically attributed to the modernity of the European Enlightenment (Connors, 2004: 208; Golden, 2004: 120).[26]

By justifying a non–Western-culture–based modernizing strategy that is still very much constrained within the imperialist, colonial, and Cold War cultural/emotional binary framework counterposing "Western, advanced, democratic countries" on the one hand and "Eastern, backward, communist countries" on the other, these countercultural discourses in East Asia contributed in some contexts (mainly in Malaysia and Singapore) to legitimizing a political system which combines economic liberalization and political authoritarianism by representing it as rooted in an Asian and Confucian-based cultural heritage in which community values such as collectivism, discipline, hierarchy, and social harmony prevail over that of individual freedom (Wang & Karl, 1998: 27–29; Guo, 2004: 72–91, 2007: 123–125; Wang & Hale 2007: 3–8).[27]

In view of Marxism-Leninism's diminishing capacity to mobilize mass opinion, the CCP aligned itself with these ideas, in what has been considered an ideological move away from the Soviet tradition toward the East Asian model (and toward a regional identity).[28] In fact, this move not only provided the CCP with an alternative ideological framework for reinforcing its political legitimacy while continuing its developmental socioeconomic plans of reform; it also facilitated the revitalizing of a Chinese-centric cultural identity in which China (and its new service-based industries) is viewed as the cultural center of the Asian Pacific market, by nationalizing Asian cultural traditions into the space-time of the traditional China (and therefore reconstituting the cultural imaginaries of the former imperialist/colonizing China) (Guo, 2007).

In sum, the three ideological junctures described in this section uncover the economic and political conditions of institutional discourses on modernization, internationalization, West/China cultural polarization, and institutional reform that emerged from the very beginning in the fieldwork carried out in the three experimental schools in Zhejiang. They point to the conformation of modernizing discourses in which economic legitimacy gains greater emphasis. However, these ideological junctures do not seem to be traversed by a linear shift from political to economic legitimacy, as has often been described in relation to the late modern contexts of Europe or North America. Rather, the discursive traces connecting the social space of the three experimental schools in Zhejiang with the wider transformations of the ideas of identity, nation, and state in China provide the backdrop to the discursive formation of a state-led authoritarian project of economic development based on economic pragmatism and cultural commodification, resulting from the specific historical conditions of modern China.

In this regard, the tensions that have been described between language and culture as commodified skills or as markers of authenticity, concerning the impact of the new globalized economy on the modern nation-state (Heller, 2011), need to be examined in the framework of this specific discursive formation. The particular ways through which these tensions emerge and are articulated in the discursive organization of the three experimental schools studied in Zhejiang will be the focus of my narrative in the remaining chapters of this book. The analysis of everyday practice in these schools, with special attention to their English-language classes, provides all the necessary elements to come back to this discussion later and to delimit the specific implications for our understanding of the issues concerning late modernity, urban schooling, English-language education, and interaction in contemporary China.

1.4   STRUCTURE OF THE BOOK

I have already put myself on the spot in the course of this first chapter, by reflecting on the extent to which my own corporeal presence in the institutional space of the three Chinese experimental schools led to social and discursive situated practices that are relevant for understanding wider and trans-local socioeconomic and political processes of change. However, I need to commit myself to this task and take this subjectivist line of enquiry a bit further. In this regard, and before getting closer to the three studied schools and to the young people and teachers who attended them, I will first try to make more explicit the theoretical and methodological choices that I made when conducting the research in Zhejiang.

Chapter 2, therefore, will step back and review these choices, which in some way inform the accounts that I have already initiated here and that I shall continue unfolding throughout the rest of the book. I will do so by highlighting the major ontological and epistemological moves experienced in the last decades in the interdisciplinary fields of social theory, linguistic anthropology, and sociolinguistics, as these underpin my critical, sociolinguistic, and ethnographic takes in the exploration of social change through linguistic practice. On the basis of these major moves, I will first describe in more detail my main methodological orientations, which result from the combination of participant observation, analysis of interaction, and critical discourse analysis. In particular, I will account for the dilemmas and opportunities that each of those orientations involved during the data collection process, leading us to an overview of the data corpus that the analysis in this book relies on.

Once these methodological aspects and concerns have been localized in the space of my fieldwork, I will take one more step and review in more detail the four specific conceptual shifts that define the theoretical and methodological approach of this book. I will begin by paying attention to the notions of language, culture, and identity, which need to be seen as discursive socially situated constructions rather than universally bounded/objective entities detached from social life. Then, I will turn to the school setting, which should be understood as a modern state institution facing the contradictions and tensions of the contemporary world instead of as a neutral space where cognitive transfer between minds occurs in isolation to what happens outside the walls of the school. Lastly, I will focus on the space of second language education, which requires a departure away from the pedagogical interest in efficient teaching-learning strategies and toward a sociolinguistic description of the processes of (re)production, legitimization, and contestation of language ideologies.

After all my research choices are made explicit, I will turn, in Chapter 3, to the three experimental schools studied. The focus here will be on the consequences of the institutional competitiveness that result from Chinese educational modernization, supposedly headed by the three schools, on their everyday life. Attention will be paid to what means to be a "good experimental school" in their everyday discursive organization. This will show how the implementation of contemporary educational reform plans in these schools is mainly concerned with the need to face the opportunities and challenges opened up by the new global market, to be achieved by increasing institutional competition at all levels. Tensions and dilemmas will arise as a consequence of the pressures for the three studied schools to adapt to the institutional demands for competition, on the basis of an official combination of curriculum centralization and economic/administrative decentralization.

These demands made each school highlight different official values in different degrees, according to the resources available to them and to their local communities; that is, they ended up emphasizing these values in different ways depending on their potential for acquiring students (clients) and, therefore, obtaining higher educational fees and school budget. The social images built up by each of the three schools will be described, with particular attention to how their students, teachers, and principals positioned themselves (and positioned myself) in such a discursive space. This will allow us to consider the continuities and discontinuities with regard to the previous modernization reforms implemented during the 20th century in the Chinese educational system, which in turn will open a window for reflecting on the neoliberalization underpinnings of contemporary reforms as well as on the potential contributions and dangers emerging from the voices of the schools' participants.

Chapter 4 will then continue the account by looking at a certain number of practices that in the three schools were discursively linked to the so-called moral education (德育), as part of the official reforms for educational modernization. During the fieldwork, these practices came to be at the core of the discourses already outlined in the first chapter, as regards a Chinese-specific educational response that is based on Chinese cultural traditions and political canons to protect Chinese students from the immoral influences of West under contemporary globalization. Thus, this chapter will examine what forms of knowledge are locally (re)produced, legitimated, and negotiated in the course of the activities linked to moral education.

Exploration will focus on the social categories about the "good participant" and "appropriate knowledge" that come out of interactional and discursive data involving these practices. Such attention will show certainties and uncertainties coming out of a discursive organization in which moral education seems to be officially oriented to institutionalizing values on social responsibility in the framework of a collectively and hierarchically structured school community. These certainties and uncertainties were discursively/interactionally built upon the overlapping of institutional authorization and interpersonal collusion in the course of verbal and nonverbal activities. These overlapping processes, while reinforcing the enduring of the official practices and discourses, may also open a window for instability and social transformation given the participants' difficulties in dealing with the rigidity of such institutional discursive organization. In fact, the tracing of the discursive emergence of these moralized discourses about the community described in the three schools in Zhejiang, in connection with the construction of a modern Chinese national curriculum, will point out the always unstable/unpredictable outcomes of the wider politics of national identity that have underpinned moral education in China.

Chapter 5 will bring us to the field of English-language education. Modernization discourses are in this field articulated around strong demands for curriculum reform and methodological innovation. Thus, shifting demands over time will be briefly explored, in connection with national policies and economic processes of change. Although this exploration will provide an initial frame for understanding how wider discourses of modernization analyzed in previous chapters get institutionalized in the space of English-language education in China, important questions will be raised about the real applicability of these extremely wide approaches to explaining what happens (or has ever happened) in everyday English-language classes. On the basis of this initial claim advocating for a closer look at the localization of wider policies in the moment-to-moment of the classroom activity, attention will be paid to what notion of "linguistic competence" emerges from the interactional organization of classroom, as a concrete manifestation of the social category of "appropriate knowledge" in the English-language classes of the three experimental schools.

As it will be argued, classroom interaction in these schools legitimated a recursive participation framework traversed by structuralist, functionalist, and collectivist principles, which points to a much more complex and multilayered scenario than the one suggested by clear-cut historical-pedagogical accounts on Chinese curriculum reforms. The analysis of these recursive interactional sequences will also show the emergence of chorus-like repetition sequences as a relevant discursive space for the negotiation of institutional, pedagogical, and interpersonal dimensions in classroom activity. Indeed, the study of the collection of sequences of choral repetition, and of the discourses circulating in the three studied schools, will reveal that they constituted a key space around which discourses and practices about modern Chinese ways of teaching/learning English were officially enacted/displayed and interpersonally rejected.

In light of all these processes emerging over the course of the book, Chapter 6 will finally consider the implications for our understanding of the ongoing cultural transformations faced by contemporary school institutions in PRC. These implications will point out the specific cultural tensions underpinning the current politics of identity in the Chinese context that leave open the discussion regarding the degree and nature of the interaction between the politics of the modern nation-state, on the one hand, and the postnational processes of commodification of language, culture, and identity, on the other. These tensions will be specifically explored in relation to the English-language educational policies and practices that are analyzed in this book. Such an exploration will identify the particular ways in which ideologies and practices tied to both modern politics of identity and commodification of identity get articulated in this field, which in turn will reveal further theoretical and methodological consequences for the study of classroom practice in this context.

2 Doing Critical Sociolinguistic Ethnography in Schools

2.1 ONTOLOGICAL ASSUMPTIONS AND EPISTEMOLOGICAL CONCERNS

I stated in the first chapter how relevant I think it is to include the researcher as part of the picture she or he is trying to portray, not just for aesthetic purposes but for theoretical reasons that are strongly related to how knowledge is locally and situationally produced and circulated within the site. I analyzed how this was the case for the research conducted in the three experimental schools in Zhejiang, where I was socially constructed by my participants in ways that incorporated the traces of wider social and discursive processes of transformation occurring in the space-time of the research site. I shall continue this line of research reflexivity by showing the extent to which the story of this book is built upon specific standpoints underpinning the framework of critical sociolinguistic ethnography as developed mainly by Heller (1999, 2002a, 2011) and Martín-Rojo (2010).

These standpoints involve certain ontological ways of understanding our social world as well as concrete epistemological decisions about how to approach such a world empirically. As regards the understanding of our social world, the analytical focus of this framework rests upon the critical, social, and discursive turns adopted in social sciences since the mid-twentieth century. In this sense, the ideas about social reality being discursively constructed, reproduced, naturalized, and sometimes revised in social interaction, in the course of large-scale historical, political, and socioeconomic configurations, are at the heart of my ontological base.

This ontological base is specifically framed within the critical and interpretative traditions developed in anthropology, sociology, and linguistics, under the influence of diverse disciplines such as pragmatics (Austin, 1962; Searle, 1969; Verschueren, 1999), microsociology (Goffman, 1967, 1974, 1981), linguistic anthropology (Gumperz & Hymes, 1972; Silverstein, 1976; Gal, 1989), sociolinguistics (Gumperz, 1982), and critical social theory (Foucault, 1970; Bourdieu, 1972, 1982, 1991; Cicourel, 1978, 1980, 1992; Giddens, 1984). The approach resulting from these traditions axiomatically assumes the following presuppositions that I summarize above (adapted from Rampton, 2006: 390):

1. Social life is discursively constructed by people (including the researcher) who are considered as social agents interacting across space and time.
2. Conventional structures configure but also constrain interactions.
3. Daily interactions can also reshape conventions, often fleetingly but sometimes in more enduring ways.
4. Social agents do not interact with each other in a context of equal relations, but within economic and political forms of organization in which symbolic and material resources are unequally (re)produced and distributed.
5. The interplay between agency, structure, constraint, and change opens up a window for analyzing the operation of relations of power.

There are two main aspects deriving from these presuppositions that need to be highlighted at this point of the discussion, in order to understand what, in my opinion, it is about critical sociolinguistic ethnography that makes it theoretically distinguishable from other approaches in social (linguistic) disciplines. On the one hand, this ontological base understands agency and social structure as mutually constitutive beyond the often-so-called micro/macro dichotomy. Instead of two different realms needing distinct analytical tools to be studied, this theoretical standpoint calls our attention to human activities as socially situated practices ordered across space and time by which human beings engage reflexively and agentively in daily activities while at the same time reproducing the conditions that make these activities possible (Giddens, 1984: 27).

On the other hand, the previously mentioned presuppositions address language as a domain where social processes are constituted, "both in the ways that it forms part of the social practices that construct social reality, and in the ways it serves as a terrain for working out struggles that are fundamentally about other things" (Heller, 2011: 49). This focus on language is particularly reflected in the study of processes of social categorization, which is a key endeavor in critical sociolinguistic ethnography. Indeed, these processes constitute valuable examples of labeling through which people construct and make sense of their social experience by means of communicative and discursive practices.

With respect to the epistemological decisions about how to approach such a social world empirically, a critical sociolinguistic ethnography like the one I have been drawn to involves the appropriation and combination of participant observation, analysis of interaction, and critical discourse analysis, these methodological contributions being based on the fields of ethnography, sociolinguistics, and discourse studies, respectively. The latter fields diverge slightly in their conceptions of what counts as knowledge or evidence of the social reality to be investigated, although they all agree on their interest in analyzing situated social practices across space-time and their consequences for the participants involved (whether short-term, in the course of the local activity, or long-term, in the event of large-scale societal processes of social change). This combination introduces different procedural disciplines but at the same time enables us to overcome some of the analytical limitations that have been pointed out with respect to the use of their methods separately (see Anderson, 1989; Hornberger, 1995; Heller, 2001).

Further clarification of this emerges if we take each of these methodological orientations in turn, not only outlining the ways by which they have shaped the book, but also acknowledging briefly the points where the solidity of their corresponding research traditions has itself been questioned.

2.2   COMBINED METHODOLOGICAL ORIENTATIONS

2.2.1   Participant Observation, from Ethnographic Studies

On the one hand, this study's epistemological framing within ethnography takes the methodological procedure of participant observation, in line with the interests of the ethnography of communication (Hymes, 1964; Gumperz & Hymes, 1972). This field of study has traditionally been concerned with the organization of communicative practices within a given community. In this regard, linguistic forms are conceptualized as symbolic resources through which people (re)constitute their social organization, instead of their being conceived as isolated units. This perspective also implies paying a good deal of attention to what people do in their daily life and to how their actions at particular moments and spaces are connected and constrained by other interactions across space and time.

In the case of the fieldwork conducted in the three experimental schools in Zhejiang, this degree of attention required me to take full part in the schools' activities and routines so as to derive their meaning and rationality from the local perspective before making any abstraction for exogenous audiences. I needed to engage fully with my participants in order to be able to trace their trajectories throughout the flow of interactions around which the symbolic and material resources of the schools were institutionally allocated, distributed, and mobilized. Thus, I had to spend time to get to know them, as well as to become known by them, in the course of everyday participant observations within the spaces and times in which each school community organized itself. Thus, the fieldwork in the three experimental schools lasted about six months and involved observation of their everyday activities both inside and outside the classroom spaces, from Monday to Saturday every week (from 7:00am to 4:30pm).

These observations did not involve a fixed/stable position to which I could accommodate myself throughout the process of data collection. Rather, they required me to take up different positions (often related to the degree of trust being built up with the participants), which often involved different methodological dilemmas. At some points, I was placed at the back of the classrooms or to the rear of activities outside the classrooms, which allowed me to concentrate on taking detailed field notes of what was going on simultaneously at different moments and spaces of the observed activities, but did not leave much room for face-to-face social interaction with the participants; at others, I was asked to teach English or Spanish language to students and teachers in the classrooms or to evaluate students in the course of activities outside the classrooms, which gave me the chance to interact differently with them in the course of those activities, but made it difficult to pay close attention to those parallel interactions that are often difficult to identify from the teacher's viewpoint.

Nevertheless, the use of participant observation does not in itself provide the necessary perspectives to give an account of the local social forms of action around which people in the social groups studied construct and negotiate meaning in a situated context. In fact, the use of observation alone has been widely criticized in sociolinguistics as privileging the study of paradigmatic relationships among communicative events within a given community as well as between different communities (Angus, 1986: 62–63; Anderson, 1989: 252–254; Erickson, 1992: 202–203). As the traditional focus in the ethnography of communication has been to characterize, compare, and contrast the communicative events around which a social group constitutes itself, this may lead to a representation of communities as fixed and bounded, and of language as a true reflection of the social order (see also Pratt, 1987). It is precisely this concern that has formed part of the argument about the capacity of sociolinguistic discourse analysis to "tie ethnography down" (Rampton, 2006: 395).

2.2.2   Analysis of Interaction, from Interactional Sociolinguistics

By making use of the analytical procedures of analysis of interaction, this book can engage with the methodological approaches pioneered by Goffman (1967, 1974, 1981), Gumperz (1982), and Goodwin (2000), who introduced the ethnomethodological focus on the routines and patterned use of language (Garfinkel, 1967; Heritage, 1984) in the fields of sociolinguistics and linguistic anthropology. Within this tradition, the analytical concepts introduced in the study of classroom discourse analysis are particularly insightful (Philips, 1972; Mehan, 1979; Cazden, 1988; Tsui, 1995; Seedhouse, 2004). In the three schools studied in China, this focus involved the audio/video recording of the recurrent activities around which the participants recursively and sequentially coordinated their social actions in the course of everyday school life.

I had to negotiate with my participants on the use of technological equipment so as to be able to recover and analyze detailed and sequential forms of social action that in many cases could not be properly recorded in writing. However, in some stages of the research the use of technology was not possible, and I had no choice but to take field notes (as detailed as possible), writing down literal fragments of conversations and depicting the forms of nonverbal communication displayed by participants in the course of their joint social activities (see Blackledge & Creese, 2010, for an illustrative example of the use of field notes in school-related sociolinguistic ethnography). When acting as a teaching assistant, and thus unable to take field notes during the observation, I even had to make use of my memory; that is, I had to recover as many as possible of the interactional details once I had left the school and was comfortably seated at home—or inside a crowded train on the way home, immediately after having left the school, as I tend to forget small items of information very soon after the events experienced, and to produce, instead, idealized, compressed, coherent, and manufactured packages of holistic stories.

In later stages of the research, however, the building of trust relationships (which are needed when we ask people to cede their image to an unknown academic audience) encouraged my participants to allow me to disrupt their lives with the chaos produced by my audio recorders, video cameras, and microphones; these technologies helped me to overcome the methodological tensions mentioned above, when I was unable to take field notes, but at the same time introduced new ones when I had to deal with often unpredictable technical aspects. In such cases, recorders did not remain outside the scene as if they were pure instruments capturing a reality out there, but rather became constructed as objects socially and semiotically incorporated by all participants within the scene—by waving and saying hello to the camera—or in the course of more complex interactions in which the camera was bodily and verbally introduced by the participants for the purposes of displaying certain social images to other participants.

Most importantly, and in line with Rampton's procedures (1995, 2001, 2006), I followed the analytical perspective of interaction analysis to become immersed in these recordings and to pay attention to the moment-to-moment of the interaction so as to follow the process whereby the participants constructed frames of common understanding. Curbed by this methodological procedure, I had to commit myself at some points to suspend all preconceived ideas and general arguments in order to work with the recorded and transcribed activities and to look at them as unique social episodes in which meaning making and context are interactionally constructed in a situated action. At such moments, I specifically looked at the linguistic/communicative (verbal and nonverbal) conventions through which participants sequentially coordinated their social actions by constructing social relations among themselves and with the surrounding material setting, in the course of recurrent everyday educational activities (e.g., turn-taking, language choice, lexical choice, proxemics, kinesics, and the use of texts in interaction).

This analytical exercise, therefore, goes beyond bounded representations of communities, being strongly oriented toward the discovery of the local-uncertain-unpredictable-changeable positioning of the participants. However, and unlike other disciplinary traditions such as conversational analysis (Sacks, Schegloff, & Jefferson, 1974; Atkinson & Heritage, 1984), I did not carry out this type of enquiry by permanently putting aside any connection between the fragments analyzed and other observed activities across the schools' space and time. Instead, I looked at each recorded and transcribed interaction as part of a web of social activities that participants developed in the course of their trajectories within the schools, in intersection with the trajectories of other material artifacts and discourses being produced and circulated at that historical moment in this geopolitical and economic domain.

The interactions recorded, transcribed, and analyzed were not selected at random, but were in line with specific research decisions about what regularities were emerging from my ethnographic observation of everyday life in the schools and about what was considered to be relevant in terms of my research goals and objectives. In relation to the regularities being revealed by the fieldwork, I paid special attention to selecting activities that were recursively considered by the participants as relevant to the social categorization of the students as "good" or "bad". This interest led me through diverse spaces within the schools, to include activities other than those taking place inside the classrooms. Although I initially intended to conduct traditional classroom observation in English-language classes, I soon became aware of the need to explore other spaces in order to understand either the kind of knowledge that was institutionally legitimated in the classroom activity or the social positioning being interactionally displayed by certain students during the lessons.

As for the decisions about the knowledge considered relevant, once I had identified the activities to be recorded and transcribed for careful further analysis, I focused particularly on those interactional moments in which the teachers and students collaborated ambiguously. I considered these potentially disruptive moments as especially rich sites for exploring the social processes by which norms and rules (frequently tacit and unnoticed as, for most of the time, they are taken for granted by the participants) are made explicit and salient. However, the combination of the ethnographic method of participant observation and the sociolinguistic one of analysis of interaction does not guarantee a proper consideration of the connections between the situated social organization of a given group of people and the wider socioinstitutional networks of social relations, goods, and discourses that such a group is linked up to. It is here where the orientations of other lines of enquiry within discourse studies have a contribution to make.

2.2.3   Critical Discourse Analysis from Discourse Studies

Finally, my appropriation of the field of critical discourse analysis draws particularly on the work of van Dijk (1987), van Leeuwen (1995), Martín-Rojo (1997, 2003) and Wodak (2000). Their analytical contributions, in combination with those from the fields of the ethnography of communication and of interaction analysis, allowed me to address the challenges of the previously mentioned view of interactions as part of a web of social activities in which people's trajectories intersect those of the material artifacts and discourses circulating at a given moment in a defined socioeconomic space.

In this field, specific attention is paid to the textual, semiotic, and linguistic resources (e.g., the management of agent/patient semantic roles, predicating strategies, lexical choice, argumentation schemata, the distribution of para-textual elements, or a combination of different semiotic codes) by which people construct, legitimate, and naturalize certain forms of knowledge (about events, social actors, and social relationships, among other aspects) under the historical and economic conditions of a given social order. In other words, this tradition explores the discursive mechanisms underlying Foucault's (1975) idea of power and knowledge as being mutually constitutive. I decided to apply this view to examine the ways by which my participants in the three experimental schools made sense of their everyday practices and of the social and moral categories emerging from these practices.

I was interested in examining the discursive traces connecting situated practices in the space of the three schools and other institutional documents and wider political discourses being produced and circulated in remote space-times beyond the school walls. For this reason, during the fieldwork I collected as many samples as possible of discourses from institutional voices, documents, and material/electronic objects. But I did not do so in disconnection from the methodological approaches outlined in the previous subsections. On the contrary, my collection of samples of discourses circulating within the schools was ethnographically and interactionally driven, which enabled me to overcome the limitations of critical discourse analysis to give a useful account of the emic processes in meaning-making construction practices (Blommaert & Bulcaen, 2000).

Thus, I paid close attention to verbal and multimodal discourses concerned with the interactional practices that were ethnographically relevant to the kind of research questions I was asking. This sometimes took the form of interviews with the participants in such practices (teachers, students, school principals), as I sought to understand specific aspects about the nature of the analyzed interactions (What meaning does a person attribute to a particular observed action or activity? What explanations does s/he provide to make sense of how such activities unfold? How do they relate to the social and institutional world in which s/he lives?). In the course of these interviews, the teachers, students, and school principals often referred to institutional discourses contained in official discourses and in the schools' policy documents—although this was always in combination with nonofficial statements and more or less unvoiced complaints, as we will see in the remaining chapters in this book.

Apart from the interviews, I also examined how daily practices were represented in the schools' official documents, where institutionally embodied discourses were often present in the form of rationalization, authorization, and moral evaluation anchored in specific references to wider educational and political discourses, slogans, concepts, and labels. This included not only school policy documents, but also all forms of multimodal objects (panels, signs, sculptures, etc.) that were widespread around the schools' material spaces and installations, in discursive coexistence/concurrence with the socially-constructed-as-key daily practices. In fact, some of my participants would mention these objects in informal conversations with me (pointing them out or even taking me directly to their locations during break times) when explaining those practices, in order to exemplify/illustrate/frame their cultural-philosophical-institutional foundations—and the fact that I was usually constructed as a "cultural other" or as "culturally distant", as we saw in Chapter 1, contributed to this pedagogical use of objects during conversations with me.

The articulation of ethnographic, interactional, and discursive analytical perspectives resulted in a broad-based data corpus, including field notes (960 pages); video/audio recordings of extraclassroom practices (19 hours) and in sixth/eighth grade English-language classrooms (52 classes of 45 minutes each); interviews with school members (principals, teachers, and students) (9 hours); questionnaires addressed to teachers (6) and students (30); e-mail communications (12); institutional documents (3); the English-language curriculum for experimental schools (1); pictures and samples of institutional spaces, objects, panels, and posters to which everyday activity was oriented (185); schools' Web pages (3); and English-language textbooks (3), workbooks (4), and complementary pedagogical resources used in the English-language classrooms studied (98).

Such a varied collection of data, obtained from the three combined analytical perspectives, has been considered by some as a good empirical base to ensure the validity and reliability of interpretations in ethnographic research (see Jick, 1979; Cherryholmes, 1988; Schensul, Schensul, & LeCompte, 1999, for a review of ways of triangulating different types of data in ethnographically oriented research). In my opinion, and as has also been pointed out by Hornberger (1995: 245–246), the articulation of these data opens up an interesting viewpoint to study how sociocultural identities, forms of participation, and social norms are (re)constructed through educational activity, in a dialogical relationship with processes of (re)production and challenge of wider ideologies and discourses in society.

These ontological assumptions and epistemological concerns that have been reviewed in previous sections rest on underlying conceptual shifts regarding our understanding of language, culture, and identity; of the school setting, and of the field of second language education. Therefore, it is worth unfolding these shifts, and their corresponding consequences for the rationale behind this book, before returning to the story of the experimental schools studied in China.

2.3 KEY CONCEPTUAL SHIFTS

2.3.1 Language, Culture, and Identity: From Universal Entities to Social Constructions

In accordance with the previously described ontological views about social reality, this book takes language, culture, and identity as social constructions that are locally produced, redefined, and challenged under the particular socioeconomic and political conditions of a situated space-time location. That is, these entities are not conceived of as natural objects that exist on their own, in isolation from the social world to which they refer; they are approached as linguistic and cultural products resulting from processes of socioeconomic and political organization (Gal, 1989; Schieffelin, Woolard, & Kroskrity, 1998; Irvine & Gal, 2000; Kroskrity, 2000). This conceptualization, therefore, makes sense within the positivist breakdown in social studies, which entails a critique of the structuralist search for universal scientific principles in linguistic and anthropological inquiry.

As Bauman and Briggs (2003: 59–69) have noted, universality was once a legitimate empirical endeavor against the importation of Darwinist ideas of language and culture in linguistics and anthropology. By claiming the existence of a universal human capacity to develop equally sophisticated languages and cultures, this principle laid down a solid foundation to challenge the representation of languages and cultures as organic entities that are hierarchically organized according to a linear scale of biological evolution.[1] That is to say, the introduction of structuralism by linguists and anthropologists, and the search for universal principles, allowed them to dismantle the discourses and categories about "primitive", "impure", or "advanced" languages/cultures that had been produced and mobilized in Europe during the 19th century to justify colonialism/imperialism in the name of modern civilization projects.[2] However, Bauman and Briggs call our attention to the role of universalism in contributing, at the same time, to naturalizing and protecting the socioeconomic interests of those who had invested in the constitution of the modern nation-states.

In the ideological framework of modern nationalism, language, culture, and identity are abstracted and represented as symbolic properties that are shared by the whole nation, constituting it as the organic body of a distinguishable sovereign state. They are conceived of as key discursive elements in the legitimization of the one language-one culture-one identity-one sovereign state equation. Most importantly, their abstraction—shared by the whole nation—is constructed as a necessary guarantee for the equitable participation of all nation members within the political structures of the state (one and the same language, culture, and identity for all). Thus, as we are reminded by those who have criticized modern nationalism, the cultural and linguistic standardization policies carried out during the 20th century were crucial for the survival of the modern nation-state (Higonnet, 1980; Grillo, 1989; Hobsbawm, 1990).

These authors have pointed out that such standardization policies have contributed to representing the modern nation-state as democratic ("liberté, égalité, fraternité"), in contrast with the supposedly autarchical (but also disordered, chaotic, and illogical) societies of premodern times, even when these cultural/linguistic standards have always been based on the linguistic and cultural practices of the bourgeoisie in each context. In this regard, the representation of language, culture, and identity as true objects of scientific knowledge detached from social dynamics (these dynamics being represented as chaotic and disturbing for our knowledge of the "real world") has contributed to exercise a "symbolic domination" (Bourdieu, 1972) through the establishment of a "regime of truth" (Foucault, 1970) that neutralizes the very processes of linguistic and cultural standardization in which the socioeconomic and political organization of modern nationalism resides. That is, their representation as separated from social structures naturalizes the cultural politics of dominant social groups by constructing these politics as "right" or "normal" for everyone, therefore legitimating these social groups' privileged position in the production, circulation, and valuation of the cultural resources (e.g., forms of language use, its varieties, accents, or even subjectivities) that allow access to the state's key social and institutional spaces.

This critique of universality in the study of linguistic and cultural life, therefore, has placed social inequality and power relations at the center of attention. In other words, critical and interpretative research in linguistics and anthropology has shifted the focus of attention away from the systematization of autonomous linguistic and cultural systems toward a close examination of the social differences that the situated fieldwork of anthropologists and sociolinguists has long documented within local social groups and communities. Under such an intellectual breakdown, structuralist concepts and metaphors for the description of language, culture, and identity are no longer suitable. The study of social processes of differentiation requires new poststructuralist concepts and metaphors that do not take for granted the existence of abstract, autonomous, static, and bounded entities corresponding to a single factor, such as language, culture, or identity.

Among alternatives proposed are the Bourdiean and Foucauldian notions of "symbolic capital" (Bourdieu, 1982), "legitimate language" (Bourdieu, 1977), or "power" (Foucault, 1984), which conceptualize language, culture, and identity as "fields", "markets", or "discursive spaces" traversed by historical processes of socioeconomic organization. In other words, these entities are represented as symbolic resources that are socially and discursively produced, attributed value to, and unequally distributed according to the restrictions of a given socioeconomic order in which people have different degrees of control over those very processes of attribution of value and circulation, as well as over their discursive legitimization.[3] In Heller's terms (2007a: 84–85),

They make sense within conceptual spaces shot through with power, within ways of understanding the world that are deeply interested, and that can be understood as regimes of truth in the Foucauldian sense: shared frames of reference and practices of signification that construct, legitimate, and mask relations of power (Foucault, 1970). The term "resources" in this sense comprises interchangeable material and symbolic practices or things, whose sense is part of the knowledge-power nexus to which both Foucault and Bourdieu attached so much importance (indeed, Bourdieu insists frequently on the role of the exchangeability of material and symbolic forms of capital in processes of social reproduction).

This conceptual shift, therefore, has implications on how we should observe the experimental schools described in this book. Apart from its impact on the decisions taken regarding data collection, selection, and analysis, this shift requires us to take careful note of the moral of the story that emerges from these schools. The exploration of such schools' everyday life is not an open window to an autonomous culture, corresponding to a geographically/temporally abstracted and unique China, to be extrapolated and compared with data emerging from other national (and unique) contexts. On the contrary, the analysis of their daily practices, as we began to see in the previous chapter, is an opportunity to identify the local discursive transformation (which may or may not be replicated in other schools inside and outside China) by which these three communities, the experimental schools in the here-and-now of the study, reconstituted themselves in response to wider discourses and socioeconomic processes of change at institutional, national, and international orders. This discursive transformation, moreover, goes beyond unifying imaginaries in that, as we will see in subsequent chapters, the spaces of the schools were by no means coherent, but were traversed by different discourses, produced and circulated in line with varied social interests and investments.

Approaching all these issues not only entails an explicit positioning in the poststructural shift within the fields of linguistics and anthropology. It also requires a sociological approach to the school setting, which constitutes another established field from which my perspectives, analyses and claims draw inspiration—in fact, this field is of interest to sociologists, and also to sociolinguists and anthropologists who pursue interests in the study of social difference and power.

2.3.2　The School Setting: From Neutral Space to Late Modern State Institution

In a critical sociolinguistic ethnography focused on the educational setting, the school is taken as an institutional space. In other words, the school cannot be detached from the social and discursive processes by which the ideological framework of the modern nation-state is institutionalized, reproduced, naturalized, and contested/transformed under late modern economic and cultural conditions. In adopting such a sociocultural stance, this book distances itself from approaches that view school knowledge construction as a cognitive (pure, nonsocially constructed) transfer between minds which occurs in a neutral space. Indeed, this stance emerges from the linguistic, sociological, and anthropological studies that since the 1960s have reacted to an observed and persistent unequal distribution of school failure among students in modern societies—regarding social class, ethnicity, and/or gender (Jacob & Jordan, 1993: 3–11).

The sociocultural theories provided to explain such an unequal distribution of school failure have, however, varied greatly over recent decades. Among them, those pointing to cultural deficit, social difference, and social domination have been most prominent. Hence, a brief review of their contributions and limitations will provide a historical and disciplinary perspective from which we may better understand the specific implications of an approach to the school as an institutional space tied to the late modern cultural and political economies of the state in the 21st century. On the one hand, the cultural deficit explanation, which has been disciplinarily linked to Bernstein's (1964) sociolinguistic work, contributed an initial vocabulary with which to describe sociocultural differences in students' academic results.

In response to those who during the first half of the 20th century posited the existence of a genetic deficit, as an explanation of the high rate of school failure among certain groups of students (see Brace, Gamble, & Bond, 1971, as an illustrative example of this argument), the cultural deficit theory referred to a social class dimension. In particular, according to this stance, a poverty culture or "restricted code" was the main reason why the children of low socioeconomic status groups performed worse, academically, in each national context (Bernstein, 1964: 62). In other words, the family socialization of the children in these social groups was taken as the main cause of their nonaccess to cultural and linguistic means of success at school:

> A restricted code is available to all members of society as the social conditions which generate it are universal. But it may be that a considerable section of our society has access only to this code by virtue of the implications of the class background. I am suggesting that here there is a relatively high probability of finding children limited to this code among sections of the lower working-class population. On this argument, the general form of their speech is not substandard English but is related to and shares a similar social origin with the restricted code I have just outlined. It is a special case where children can use one and only one speech system. What this code makes relevant to them, the learning generated by apparently spontaneous acts of speech, is not appropriate for their formal educational experience. (Bernstein, 1964: 62)

Although this approach constituted a starting point in the search for social models explaining educational inequality, it ended up being strongly criticized as ethnocentric—often unfairly, as a result of a misinterpretation of

Bernstein's early work, possibly related to some of the unfortunate concepts he used to support his ideas. The cultural deficit approach was taken as relying on middle-class experiences and views, in that it represented the working class culture as monolithic in contrast to a supposedly culturally homogeneous elite social class that might be misunderstood as the norm. Indeed, the work done by other sociolinguists in the 1960s highlighted the richness and complexity underlying the linguistic practices of those social groups attributed to a taken-for-granted deficit culture (see Labov, 1969, 1972; Wolfram, 1969).

On the other hand, the social difference explanation provided by American sociolinguists and anthropologists such as Gumperz (1982) focused on the interactional processes of socialization by which different social groups build up their culturally ritualized conventions. From this perspective, school failure is viewed as the result of an institutional process of evaluation in which one social group sanctions the conventions of others according to its own, and whereby conventions are conceptualized as agreed social norms that enable common understandings and shared frames of interpretation:

> Independent ethnographic evidence from work in urban school settings highlights the importance of some of the interpretative issues illustrated here. Note that [. . .] "help me" [. . .], [. . .] "I don't wanna read" [. . .] and [. . .] "I don't know" [. . .] have similar formulaic interpretations which are specific to black cultural traditions. They all tend to be understood as requests for cooperation which may be motivated by no more than a desire for company, or friendly support. The formulaicness of such utterances is marked syntactically by phrases like "I don't", "I can't" followed by a predicate and prosodically by a characteristic intonation contour. This contour accents the predicate and thus serves to identify the formula. Other American listeners, however, who are not attuned to these cues tend to rely on their own system to interpret these phrases as confessions of inability to perform the task at hand or expressions of helplessness and indirect requests for assistance. (Gumperz, 1982: 149–150)

In other words, school failure is explained as the consequence of the co-existence of different social groups that, while socialized in the framework of different cultural conventions, have to accommodate themselves to those of the group(s) controlling the institutional spaces of the state. In the school space, this is reflected in the organization of everyday routines, which are based on the cultural conventions and assumptions of the dominant group. In this way, the social categorization of students as competent or incompetent depends on the (majority and minority) students' degree of knowledge about these conventions (Gumperz, 1986: 47).[4] The present approach represents an attempt to take Bernstein's work further and to avoid some of the criticisms addressed to him, although it has often been pointed out that it is necessary to extend it and incorporate power relations into the processes whereby school failure is unequally distributed.

In fact, analysts of the social difference explanation have observed that this approach can easily lead to a simplifying culturalism. In particular, it has been associated with a representation of ethno-cultural groups as being unified and static, in a transversal model in which cultural and communicative differences and school failure are syntagmatically equated, and where the socioeconomic and institutional conditions under which certain social groups are disadvantaged are not sufficiently taken into account (Kandiah, 1991; Meeuwis & Sarangi, 1994).

Finally, the domination explanation relies on statistics showing that in each nation-state there are particular social groups that, in the educational space, have historically failed. On the basis of these statistics, it is argued that communicative differences in socialization practices between majority and minority groups are not enough to account for the complexity of the social issues involved in the unequal distribution of school failure. Indeed, from this standpoint, the use of cultural difference to explain this unequal distribution may be viewed as dangerous, in that it contributes to the ideological justification of established forms of social organization. If the lack of incorporation of minority social groups' cultural knowledge in the school is considered to be the cause of their high rate of school failure, then the solution seems to be of a pedagogical nature rather than one requiring a more profound consideration of socioeconomic structures.

On the basis of this objection, the domination approach developed by sociologists like John Ogbu (1992) states that formal education is tied to a social structure of unequally distributed economic opportunities, which tend to produce differentiated cultural identities and social strategies in accordance with the degree of trust that different social groups place in the school system. The historically disadvantaged position occupied by some groups in the socioeconomic order, such as Afro-Americans in the United States or Roma in Europe, is related to the conformation of a collective identity constructed upon a lack of investment in formal schooling and forms of certification as well as upon a resistant attitude to hegemonic cultural practices by the state. On the contrary, the voluntary incorporation of some social groups in the latter social position, as a means of working for a better future, an attitude that is adopted by certain migrant groups in diverse countries, is related to a collective identity where investment in formal education and acculturation is seen as necessary for social mobility (Ogbu, 1992: 13).

This explanation proposes a more complex interrelationship between cultural difference and social inequality, in that the former is not unequivocally represented as the cause of the latter; on the contrary, it is the consequence. In other words, cultural difference is problematized and placed at the center of wider social processes involving economic structures, collective identities, and strategies of contestation/cultural reproduction. Yet there are important issues lacking, as remarked by those who are concerned by the social representation of the school as a "black box" space between students' lives and hierarchical socioeconomic divisions, as suggested in this approach (Cazden & Mehan, 1989; Erickson, 1993).

With respect to this domination approach, particularly useful work was done by Bourdieu and Passeron (1977), going beyond issues of trust in social reproduction theory to shed light on the institutional processes by which the cultural practices/values of the bourgeoisie in the modern nation-state are legitimated and naturalized on the basis of a meritocratic representation of the educational institution. Bourdieu described how the moral categorization of students (as "good" or "bad") emerges from a specific logic of practice around which knowledge is arranged and normalized in everyday life. Nonetheless, he has also been criticized because, although oriented to dialectically transcend the opposition between objectivism and subjectivism, his approach is still considered essentially deterministic and circular (Jenkins, 1982).

These three sociocultural explanations, with their respective strengths and weaknesses, constitute the frame of reference within which this book examines the three experimental schools studied in China. Thus, the school is conceptualized as a key institutional space for the cultural reproduction of an "imagined community" (Anderson, 1983: 6) which contributes to the socioeconomic and political interests of the social groups that seek to establish it and benefit from it.[5] However, these processes of sociocultural reproduction are not considered as being achieved by unconscious domination or social consensus. Probably, they never were, although the increasing conversationalization (Fairclough, 1992) resulting from contemporary processes of democratization, neoliberalization (marshaling of the state), consumerism, and technologization is bringing about new conditions that make institutional authority and imposition harder to work.

Under these new conditions, it may be more useful to look at the school as a discursive space traversed by local processes of uncertainty, negotiation, and discontinuity where dense social relations and learning are built up in complex and unexpected ways—sometimes in line with official goals, sometimes in confrontation with them, sometimes aside from them (see Jaspers, 2005; Bucholtz & Skapoulli, 2009; Chun, 2009; Harris & Rampton, 2009). Local processes of uncertainty and discontinuity may vary depending on the institutional context being examined. For this reason, in this book I do not take it for granted that what has been extensively described for the educational contexts of Europe and North America is likely to be found in the same nature, intensity, and form elsewhere.

Late modern conditions, as emphasized and illustrated in Chapter 1 with regard to the intersection between modernity and coloniality in China, may involve specific economic, political, and historical factors that need to be taken into account if ethnocentric (and potentially neocolonial) interpretations are to be avoided. Thus, careful precautions are taken in the subsequent chapters to avoid creating a picture of the three experimental schools in China in accordance with processes found in other contexts where late modernity is linked to liberal democratization.

Apart from the school setting, these social and discursive approaches also have implications for the conceptualization of the classroom activity within the domains of each curricular subject, such as that of second language education, which is a prime focus of this book.

2.3.3 Second Language Education: From Pedagogical Concerns to Language Ideology

Taking a social and discursive stance in the field of second language education is often misunderstood as being concerned with critiquing the everyday pedagogical activities of second language teachers and with opening their eyes by providing them with new and more effective teaching-learning strategies. However, sociolinguists doing critical ethnography in the educational setting do not seek to tell teachers what to do in their own environments; for one reason, their research interests (and knowledge expertise) are not oriented to designing teaching methodologies. Instead, they wish to analyze how certain educational arrangements of classroom activity and official discourses about those arrangements are socio-institutionally constructed on the basis of particular views of languages and how to teach/learn them in a way that makes sense under specific socioeconomic, historical, and political conditions.

Such a conceptual shift, from pedagogical concerns toward socioeconomic/political issues, is anchored in two concrete poststructural moves in second language education studies that involve scrutinizing the notion of method in pedagogy, on the one hand, and incorporating language ideologies as a relevant dimension to understand the institutional organization of classroom activity, on the other. Regarding the educational notion of method, this has been questioned in connection with critiques of the search for universal principles in social sciences, as reviewed in Section 2.2.1. Thus, a social/discursive approach to language education entails a total rejection of the representation of method as ideologically free, as it is considered to be a form of knowledge that is socially (historically, politically, economically) situated (Apple, 1979, 1986; Harris, 1979; Popkewitz, 1984; Simon, 1987; Giroux, 1988; Giroux & McLaren, 1989).

In contrast to the positivist educational philosophy from which the very concept of method emerges in pedagogy, this approach rests on the concerns of those who have pointed out that the modern ideas of progress, rationality, and objectivity that underpin educational methods in second language teaching have resulted in the legitimization of relations of social inequality between American/European scholars (and related language teaching industries) who propose prescriptive models (and textbooks) for the organization of classroom activities and language teachers in the rest of the world who are supposed to implement (buy) them (Phillipson, 1988: 348). Indeed, these prescriptive models have been disciplinarily constructed as more or less "progressivist" in relation to a supposedly linear (evolutionary) scale in which the different educational methods are categorized, between traditional/old-fashioned and modern/advanced, depending on their degree of fit to the sociocultural and economic standards (values) sanctioned by the social actors in Anglo-Saxon contexts:

> The Method construct that has been the predominant paradigm used to conceptualize teaching not only fails to account adequately for [. . .] historical conditions, but also is conceptually inconsistent, conflating categories and types at all levels and failing to demonstrate intellectual rigor. It is also highly questionable whether so-called methods ever reflected what was actually going on in classrooms [. . .] if the argument has been that all knowledge is interested, we may indeed want to ask what interests are served by particular forms of knowledge. It is therefore important both to understand the construction of the Method concept within an apolitical, ahistorical, positivist, and progressivist orientation to education, and to investigate the effects of the production of that knowledge. This knowledge, then, should be seen within its political context and, more specifically, in its relationship to the political economy of textbook publishing, the hierarchical nature of knowledge production, the gendered issue of teaching practice, and educational imperialism in the teaching of English as an international language. (Pennycook, 1989: 608–609)

In line with this critique, the focus of research in classroom discourse studies has shifted in recent decades, from prescriptive to descriptive models. Thus, an increasing body of literature has emerged whereby greater emphasis is placed on making a detailed analysis of the situated practices between teachers and students in classroom activity (Sinclair & Coulthard, 1975; Mehan, 1979; Cazden, 1988; Tsui, 1995). This changing focus of attention has played a crucial role in the incorporation of language ideologies as a relevant dimension of study, which is the second aspect mentioned above in relation to post-structural developments in research into second language education.

The work done by those who have focused on the systematic description of situated classroom practices has enabled comparisons to be made across different contexts. In turn, this has highlighted the institutional order in the organization of what happens in the classroom within each curricular subject. Teachers and students negotiate meaning in unexpected ways in the course of their joint social actions in classroom activity; however, as Seedhouse (2004) pointed out, these social actions are constrained by institutional arrangements (physical settings, the distribution of students across levels/classrooms/subjects, educational systems/structures, teaching materials, etc.) and official goals (e.g., educational objectives or curriculum designs) that are ultimately related to regional, national, and international policies, in areas such as educational laws and guidelines, economic provisions, market demands, and international cooperation agreements.

In the case of second language education classrooms, all these interrelations are enacted in the terrain of language. In this regard, the institutional organization of classroom activity cannot be detached from the language planning policies that are locally implemented in response to socioeconomic conditions at local, national, and international orders. More specifically, the dynamics of social change in institutionalized second language education cannot be properly apprehended if we do not take into account the fact that views on what is considered to be language competence, bilingualism, or multilingualism have changed over the course of history in accordance with shifting local and global socioeconomic conditions (Heller, 2007b).

As Pujolar (2006) remarked, the contemporary development of transnational markets, networks, and mobilities is bringing about new conditions where fixed borders, uniformized groups and standard languages as a whole are called into question, in contrast to the conditions of early modernity when language was located at the heart of the legitimating discourse of the nation-state (again, one language, one culture, one nation, one state). Under these late modern socioeconomic conditions, languages are thus coming to be represented as necessary skills for successful participation in the new postindustrial and globalized economy; that is, languages are being socially and institutionally represented as a necessary capital in the process of economic (delocalized) production (where communication is crucial to the organization of economic activity in each and every sector) rather than as a product (as in the industrial, localized, and Fordist economy, where communication plays a less important role).

Nevertheless, as Cameron (1995) reminds us, old ideas about languages remain in contemporary life, as nation-states continue to be key actors in the socioeconomic organization of people (and markets) at both local and global orders (see also Gal, 1995; Blommaert, 1999; Blackledge, 2005). This is why, for example, discourses on multilingual skills are constructed today in ways that still represent bilingualism and multilingualism as parallel (separated, bounded, uniformized, fixed) monolingualisms that allow for the reproduction of the social order within each nation-state (Moyer & Martín-Rojo, 2007; Pujolar, 2007; Codó, 2008; Márquez-Réiter & Martín-Rojo, 2010). In other words, these new discourses on the importance of bilingualism and multilingualism for participation in the international market still restrict access to each of the national markets involved as they continue to legitimate the monolingual linguistic practices of native speakers against the plural and hybrid ones of those who are not.

Thus it can be seen that ideological transformations concerning the conceptualization of languages do have an impact on what counts as appropriate ways of teaching/learning languages in institutional settings. Comparative educational research, from a sociolinguistic/discursive perspective, has shown the extent to which second language teaching practices are locally configured from the distinct constellations of old and new language ideologies at regional, national, and international orders (see Heller & Martin-Jones, 2001; Block & Cameron, 2002; Lin & Martin, 2005; Kubota & Lin, 2009). In other words, these studies make it possible to identify how local teaching practices are connected with the linguistic views about bi- or multilingualism emerging from how regional, national, and international interests are played out in the course of historical developments in each particular context—these historical conditions being regarded in connection with processes of social stratification that in turn are linked to globalization, colonialism, postcolonialism, or nationalism.

Wider pedagogical discourses about suitable teaching models and materials have also been linked to these historical shifts in views on language (see Dendrinos, 1992, for an ideological overview of the different language education methods, from traditional to contemporary approaches). Thus, changes in methodological emphasis, from grammatical structures (e.g., traditional and audio-lingual methods) to oral communication (e.g., communicative language teaching) should be contextualized within the wider socioeconomic and linguistic needs arising from the changing forms of political economy in each space/time—from the role of written texts and translation activities in the industrial economy of modernity to the importance of face-to-face, interpersonal, and multimodal communication in the postindustrial globalized economy of late modernity.

In the vein of this socioeconomic/political shift in the study of second language education, the consideration of the interplay between (a) these socioeconomic processes of change at local/national/international orders, (b) the ideas about languages, and (c) the discourses/practices of teaching-learning them warns us to avoid simplistic perspectives regarding issues of power relations. This is particularly the case of the institutionalization of teaching/learning English across the world, which, as noted by Lin and Martin (2005), has long been associated with unilateral and monolithic imperialisms by certain nation-states over others. Although this perspective has allowed us to identify and criticize the language policies by which colonialism was historically constructed and naturalized for the benefit of small social groups in the metropoles of the 19th and 20th centuries, it fails to make sense of the new processes of social restructuring by which local social elites position themselves in each context under the conditions of contemporary economic globalization in the postcolonial world:

> The forceful, legitimate (and delegitimized) "return" (if it has ever departed, perhaps only temporarily, as in the history of postcolonial Malaysia) of English as a dominant language and/or medium of instruction in the education system to postcolonial contexts riding on new wings of global capitalism cannot be described simply as "the Empire strikes back"—for this time the "Empire" is both invisible and non-monolithic, as it is dissolved into the "Globe" taking the form of various (sometimes conflictual) forces of globalisation, and it is not necessarily one-sidedly against national and local community interests (as seen in the postcolonial governments' and local communities' growing desire for English for both national and personal interest [. . .] English is neither a Western

monolithic entity nor necessarily an imposed reality, and local peoples are capable of penetrating English with their own intentions and social styles. English as appropriate by local agents serves diverse sets of intentions and purposes in their respective local contexts. (Lin & Martin, 2005: 4–5)

Taken together, the three key conceptual shifts discussed in the preceding text provide an account of the kind of approach adopted in this book to the study of English-language education in the three experimental schools studied in China. As we will see in Chapter 5, the study of English-language teaching in these schools is not intended to convey a pedagogical description of classroom practices in order to classify China's contemporary English-language education as fitting into one or another methodological (abstracted, idealized) tradition. On the contrary, the goal of this study is to understand those classroom practices/discourses as being closely bound to the institutional transformations that contemporary Chinese national education is undergoing (and which will be described in Chapters 3 and 4), in response to the national and international processes of economic, political, and sociocultural change discussed in Chapter 1.

However, these shifts do not imply that teachers align with the official discourses univocally; nor that they are unaware of the links between official practices/discourses in their local contexts and the wider (interested) social processes of change outside their schools. In an attempt to overcome this kind of narrow focus, I have sought to prioritize teachers', school principals', and students' social actions/voices, to shed light on the local tensions they all face in the context of institutional transformations. That is to say, I wish to avoid any conceptualization of discourse as a monolithic entity projected from the top down that can only be identified by the expert/analyst for the benefit of the whole world (including his/her participants). Instead, my theoretical positioning is aimed at providing a more nuanced description of school practices, in general, and of English-language teaching, in particular, viewing these as forming a kaleidoscopic social space where multiple perspectives (individual, interpersonal, and institutional) can coexist in complex but describable ways.

These are the ontological views and epistemological concerns that characterize the theoretical and methodological options of the critical sociolinguistic ethnography on which this book is based. It is now time to return to the analysis derived from these concerns, and to continue the story begun in Chapter 1 about the Chinese experimental schools in Zhejiang province. The following chapters, therefore, describe the discursive transformations taking place in their daily institutional life, starting with those concerning the social images each school had to display in response to contemporary Chinese national demands for modernization. Chapter 3 focuses on this particular demand and on the resulting tensions experienced by all involved.

3 Three Social Images for Three Competitive Schools

3.1 BEING A "GOOD" EXPERIMENTAL SCHOOL

After my first visits to the three schools studied in Zhejiang province, I spent a considerable time coming to understand the specific implications of the institutional category of "experimental school" (实验学校) on their everyday discursive organization. As noted in Chapter 1, Section 1.1, this categorization is directly linked to institutional and discursive changes regarding national education modernization under the socioeconomic and political conditions of late modern China; that is, these institutions are undergoing far-reaching transformations—as pioneers, preceding all other schools in China—in response to current guidelines and policies aimed at adapting the Chinese educational system to the new globalizing economy.

These guidelines and policies, as we saw in the description of how I was socially constructed during the fieldwork (see Chapter 1, Section 1.2), set out the conditions for the institutionalization of discourses of internationalism, West/China interculturalism, and institutional excellence. Accordingly, the schools in question referred to these discourses in order to represent themselves as "excellent" institutions, putting into practice innovative actions to incorporate Western languages and cultures into their educational communities without losing their presumed Chinese educational specificity. However, one question remains to be answered, regarding the specific transformations faced by these schools: what are the particular criteria they had to meet in order to acquire and maintain the institutional category of experimental school?

To understand the institutional logic underlying the current modernization reforms, we must focus closely on how these three schools evolved to meet the requirements to be considered "good" experimental schools. Exploration of the social construction of what was involved in this adaptation provides a useful insight into the discursive reorganization by which the schools adjusted to the new resources (symbolic or material) being nationally distributed/allocated. With the goal of addressing these local/institutional/national processes, I posed explicit questions in this respect in the course of the interviews, particularly with the heads of the schools. See, for example, the interview conducted with Mr. Wang (Extract 3.1), who talked about some of the characteristics that he believed made his experimental school outstanding in Hangzhou city:

Extract 3.1 "This Is a Flagship School in Hangzhou"

Wang: 这个学校在杭州那是一流的 / 为什么是一流呢？
this is a flagship school in Hangzhou / why flagship?

Miguel: 为什么？[laugh]
why?

Wang: 一 / 他的教师队伍 / 教师的素质比较高 // 那么我们学校的老师 / 在杭州市 / 基本上都是很有威望的 // 那这是最主要的 // 第二 / 学校也比较漂亮 / 它设施也比较好 // 我们学校的这个教学的设备 / 在中国乃至于在全世界都还是算好的 / 像我们有很多的活动的场地 / 体育馆就有两个 / 我们有篮球馆 / 有游泳馆 / 有羽毛球馆 / 我们什么都有 / 让学生- 孩子在这里学习他有一个很好的发展的空间 // 第三 / 我们学校的这个 管理 非常的 规范 // 学生 / 你去看 / 他的这个形象 / 他的表情 / 他的气质都看上去都是非常活泼的 // 当然这是第三 / 第四 / 那么我们通过这个几年的这样一种奋斗 / 那么已经形成了我们中国人非常重要的一个指标 / 就是教学的质量 / 就是学生考高一级学校的那种比例 / 比较高 // 第四呢 / 我们跟其他学校比呢 / 他这个学校很有特色

*first / its teaching staff / the quality of the teachers is higher // so our teachers / in Hangzhou / basically they are all top rank // so this is the most important // second / the school is also nicer / the facilities are better as well // these teaching facilities of our school / are considered good in China and even at a world level / like the various sport venues that we have / there are two gymnasiums / we have a basketball court / swimming pool / badminton court / we have everything / it has a good atmosphere to let students—kids learn here // third / our school's MANAGEMENT is very highly REGULATED // the student / go and have a look / his image / his facial expression / his temperament everything looks magnificent everything is lively // of course this is the third / fourth / this type of struggle that we have gone through during the past few years / has become a very important indicator for us the Chinese / just quality of education / just the proportion of the students who succeed in the National Higher Education Entrance Examination and enter high-level educational institutions / is higher / then the fourth / compared to others our school / this school is quite distinctive *

(Interview with a head of school; recording code: 23dp_Zh_S07122006E)

In a conversation with Mr. Wang about the characteristics of good experimental schools in China, he states that his is a "flagship" school in the city of Hangzhou and goes on to ask a rhetorical question (immediately reinforced by my own request) that opens up a monologue in which he provides specific arguments in support of this claim. The monologue belongs to the argumentative genre, where a clear structure of separated, enumerated, and well-delineated reasons is constructed in what seems to be a solid explanation based on clear-cut institutional and bureaucratic criteria. These criteria are concerned with organizational elements at different levels involving the hiring of prestigious teachers, the allocation of multifunction teaching facilities, the implementation of a regulated management apparatus, the ensuring of high student pass rates for the (nationally centralized) university entrance examinations, with very good results, and the performing of a distinctive role.

These different elements were recursively elicited during my interviews with the heads of the three schools. As a concrete manifestation of the latest modernization reforms they have had to adjust to, their schools are expected to achieve "quality education". This broad educational goal implies their commitment to the previously commented criteria, which in turn determine their institutional recognition as "experimental" and grant a prestigious position among state schools. Indeed, their labeling as experimental increases their public visibility, with their inclusion in the official ranking of the most innovative public educational institutions at municipal, provincial, and national levels in China.[1]

As part of an educational model in which registration fees are not fixed, and where parents have the right to choose the school for their children at the municipality level, this social prestige enables these schools to attract higher numbers of students, at higher fees, with which to continue funding state-of-the-art teaching facilities and hiring teachers graduated from the best universities in the region—whose higher salaries must be partially met by the schools themselves. These teachers are in fact selected by the experimental schools even before they finish their degrees; as is often recognized, "[他们]去到学校里面去选今年毕业的学生/ 我是被选中的" (they go to the school to select those who just graduated / I am selected).

In addition, the fact that experimental schools receive more entry applications allows them to choose only those students with the best educational records, therefore ensuring higher rates of successful students accessing higher education. Maintaining recognition of their status, therefore, is regarded by the school heads as crucial in this financially decentralized system that impels schools to compete for students' registrations in order to cover part of their educational budgets. However, these three experimental schools seek to preserve their institutional recognition by diverse means, in line with the official requirements to conform to the prescribed guidelines without losing uniqueness. Furthermore, in my interviews, it was not always easy to identify these different ways of responding to institutional demands, as the information received proved to be insufficient to account for all the transformations observed.

In contrast to the common assumption that interviews by themselves give direct access to the participants' thoughts and therefore to an abstract truth that is "out there" waiting to be captured by the researcher, in reality they constitute a social practice that must be considered in the interplay between the social relations and identities being negotiated in the course of the conversation. The clear structure of separated, enumerated, and well-delineated principles that emerges from Extract 3.1, for example, must be placed in the context of a formal interview between an academic researcher and a school principal that is taking place in the latter's office. In fact, the observation of everyday life in schools often reveals greater complexity and uncertainty than do official accounts. This was certainly the case with my fieldwork in Zhejiang; whereas the previously mentioned requirements were recursively elicited in the interviews with the school heads, a multisite observation of their institutions' daily life revealed important discontinuities regarding their discursive organization as spaces of educational excellence.

These institutions engaged in the discursive production of different social images, each of which was pervaded by internal contradictions and paradoxes. In the following sections of this chapter I will provide a more detailed ethnographic description of how these distinct social images emerge from the constellation of discursive practices/products circulating within the schools' social spaces, including the specific and differentiated forms of collaboration coconstructed between the participants and myself in the course of the fieldwork carried out at each site (Section 3.2). The analysis of these differently coconstructed social images, with the resulting tensions and dilemmas for the social actors involved in each case, provides a more nuanced account of the local impact produced by the institutional reforms resulting from the national call for educational modernization. This will lay the groundwork to discuss, in the last section (Section 3.3), the continuities and discontinuities with respect to previous education reforms undertaken during the process of modern nation-state building in China since the early 20th century.

3.2 LOCAL ADAPTATIONS TO NATIONAL DEMANDS: BILINGUALISM, HISTORICAL PEDIGREE, AND SOCIAL COHESION

To begin this three-part story I will examine Hangzhou Primary School,[2] which invested a great deal of discursive work in constructing English/Mandarin bilingualism as its main asset. I then continue with Hangzhou Secondary School, focused on the construction of its historical pedigree as a paramount feature to be exhibited. Finally, I consider Wenzhou Secondary School, where social cohesion played a very important role in everyday life.

3.2.1 Hangzhou Primary School and the Value of Bilingualism

Hangzhou Primary School (see Figure 3.1; note that parts of the real names in the pictures have been deleted to ensure the anonymity of the schools) is located near the central district of Hangzhou, a city renowned for its historical, cultural, and commercial values since ancient times.[3] It is the capital of Zhejiang province and, due to its location at the delta of the Yangtze River, its main economic activities are maritime commerce and tourism.[4] As an educational institution affiliated with one of the main universities in Zhejiang province, the school, at the time of data compilation, was characterized by spacious outdoor installations and technological facilities, as described in Chapter 1, Section 1.1, when referring to some of the commonalities of these three experimental schools.

With regard to the outdoor installations, the main school building was constituted of three 5-floor units in a U-shaped configuration around the main entrance, such that immediately on entering, the visitor was able to see all the classrooms (Figure 3.1). This physical arrangement provided space for more than 1,300 students, in classes with an average size of 50 students. There was also space for a standard synthetic athletics track and various basketball courts, used also for physical and leisure activities during break times (Figure 3.2)

With respect to the technological facilities, the school had an electronic panel sited at the entrance (Figure 3.1) welcoming students every morning and announcing upcoming events of interest to the school community (parents' day, open days, exams, tutorial timetables, notices about staff meetings, extracurricular activities, etc.). In addition, all the teachers' offices contained desktop computers, assigned on an individual basis, and the classrooms were equipped with wide-screen TVs connected to a computer controller at the teacher's desk. One of the most distinctive features of this

Figure 3.1   Entrance to Hangzhou Primary School

school was the significant role played by English, in both material and symbolic spaces. Thus, all the texts displayed in the main entrance, along the corridors, and inside the classrooms were Mandarin/English bilingual signs, providing information about: (a) the institutional affiliation of the school (Figure 3.3); (b) the distribution of the classes, labs, and teachers' offices on

Figure 3.2 Outdoor facilities at Hangzhou Primary School

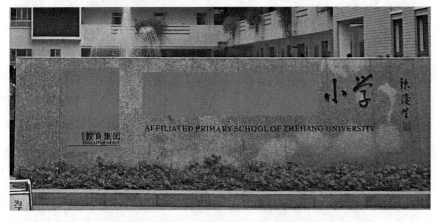

Figure 3.3 Bilingual texts at the entrance, in the corridors, and inside classrooms

each floor (Figure 3.4); and (c) the core educational values of "solidarity", "cooperation", and "politeness" (Figure 3.5).

The school's website also placed strong emphasis on constructing the social image of an institution pursuing Mandarin/English bilingualism. Extract 3.2 is taken from a report published in English by a Chinese journalist who visited the school shortly after the data collection, which was later uploaded verbatim to the school's website. This report makes clear the importance of English in the school as part of an institutional agenda centered on the consolidation of a partnership with an elementary school in California (USA):

Figure 3.4   Bilingual texts at the entrance, in the corridors, and inside classrooms

Figure 3.5 Bilingual texts at the entrance, in the corridors, and inside classrooms

Extract 3.2 "He Has Plans for a Job on Wall Street When He Grows Up"

While kids have work to do, they still have spare time. They like to play, just like kids in America. Video games and Hollywood are not new concepts in China. Harry Potter is a favorite in both countries. When he has time, Hao, a student (. . .), plays video games. "I like to play Game Boy and computer games with my friends," he says. "I have a Nintendo Wii, too." Some of these kids have had the opportunity to visit America. Each year, 30 students from [the school] are selected to go on a summer camp exchange program to visit an elementary school in Palo Alto, California. Yinan participated in the summer program. After seeing America, he has plans for a job on Wall Street when he grows up. Many Chinese parents want to send their children to America to go to school there. In preparation for that, most kids take English as an extracurricular class. This is in addition to the English classes they take in school three times a week starting from third grade.

(Journalist report on the school, later uploaded to the school's website)

The special significance of English was apparent not only in the management of language choice and institutional content in signs and panels within the physical/electronic spaces of the school; it was also salient during the informal conversations I had on a daily basis, when conducting the fieldwork. Although all three schools coconstructed my presence as a resource for them to present the public image of an international institution (see Chapter 1, Section 1.2), the teachers and students at Hangzhou Primary School were particularly focused on the interactional enactment of a supposed Mandarin/English bilingualism. Thus, intense discursive work took place in this school to perform bilingualism as part of everyday life, in contrast to the other two schools, where all my everyday informal conversations took place in Mandarin. Extract 3.3 provides a representative example of the occasions on which teachers and some students collaboratively negotiated these types of performing practices when addressing me during the recess periods, outside the space of the classrooms:

Extract 3.3   "Can I Speak Chinese?"

1 {It is break time between two class periods. 1 I am taking pictures of the athletics track from one of
2 the corridors on the fourth floor while most of the students are playing around. At one point, Shaonan,
3 a sixth-grade student who is not part of the groups I observed, approaches me.}
4 **Shaonan:**   hi!
5 **Miguel:**   你好! {I continue taking pictures without looking back}
6   *hi!*
7 **Shaonan:**   where are you from?
8 **Miguel:**   Spain {I continue taking pictures without looking back}
9 **Shaonan:**   ah! / Spain / that's far away from China
10 **Miguel:**   [laugh] {I stop taking pictures and look back to the student} oh! / you know Spain! A
11   re you from Hangzhou?
12 **Shaonan:**   yes / but I also lived in America one year / I was in California
13 **Miguel:**   oh! / really? / and why is that?
14 **Shaonan:**   because my parents were living and working there and they took me with them
15 **Miguel:**   ah! / interesting / and did you like it?
16 **Shaonan:**   yes / because I could learn some English
17 **Miguel:**   oh yeah! / your English is good
18 **Shaonan:**   yes / eh (4–5") oh! / thank you!
19 {a group of students crowds around Shaonan and me}
20 **Lanqing:**   {to Shaonan} 他听得懂中文吗? &
21   *does he understand Mandarin?*
22 **Miguel:**   & {to Lanqing} 对 / 我听得懂
23   *yes / I do*
24 {Lanqing looks surprised at the student next to him and laughs}
25 **Shaonan:**   what are you doing here?
26 **Miguel:**   I'm- 我听课
27   *attending classes*
28 **Yonjing:**   {to Miguel} 你是中文学生吗?
29   *are you student of Chinese?*
30 **Miguel:**   不是 / 我在西班牙学过中文 / 在这儿浙江大学我是研究生
31   *no / I studied Chinese in Spain / here I am a researcher at Zhejiang University*
32 **All:**   oh! / [laughs]
33 **Shaonan:**   my mother also works at Zhejiang University / she is a teacher
34 **Miguel:**   oh / really? / what is she teaching?
35 **Shaonan:**   eeh // can I speak Chinese?

36	**Miguel:**	sure!
37	**Shaonan:**	她在这大科学系 / 不太清楚什么棵但是她的专业跟化学有关系
38		*she works at the Science Department / I am not very sure about what subject but her
39		specialty has to do with chemistry *
40	**Miguel:**	啊！/ 明白
41		*ah! / I understand*
42	**Shaonan:**	and what are you studying here?
43	**Miguel:**	我学习中国的教育怎么样
44		*I study what Chinese education looks like*
45		{music sounds from the speakers placed in the corridors indicating the beginning of the next
46		period. Miss Laura, the English-language teacher for sixth grade approaches us on her way back to a
47		classroom.}
48	**Shaonan:**	oh! / Spanish education must be a lot better than Chinese?
49	**Miguel:**	better? / why?
50	**Shaonan:**	because it's more fun / I was in Germany
51	**Miguel:**	really? / when?
52	**Shaonan:**	yes / I was there and students just have &
53	**Laura:**	& {to Shaonan} WHEN?
54	**Shaonan:**	eeh {counting with his fingers} / this year
55	**Laura:**	but WHEN? which month?
56	**Shaonan:**	eeh {counting with his fingers} / July
57	**Laura:**	啊！
58		*ah!*
59	**Shaonan:**	{to Miguel} I was there and students just have classes in the morning and then in the
60		afternoon they have fun

(Informal conversation with students in the corridors. Notebook 2, pages 9–12)

Shaonan cannot be said to be a representative student of the school in terms of English-language repertoire. In fact, few students had lived outside China at the time of the data collection, and apart from the students taking part in exchanges with the U.S. school, most of the other participants, including many teachers, were unable to hold a brief informal conversation in English. However, the encounter illustrated in Extract 3.3 shows a recursive phenomenon that I faced in my everyday life at Hangzhou Primary School, namely that I was approached exclusively in English, by all concerned, even when they knew I could speak Mandarin Chinese—except for Miss Laura, the focus teacher of my observation at the school, who would shift to Mandarin during our private conversations within the school or in the course of our meetings and chats outside the school building.

In other words, there seemed to be an established sociolinguistic order in the school that made my participants feel obliged to interact with me in English. This often resulted in conversations like the one shown in Extract 3.3 where meaning, participation management, and social relations are all built up around the continuous (never taken for granted) negotiation of language choice, given my non-full aligning with this sociolinguistic order. A close look at the interaction reveals some of the related tensions for all involved, from the opening of my conversation with Shaonan (lines 4–11) to the topicalization of the theme of living in America (lines 12–18) to the discussion on professional activities in front of newly arrived participants (lines 19–44) to a subsequent teacher-guided turn-taking about the issue of studying abroad (lines 45–60).

Shaonan initiates the first exchange by greeting me in English, which is followed by my replying in Mandarin (lines 4–5). Nonetheless, this reply does not yet seem to imply the opening of a conversation, as my attention remains on the action of taking pictures of the athletics track. A possible explanation for this lack of body engagement is that I was accustomed to these kinds of short exchanges in which my participants ventured a brief greeting in English but were not willing (or able) to take those exchanges further, to have an extended conversation. After many instances in which I had tried to interact in English or switched into Mandarin to ensure the continuation of an initial conversation, without any success, I learned to perform these brief exchanges without expecting any subsequent development. However, Shaonan challenges this expectation in the example given in Extract 3.3.

The student follows up the initial exchange by posing a question about my origin, in English, which I answer in English without interrupting my picture-taking activity (lines 7–8). He finally gets my full attention by extending the previous exchanges with a comment on how far Spain is from China. I am driven to interpret this comment as a cue of his availability to hold an extended conversation, which leads me to address a first information request (lines 9–11). Once the frame of a conversation with both of us speaking English is set up, Shaonan replies to my question on his origin by mentioning his previous experience in America, in what constitutes the opening of a coconstructed development of the topic of him arriving there and learning English (lines 12–18).

At one point in the interaction, other students crowd around us and address Shaonan, asking him in Mandarin if I understand Chinese (lines 19–21), thereby introducing a new frame of action that requires the renegotiation of the rules and the topic of conversation. Under this new frame I feel that I am pushed to the participant status of *bystander* (Goffman, 1981) as my participants are talking about me as if I were not there. Thus, I immediately reply in Mandarin to the question addressed to Shaonan, without giving him the chance to answer, so as to make clear that Chinese can also be the language of conversation for all the participants involved (lines 22–24). This does seem to have an impact on the ongoing interaction, as language choice comes under negotiation.

Shaonan then retakes the floor and shifts to English through a new question on the reason why I am at the school, to which I reply in Mandarin referring to my observation of the classes (lines 25–27). This is taken up by Yonjing, one of the students newly arrived to the conversation, who asks me in Mandarin if I am a student of Chinese, in what appears to be leading to a new topic about professional activities related to Zhejiang University (lines 28–32). The code-switching from English to Mandarin is then counterbalanced by Shaonan in the course of developing the new topic, as he restores the previous pattern of interaction by initiating an English-dominated turn-taking between him and me regarding his mother's occupation as a teacher at Zhejiang University (lines 33–35). Nevertheless, this restoration is challenged as soon as Shaonan realizes he cannot continue the conversation in English.

As he is unable to provide a further explanation in English of his mother's work when asked to do so, he makes an explicit request for permission to use Chinese, which I grant (lines 35–36). At that point, the interaction develops in Mandarin Chinese concerning my professional activities and those of Shaonan's mother (lines 37–44), although the common achievement of this frame of understanding again becomes uncertain when the English teacher, Miss Laura, approaches us on her way back to the classroom (lines 45–47). Her arrival is accompanied by a fresh code-switch to English by Shaonan, who reintroduces the topic of being abroad by referring to his experience in Germany (line 48-50). This opens up a new teacher-guided frame of action in which, while the rest of the students listen, Shaonan's answers to my questions about this experience are scaffolded by the teacher in what seems to be an interactional strategy by Laura to ensure that Shaonan replies in English to give the specific information I am requesting concerning the time he was living in Germany (lines 51–60).

All in all, this interaction shows the extent to which speaking English in front of me was an activity that required some degree of complicity between teachers and students outside the space of the classrooms. This activity was usually initiated by those students who felt more confident with their English, but it also relied on the interactional work of their peers and teachers, who would often position themselves as unofficial or *non-ratified participants* (Goffman, 1981) who nonetheless were able to participate incidentally across the boundaries of the dominant encounter between the first student and myself, addressing him either by asking him in Mandarin about information on the ongoing encounter (thereby relegating this language to the margins of the dominant encounter unless I challenged it by code-switching, as in lines 24–34) or by scaffolding him in the replies to my questions.

In line with all these discourses and everyday practices concerning the material and symbolic spaces of the school, the negotiation of my own contribution to the community being researched was also socially constructed in relation to English/Mandarin bilingualism as a distinctive feature. As in the case of the other schools studied in Zhejiang province, I was asked by the principal of Hangzhou Primary School to help the English teachers by supporting them in class and by giving feedback to help improve their pedagogical practices. However, at this school I was specifically asked to provide an institutional evaluation of this collaboration with the teachers in class, that is, an assessment by a Spanish/English bilingual linguist. Thus, my expertise as a Spanish speaking scholar based in the disciplinary area of linguistics and interested in English-language education was constituted in this site as a source of authority. Figure 3.6, translated in Extract 3.4, shows the extent to which this form of research collaboration was discursively exhibited by the school through its website:

附小英语:欢迎来自西班牙的朋友——米盖儿

近一个月来,浙大附小六年级的英语课中多了一位新朋友,他是来自西班牙的米盖儿老师。为了更深入地研究中国教育,体验中国文化,他走进了我们的英语课堂,和孩子们一起学习,了解中国孩子是如何学习外语的。浙大附小的朱红校长和英语组林娴老师热情地接待了他。经过近一个月来的听课,米盖儿进一步了解了中国小学英语教学的状况。他对附小孩子们现有的英语学习能力给予了高度的评价。今天早上,他精心地准备了一节别开生面的外语课,他制作了精美的PPT,向同学们介绍了关于西班牙文化、教育等方面的知识,还教了一些简单的西班牙问候语,老师教的生动有趣,学生学的不亦乐乎。这位来自异国的老师深深的吸引着我们的学生。

Figure 3.6   Linguistic evaluations in English-language education

Extract 3.4   "He Has Also Given a Very Good Evaluation"

Welcome Miguel, our Spanish friend (title). In the last month, the English language class in sixth grade has a new friend who came from Spain, teacher Miguel. In order to investigate in depth Chinese education and to personally experience Chinese culture, Miguel has entered the English class to learn from it together with the students so that he can know how Chinese boys and girls learn foreign languages. After a month of observation in the classroom, and after a warm welcome from the head of the school and the English teacher, Miguel knows a little bit more about the situation of English language teaching in Chinese primary education. He has also given a very good evaluation of the ability of our school's boys and girls to learn English. This morning he prepared a spectacular foreign language class. By means of a nice Power Point presentation, he introduced to the students notions on Spanish culture and education. With a very enthusiastic style that the students enjoyed very much, he also taught some greetings in Spanish language. This exotic teacher is attracting profoundly our students' attention.

(Translation of text in Figure 3.6)

My background as a Spanish linguist was not remarked on at all in the other school that I studied in Hangzhou city. In this other school, the forms of research collaboration that were required and applied must be understood within the frame of its own historical background.

3.2.2   Hangzhou Secondary School and the Burden of Historical Pedigree

Hangzhou Secondary School is located in Hangzhou's central district. Like the school described previously, this school had remarkable installations and technological facilities when the fieldwork was carried out. Here, too, the main entrance was equipped with an electronic panel (see Figure 3.8), the teachers were each assigned laptops that they carried from class to class during the day, and the multifunction sports amenities were located around a well-maintained synthetic athletics track. Nevertheless, there were some differences with respect to Hangzhou Primary School. On the one hand, the school was considerably bigger, as it offered all preuniversity educational stages as part of its curriculum; its 3,000 students and 180 teachers were distributed in various groups of five-floor buildings separated according to the different educational levels (primary education, junior secondary education, and senior secondary education).

On the other hand, English did not play such a significant role in the school's everyday discursive organization. Unlike in Hangzhou Primary School, English language was not present either in its physical spaces or on its official website; all institutional panels and signs were displayed only in Mandarin Chinese (see Figures 3.8 and 3.9). Even the main entrance featured exclusively Mandarin Chinese (see Figure 3.7). In this case, all discursive work was oriented to the construction of the school's social image, where its outstanding historical trajectory and high academic prestige occupied the most prominent positions.

The discourses mobilized for the construction of this social image were circulated through different material and symbolic spaces in the school. Figure 3.10 corresponds to a picture of the school's emblematic sculpture, a stone placed in one of the patios near the building containing the school's offices. This stone has an inscription briefly describing the founding of the school (see translation in Extract 3.5). This inscription helps identify some of the key discursive elements that contribute to the social image, where the school's historical pedigree plays a constitutive role in its institutional profile.

Figure 3.7   Entrance to Hangzhou Secondary School

Figure 3.8   Signs and posters in Mandarin Chinese

Figure 3.9   Signs and posters in Mandarin Chinese

Extract 3.5   "Founded on the 4th of September 1949"

The primary school was founded on the 4th of September 1949 as the Zhejiang General Government School under the direction of Tan Zhenlin, the head of the military Commission of the Provincial Government at that time. Initially composed of the Preschool and Primary Education divisions, the school had 180 students in its first year, all of them from families of the military cadres of the Nanxia Party, the Clandestine Party, and the Revolutionary Martyrs. The teaching staff was also composed of military personnel and members of the Clandestine Party. Some of them had joined the Long March and others came from the Yan'an revolutionary base. In February 1951, the Primary Education division was separated off to form the Primary School of the Provincial Government, moving to its current location in 1955. Later, the head of the Provincial Education Office renamed the school as the Primary Education School. In September 2001, the Secondary Education division was added to the school constituting the Experimental School. This is the place where the original building, built in October 1954, was located. It comprised a total area of 2,800 square feet and was later demolished in 2001.

(Translation of text in Figure 3.10)

Figure 3.10   Sculptures as discursive emblems

Under the heading of "honorable history" (光荣的历史), the text inscribed on the sculpture gives an account of the different stages undergone
by the school since it was first built. This account is based on the linguistic resources that are typically found in historical biographies, a particular
genre in which the use of dates, places, leading figures, institutions, and

statistics provides an objective character to what is being told. In particular, the text represents the school in close association with institutions and events that are linked to the official narratives on the national founding of the People's Republic of China in 1949. Thus, the school is discursively represented as the recipient of actions referring to building, composition, and renovation where the agents are military officials as well as members of governmental offices and parties who played a key role in the victory of the Chinese Communist Party (CCP) during the Chinese civil war.[5]

The school is therefore discursively linked to these grand narratives and to the education of the children of those officially constructed as national heroes by the CCP. But the historical pedigree of the school was not only regarded in terms of its association with these national narratives, it was also related to the institutional stress on high academic demands. This is well illustrated in Extract 3.6, which is taken from the school's official website. In this example, reference to a glorious past closely bound to the CCP is explicitly related to an institutional profile of the highest academic requirements:

Extract 3.6 "Extraordinary Results in the Teaching of Disciplines"

原保俶塔小学创建于 1949 年 9月, 经过 50 多年的发展, 取得了显著成绩, 是行为规范示范学校, 精神文明单位, 全国红旗大队、先进学校。学校有较高的教学质量, 学科教学成绩显著, 在国家、省、市竞赛中名列前茅

The Primary Education School, which was founded in September 1949 and has obtained extraordinary results after 50 years of development, is a standardized model school, a unit of spiritual civilization, an excellent National Red Flag Brigade, an advanced school. The school has the highest quality of teaching, extraordinary results in the teaching of different subjects, and is among the best in municipal, provincial, and national competitions.

(School's website)

In line with the type of representations constructed in the stone's inscription, Extract 3.6 also constructs the school's social image upon a long history associated with the year of the foundation of the People's Republic of China, and also with the CCP, through references to its contemporary political slogan on "spiritual civilization" (see Chapter 1, Section 1.3) and to the brigade of young pioneers who have always been officially inspired to construct socialism and communism in the schools (Price, 1970). The example shows that this social image is also attached to discourses of educational advance, extraordinary results, high quality, and excellence at municipal, provincial, and national levels in China.

This role as an institutional reference bonded to great history and academic rigor was regularly cited by the head of the school, by the teachers, and by the students as the main cause of the pressures and tensions they faced in their daily life. These concerns were made explicit through ambiguous forms of discursive positioning. For the head of the school and the teachers, this ambiguity was enacted in the form of general statements about the Chinese educational system that functioned as the background from which the related difficulties in their school were to be inferred. Extract 3.7 is part of an interview conducted with Mr. Wang, the head of Hangzhou Secondary School.

Extract 3.7   "Too Much Pressure"

Miguel: 你可以那个跟我说- 校长有一些好处 / 校长也有一些那个 。。。/ 坏处 / 什么东西你喜欢什么东西你不喜欢?

could you tell me- the head of the school has some advantages / and the head of the school has also some uuh / disadvantages / what things you like and what you don't?

Wang: 我们这里校长都是政府任命 / 不是选举的 // 政府觉得这个人有能力 / 他说你到这里 / 他到那里 / 她到这里 // 明年可能我在那里 / 他到那里 / 经常要调整 // 一般在一学校是三到五年 // 五年 / 那么有的长一点 / 十年也有 // 我在这个学校第六年了 / 我到 / 五年之前 / 六年之前我不在这里 / 我在另外的学校 / 那么校长 / 你说中国的校长很累 / 因为我要上课啊 / 我要管理 / 对吧? / 不像这个我们去年到德国 / 我们在德国 / 我带了 50 个学生到德国去看 / 校长就是校长 / 就搞管理 / 是吧? / 哎中国校长累 // 一个我觉得不喜欢我觉得太累 / 第二 / 压力太大 // 压力 / 压力大怎么呢? / 就是我们现在竞争很激烈 / 你这个学校好不好关系到你明年招生能不能招 / 招多少 / 那他的压力很大 // 第三 / 也有一些烦恼啊处理有中国的教育 / 自主的权利不大 // 我这个校长 / 我课程啊什么我没有权去弄 / 我总要上面同意 / 怀疑的 // 那么有时候呢你要按照你自己的想法去做 / 那会有一些困难 // 哎。。。当然也有些开心 / 开心看到学校发展 / 学校在变化 / 很多老师成长了 / 很多学生优秀了 / 那你就很开心

we the HEADS OF SCHOOL are here selected by the GOVERNMENT / we are not elected by vote // the government believes this person is capable/ says you here / him there // next year I might be there / him here / there are adjustments all the time // most spend between three and five years in the same school // five years / some a bit longer / ten years as well / this is my sixth year in this school / I arrived / five years ago / I was not here six years ago / I was in another school / so the head of school / you say that heads of school are tired / because I have to teach / I have to do management / right? / it was not like this when we arrived in Germany last year / we in Germany / I took 50 students to visit Germany / the head of school is just a head of school / just management / right? / ah! / being head of school in China is tiring // something I think what I don't like is that I think it's too tiring / second / too much pressure // pressure / how is that? / it is just we are now very competitive / depending on how well or bad you do in this school has an impact on your ability to enroll students next year / number of registrations / so the pressure for him is great // third / there are also some problems concerning education in China / the right for autonomy is not great // I am uh the school principal / I have no authority to do things my way on any aspect of the curriculum / I always have to agree with people from above // so sometimes you have to do according to your own view/ and then you have problems // heey! of course there is also enjoyment / enjoyment from seeing the school developing / the school is changing / a lot of teachers are grown up / many students become excellent / so you feel happy*

> (Interview with the head of school; recording code: 23dp_Zh_S07122006E)

As explained by Mr. Wang, the general institutional procedure for the assignment and rotation of heads in schools in China imposes a great responsibility on them. He answers the question on the advantages and disadvantages of being head of school with a detailed description emphasizing the specific difficulties involved in his position, and making only a very brief and general statement on the positive aspects of his work at the very end of his turn. The difficulties identified are fundamentally tiredness, pressure, and lack of freedom. Although this description seems to point to general concerns affecting all heads of school in China, they should be considered taking into account the specific implications of the previously mentioned concerns in the particular circumstances of the Hangzhou Secondary School, as described by Mr. Wang in the course of subsequent conversations and interviews.

First, the description of his duties as teacher and manager in terms of excessive tiredness must be placed in this specific context, where the management duties involve all the preuniversity education divisions—which is not necessarily the case of other schools. Second, the point regarding the high degree of pressure arising from the official evaluation, on the basis of its impact on the prestige of his school, is a particularly sensitive issue under these conditions, in which his school is socially constructed as highly prestigious; in other words, Mr. Wang's future depends on his capacity to maintain this high prestige, which in turn means that for him there is more to be lost than gained. Finally, the lack of freedom to take his own decisions is especially significant in relation to the forthcoming official examination of schools that, like the Hangzhou Secondary School, are considered as outstanding historical references to be followed by the other schools in the area.

As remarked previously, the same ambiguous positioning was to be found in the teachers' discourses, as shown in Extract 3.8, corresponding to an informal conversation with Ms. Zhu, a 25-year-old English-language teacher whose teaching experience comprised the three years during which she had been working at this school.

Extract 3.8   "I Have to Put In a Lot of Effort"

Miguel: 你很辛苦啊！每天白天的话在学校里面上课 / 下班以后还有家教！/ 你太忙!

you work very hard! / you teach every day here in the school / and then you do tutoring at home after class! / you are TOO BUSY!

Zhu: 当老师很辛苦但是我还很喜欢我工作 / 我喜欢帮我的学生 / 中国的教育很竞争的因为学生太多 / 小学和中学很多但是大学不够 / 就是一些上大学 / 那么我应该帮助他们 // 我要很努力还有这边压力很大

being a teacher is hard but I still like my job / I like helping my students / education in China is COMPETITIVE because there are too many students / there are too many primary and secondary schools but not enough universities / only some students get access to university / so I have to help them / I have to PUT IN A LOT OF EFFORT and the PRESSURE here is great

(Informal conversation; field notes, notebook no. 4, p. 39)

In response to praise for her hard work, Ms. Zhu enumerates her duties as a teacher in China, which are explained in terms of the difficulties posed by a pyramidal educational system in which only small numbers of students have access to higher education. Thus, the hard work to which the praise refers is discursively represented as a necessary means to prepare her students to succeed in such a setting (I have to PUT IN A LOT OF EFFORT"). This attitude is expected from all the teachers at the three schools studied, to the extent that their salaries in all cases vary according to their students' results, although this aspect is heightened in Hangzhou Secondary School, where there is particular pressure on them in this respect ("and the PRESSURE here is great").

In the case of the students in this school, the ambiguous discursive positioning regarding their discontent with the school's stress on historical pedigree and academic rigor was mostly reflected in interactional ambivalence on the negative and positive evaluations of their school. Extract 3.9 is an example of this ambivalence, as part of a research interview conducted with two students in the school:

Extract 3.9 "Rules Are Too rigid"

1 **Miguel:** 你们告诉我一个。。。/ 那个这个学校一个很好的地方- 最好的地方和不好的地
2 方
3 *tell me oone / uh one positive aspect about this school –the best aspect and one
4 negative aspect*
5 **Chunhua:** 我觉得 - 这里啊/他管理比较严/ [而且特别严]
6 *I think- here /its management is more strict / [it's particularly strict]*
7 **Miguel:** [比较严]
8 *[more strict]*
9 **Chunhua:** 但是相比来说呢 / 也是挺规范的 // 跟其他学校比的话 / 因为我们七八九班他们以
10 前小学是跟我们不一样的 / 但是呢 / 明显进来以后相处一段时间以后就觉得我们
11 这里的学生要稍微比他们 / 规矩要稍微比他们好一点 // 因为是从小就开始训练
12 的嘛/所以应该是学校抓的严比较好
13 *but comparatively speaking / it's quite normative as well // compared to other
14 schools / because here we have seventh eighth and ninth grade students they in the
15 Primary school were different than us / but / obviously after entering – after a while
16 together we the students here have to be a bit more than them / we have to be a bit
17 more disciplined than them // because we started to be trained when we were small //
18 so the emphasis on being a strict school is necessarily better*
19 **Miguel:** 啊。。。/这是那个。。。/最好的地方↑
20 *uuh / this is uuh /the best aspect↑ *
21 **Chunhua:** 最好的地方就是学校管理比较好
22 *the best aspect is simply that the school management is the best*
23 **Miguel:** 啊。。。/你呢？/你觉得最好的地方？
24 *uuh / and you? / which one do you think is the best aspect? *
25 **Jianyu:** 和她一样的
26 *the same as her*
27 **Miguel:** 嗯//那个。。。/最不好的地方？
28 *ok // uuh / and the worst aspect?*
29 **Chunhua:** 我觉得没什么特别差的地方
30 *I don't think there is a particularly poor aspect*
31 **Miguel:** 啊。。。&
32 *uuh*
33 **Chunhua:** & 都蛮好的
34 *everything is quite good*
35 **Miguel:** 啊/还有那个。。。&
36 *uuh / and uuh*
37 **Chunhua:** & 如果和中国学校相比
38 *compared to Chinese schools*
39 **Miguel:** 就是什么？
40 *what? *
41 **Chunhua:** (( )) / 而且。。。/ 嗯。。。/ 就是感觉有时候太 / 有时候是比较严 / 嗯。。。/ 严
42 厉是好的 / 但是有时候 / 有时候就是太死板了 / 规矩太死板了 / 就不是什么好事
43 情
44 *furthermoore / uuh / it's just that I think sometimes it's too / sometimes it's a bit
45 strict / uuh / severe is good / but sometimes / sometimes it's too rigid / rules are too
46 rigid / it's simply something that is not good*
   (Interview with students. Recording code: 22dp_Zh_S24112006E)

The content and forms of participation provided by Chunhua and Jianyu in this example must be framed in the context of the research question posed at the very beginning ("tell me oone / uh one positive aspect about this school—the best aspect and one negative aspect"). This question opens up a frame of participation/interpretation focused on the negative and positive characteristics of the school, a frame which can place the students in a very difficult position, given the fact that this is not an ordinary conversation taking place just anywhere but a research interview between a university researcher (with the authority associated with this status) and two students, that is being conducted within their school. This difficult position may indeed explain Jianyu's reluctance to participate as well as Chunhua's ambivalence in assigning a positive or negative value to the school's profile.

When the previously mentioned question is asked, Chunhua first mentions strict management as a distinctive feature of her school, which is repeated by me in overlap (lines 5–8). My repetition of "more strict" seems to be interpreted by the student as remarking on a negative aspect, as she immediately takes back the floor and introduces a counterargumentation ("but comparatively speaking") followed by a monologue on the normative character of the school compared to others, which finally seems to be formulated as a positive aspect ("so the emphasis on being a strict school is necessarily better") (lines 9–18). The combination of the counterargumentation together with the positive formulation of the normative aspect somewhat confuses me, as reflected in line 19 in the linguistic form of a dubitative affirmation of what she has just said as a positive remark ("uuh / this is uuh /the best aspect ↑ ").

The student, however, reframes my affirmation by stressing that the positive aspect is the good school management (line 21), which seems to leave the negative nature of the attributes "strict" and "normative" as inferred. Nevertheless, to a later question asking more explicitly about a negative aspect of the school Chunhua replies first that there is no particular negative aspect (lines 27–30) and then that "everything is quite good" (line 33), although this is then contradicted in line 46 by an evaluation of the strict nature of the school as something negative ("severe is good / but sometimes / sometimes it's too rigid / rules are too rigid / it's simply something that is not good").

Thus, the interactional efforts to reach a common understanding on the social meanings attached to the characterization of Hangzhou Secondary School as a strict institution reflect the shaping of a discursive space in which institutional and interpersonal positioning coexist in complex and not necessarily coherent ways. The official and unofficial dimensions of the social image of this school as an institution with a distinguished pedigree also pervaded my fieldwork there. My own presence as a researcher was constructed so that this representation should be divulged, but at the same time it increased the related tensions experienced by teachers and students in their daily life. Accordingly, the request that I should contribute to the school by collaborating in the preparation of some English-language lessons, which was publicly announced in the school's newspaper and referred to as an opportunity for its English teachers to learn from Western language teaching methodologies, encountered some resistance from Ms. Zhu, the teacher involved.

Ms. Zhu had always supported my research and collaborated with me very enthusiastically, and was aware of the benefits of the publicity organized by the head of the school regarding my own contributions to the English-language education division. However, she also felt this added to the institutional pressures on her to achieve high success rates in the year-end examinations, as my teaching plans were not oriented to those examinations but to "spectacular" lesson delivery.

Under the pressure of expectations to be different, as announced in the school newspaper, as a result of which my lessons were observed by all the English teachers in the school (as well as by other subject teachers), I decided not to follow the textbook. Instead of beginning with vocabulary lists and grammatical structures before proposing practical exercises, I arranged my lessons on the basis on working-in-groups activities in which students were given collective tasks (e.g., making a recipe) that required them to seek the necessary resources on their own (including activities of interchange with other groups), without much attention to worksheets. This approach led Ms. Zhu to feel that her students were not being provided with the activities and materials that she thought best suited her students' needs in terms of preparing for the final exams. Like it or not, these demanded that a great deal of attention be paid to learning vocabulary lists and grammatical structures (see Chapter 5 for an in-depth exploration of everyday practice in the English-language classes at the three schools studied).

Thus, the dilemma presented by having to engage in the public construction of the social image envisioned by the head of the school, by allowing my teaching assignment, while having to continue with her teaching agenda so as to meet the institutional pressures regarding students' success rates in the final examinations, led her to allocate extra classes (sometimes without letting me know), over and above the official timetable. As a result, I found on many occasions that, on entering the school to teach the first period of the morning (at 7.40), Ms. Zhu and all her students were already in the classroom reviewing the vocabulary lists and the grammatical structures for the lesson I was about to teach. These extra classes were not only promoted by Ms. Zhu, but also requested by many of her students, who did not find my methodology useful for training the type of skills they were expected to display in their final tests, as the teacher admitted later on when asked why they were already in class.

Bilingualism and pedigree are not the only forms of localization by means of which the three schools adapted to the wider institutional guidelines for educational modernization so as to be considered good experimental schools. The third school, which represents an interesting contrast with the other two in terms of geographic and socioeconomic conditions, offers a different image, where heterogeneity and its related challenges are much more prominent.

3.2.3 Wenzhou Secondary School and the Potential of Social Cohesion

Wenzhou Secondary School is located at the heart of Longgang, a relatively small town linked to Wenzhou city (see Figure 3.11). More than nine hours' drive to the south of Hangzhou, this school offers a great contrast to those described previously. It had no connections with any famous university nor did it have a glorious history of academic excellence. Rather, it was a normal school located in a very ordinary neighborhood with no spectacular resources to attract attention.

In line with the considerable socioeconomic differences between Hangzhou and Longgang,[6] the Wenzhou Secondary School had very limited facilities. This is reflected in the material spaces (see Figure 3.12): the athletics track was not synthetic, the buildings were old, with no electronic panels, the classrooms were old-fashioned and crowded, with up to 60 students in each, and there was a notable scarcity of personal computers (desktops and laptops)—each office had only one, to be shared by all the teachers in it.

Apart from its material resources, Wenzhou Secondary School also differed in its marked emphasis on social cohesiveness, which was discursively

Figure 3.11 Entrance to Wenzhou Secondary School

Figure 3.12 Outdoor installations in Wenzhou Secondary School

constructed on a combination of academic excellence and of leadership in other activities involving the school community as a whole. Extract 3.10 shows how this social image is made apparent in the "school profile" section (学校概况) of its official website.

Extract 3.10 "Advanced Collective"

办学质量一直名列全县前茅，尤其是 2004 年中考 4 门主科总成绩全第一，4 人考取温州中学，38 人考取苍南中学，近 100 人考取省重点高中。2005 年中考 4人考取温州中学，再居全县第一。近年在获得 "市教学研究工作先进单位"、"市先进教工之家"、"市城市绿化先进单位"、"市贯彻体育条例先进集体"、"市安全文明示范学校" 等称号，并被列为浙江师大教育实习学校，被中国教育报社编入 《中国名校600家》.

The quality of the school has been ranked among the best in the county, and especially so considering the total results in the four main subjects of the entrance examination in 2004, with a total of four people accessing Wenzhou secondary schools, 38 entering Cangnan secondary schools, and 100 being accepted in key provincial high schools. In the 2005 entrance examination four people accessed Wenzhou secondary schools, and it was again ranked among the first in the county. In recent years, it has been designated an "advanced teaching and research unit", "advanced teaching center", "urban greening unit", "advanced collective in the regulation of physical education", "model school of safety" among others; it has also been listed as a teaching practice school affiliated with Zhejiang Normal University, and it has been included among the 600 elite schools in China by China Education Daily.

(School's website)

In addition to highlighting the school's rating as one of the best in the county concerning the progression of its students to postcompulsory education, the website also emphasizes other merits, in relation to environmental education, collectivist physical education, and safety. These other values were in fact explained by all the school population as a necessary means of facing the challenges posed by the students' heterogeneity, with particular respect to their academic level.[7] This was repeatedly mentioned by the teachers at Wenzhou Secondary School. In contrast to the Hangzhou school, their complaints were not limited to the stress produced by their responsibility to ensure their students' academic success. They also emphasized the dilemma of having to achieve this institutional goal in the context of an overcrowded school with a diverse profile of students in terms of academic interests and future prospects. Ms. Chen, an English-language teacher, expresses this in Extract 3.11, in an informal conversation that took place in a school corridor just after the observation of her class:

Extract 3.11   "The Difference in the Level of the Students Is Huge"

1 **Chen:**   你在这儿听英语课的话感受怎么样 / 比西班牙没有什么好 / 是吗?
2   *what impression did you have while attending the English class here? / it is not as
3   good as in Spain / right?*
4 **Miguel:**   哈哈 / 不是不是 / 那个 / 不是比西班牙没好 / 比西班牙就是不一样的!
5   *haha! / no no / uh / it is not worse than in Spain / it is simply different compared to
6   Spain!*
7 **Chen:**   不过那里的英语水平比较好 / 学生比较 active / 这里是 teacher-centered / 那比较
8   passive / 是不是啊?
9   *but the level of English is better there / students are more active / here it is teacher-
10   centered / so it is more passive / isn't it?*
11 **Miguel:**   我不是觉得这里的学生更 passive / 这里学生跟老师合作不一样的
12   *I don't think students are more passive here / here the forms of collaboration
13   between teachers and students are different*
14 **Chen:**   对 / 因为在这儿班里面学生更多
15   *right / because here there are more students in the classrooms*
16 **Miguel:**   是的 / 在西班牙有一个法律 / 那个 / 它说每个班不能有二十五个学生以上
17   *yes / in Spain there is a law / uh / it says that there cannot be more than 25 students
18   per classroom*
19 **Chen:**   真的吗? / 在这儿太多 / 每个班六十个学生 // 上大学很难 / 就是一些会上大学所
20   以竞争很大 / 那么学生水平差别很大 // 这个是对我们老师说这所学校最重要的
21   问题
22   *really? / here there are too many / each classroom has 60 students // access to
23   University is hard / only a few will enter University so competition is high / so the
24   difference in the level of the students is huge // for us teachers this is the most
25   important problem in this school*

(Interview with English language teacher. Field notes. Note-book no. 3, page 75)

As someone who has been observed, Ms. Chen wants feedback about her performance. But she frames this within a discursive contrast between "here" and "Spain" in which the latter is considered a place where English-language teaching is better (line 1). By doing so, she positions me as a legitimated institutional evaluator with more expertise and, therefore, qualified to provide assessment and advice for improvement. However, I refuse this frame of action/interpretation by invalidating her premise for the comparison in terms of better/worse (line 4), which in turn alleviates my own personal tension in having to provide an assessment as a legitimate English-language speaker despite the fact that I have long experienced a profound complex regarding my own English-language competence (see also Chapter 1, Section 1.2). This refusal is followed by another exchange in which Ms. Chen and I insist on our initial positions (lines 7–13), but finally reach a common understanding, agreeing on the different forms of collaboration between students and teachers in the two contexts.

This common frame of interpretation is interactionally constructed through different turns (lines 11–16), from my explicit statement about the different forms of collaboration, which is immediately accepted by Chen ("right"), to her reframing of the comparison in terms of the numbers of students in the classroom, which is immediately accepted by me ("yes"), and further elaborated by reference to legislative accounts ("in Spain there is a law / uh / it says that there cannot be more than 25 students per classroom"). However, the significance of this extract in the course of the argument developed in this subsection is that this coconstruction of a shared understanding is finally expanded by an explanation provided by Chen in which she introduces the topic of competition in Chinese education as a result of the pyramidal shape of the educational system ("only a few will enter university so competition is high"), justifying her concern about the difference in the levels of the students at her school ("so the difference in the level of the students is huge // for us teachers this is the most important problem in this school").

The representation of the difference in the level of the students as a problem should be viewed in relation to the specialization of the school as a "Junior Secondary School". In contrast to Hangzhou Secondary School, which included all preuniversity educational stages, and to Hangzhou Primary School, where students did not have to face a nationally standardized test at the end of primary education because of the nine-year compulsory education scheme, the students at Wenzhou Secondary School were under extra pressure in that they had to compete among themselves to ensure access to a good postcompulsory education institution. The students not only needed to pass the national examinations to obtain their graduation certificate, they also needed high marks in order to be accepted by prestigious senior secondary schools in the province.

The teachers here often referred to this extra pressure to emphasize the increasing difference of level between those students willing to carry on studying and those who had decided from the outset that they did not want to enter higher education. As a result, the teachers' main concern at Wenzhou Secondary School was to provide the best resources to enable students' access to postcompulsory education while building a sense of community among those who were not interested in this option. And it is in this space where the "integrated gymnastic exercise competition" (广播体操比赛综合) played a key institutional role in the organization of everyday life, being discursively aimed at counterbalancing the previously mentioned challenges by promoting social cohesion among the school members. Lianfang, a student in eighth grade, makes sense of these competitions within the social space of his school in Extract 3.12, as part of an e-mail conversation.

Extract 3.12   "They Can Increase the Spirit of Collaboration and Unity"

Miguel: 你喜欢广播体操比赛综合？为什么？ 对你来说，在你的学校广播体操比赛综合有什么目的

Do you like the integrated gymnastic exercise competitions? Why? According to you, what is the aim of the integrated gymnastic exercise competitions in your school?

Guofang: 我以前参加过广播体操比赛综合,认为很有意思,它可以增加班级的团结协作精神. 它的目的是让大家更加都有团结协作的精神.

I participated before in the integrated gymnastic exercise competitions. I think they are very interesting. They can increase the spirit of collaboration and unity. Their aim is to let everybody join the spirit of collaboration and unity.

(E-mail communication with an eighth-grade student. Date of reception: August 30, 2007)

Indeed, the students and teachers at Wenzhou Secondary School often mentioned the high reputation of their school at municipal, provincial, and national levels regarding preparation for the collectivist sports competition. Everybody gathered around the athletics track, once a week, to prepare these collectivist sports; internal competitions were held among all the class groups, each semester, with the best classes being designated to represent the school at the municipal and provincial competitions. During these internal competitions, the only occasion on which the students wore school uniform (in contrast to the other two schools, where all students wore uniform every day), each class group had to perform the same exercise in front of an evaluating committee of teachers and the school principal. The exercises involved the performance of a specific choreography by all the class members, guided by the group director standing at the front (see Figure 3.13).

Therefore, the importance of these practices and the values attached to social cohesion informed my fieldwork at Wenzhou Secondary School. Here, I was not required to act as a Spanish/English bilingual scholar affirming the value of the school's English-language teaching practices, nor was I asked to deliver "excellent" classes with a taste of the Western style of English-language teaching. Rather, I was encouraged to engage in the preparation of the integrated gymnastic exercise competitions, and this form of collaboration was widely communicated through the school's website and in local newspapers. Apart from my support, as needed, for the English-language teachers I was observing, the school's head asked me to participate actively as part of the panel evaluating the exercise competitions held during the semester in which I compiled my data. Thus, I became involved in selecting the class groups that would represent the school in the municipal and provincial competitions later that academic year.

These three differentiated discursive spaces in which a unique social image was constructed in response to a shared institutional framework of educational modernization, including the dilemmas and tensions affecting all school members and also myself as a researcher at these three schools, reveal aspects of importance to our understanding of the experimental

Figure 3.13 Integrated gymnastic exercise competition

reforms being addressed. Let us now consider these underlying processes and their implications. In doing so, I shall focus on what these localization processes tell us about the continuities and discontinuities with earlier education modernization reforms in China.

3.3   EDUCATIONAL MODERNIZATION AND NEOLIBERALIZATION IN CONTEMPORARY CHINA

An overview of the three ways by which experimental schools attempted to cope with the institutional demands for educational modernization provides an impression of the here-and-now of China's education reforms. In particular, we see three schools having to conform to official state guidelines while remaining sensitive to local conditions. They were expected to comply with national agendas, but at the same time these agendas had to be adjusted creatively (read: "unpredictably" or with insufficient support from the state) to specific contexts by using the schools' own resources. More specifically, they had to apply *centralized* policies and *standardized* practices of institutional evaluation within a *deregulated* economic/bureaucratic system where *flexibility* and *competition* for scarce resources ensures an *efficient* implementation of the official guidelines at all levels—school management, teachers, and students.

Regarding management, all three schools enjoyed considerable autonomy in aspects other than the official curriculum, particularly in their responses to institutional pressures for educational innovation. Nevertheless, insufficient funding, together with the parents' freedom to choose a school in their local area and the existence of a nonfixed registration fee scheme, pushed these schools to orient their autonomy to compete with other schools. Thus, they competed for students' registrations by discursively constructing unique social images (and innovative practices) that, while conforming to the official requirements of excellence, by maintaining high student success rates in the standardized national tests, were adapted to local socioeconomic conditions.

On the one hand, Hangzhou Primary School, which is associated with (and is adjacent to) an internationally prestigious university whose staff send their children to this school, emphasized a profile centered on English/Mandarin bilingualism. On the other hand, Hangzhou Secondary School, located in the city center (a very prosperous area in the Zhejiang region), stressed its historical pedigree, citing national narratives about the foundation of the CCP (and of the People's Republic of China), together with high academic demands and extraordinary results at municipal, provincial, and national levels. Finally, Wenzhou Secondary School, located on the outskirts of a small industrial town near Wenzhou, highlighted its potential for combining academic excellence and leadership in collectivist sports competitions among an academically diversified school population where not all students were willing to continue their education beyond compulsory studies.

However, things appear to be much more complicated for teachers, school heads, and students in terms of the practical implementation of these institutional images, which gave rise to various paradoxes in everyday life. Sometimes, these paradoxes arose when these images were applied in ordinary interactions, as in the case of the English/Mandarin bilingualism in Hangzhou Primary School. Although some of the students in this school had travelled to the United States or Europe, whether in the form of exchange programs with other schools abroad or through life experiences related to their parents' occupations (as, for example, the children of university teachers moving to other countries for short research stays), most of the students did not enjoy those opportunities. Thus, the interactional display of bilingualism as two separate monolingualisms was difficult to maintain on many occasions in which the students were supposed to perform only in English.

When these students encountered me in front of their English-language teachers and their peers, bilingualism was collaboratively constructed as a fictional space where only those students who had travelled abroad acted as official participants of the interaction, while the rest positioned themselves as non-ratified participants on the margins of the dominant interaction. In other words, English/Mandarin bilingualism, although officially representative of the school's profile, became, ironically, a space where not everyone's linguistic repertoires fitted, and so my presence (that of someone socially constructed as a "Westerner") actually heightened tensions and linguistic insecurities and anxieties.

On other occasions, paradoxes took the form of discrepancies with the official images being discursively constructed by the schools. These mismatches were made explicit by the school heads, teachers, and the students themselves; thus, at Hangzhou Secondary School, not all the participants agreed with the stern demands imposed by their school, while at Wengzhou Secondary School, the teachers were worried about the widening gap between students competing to enter higher education and those not motivated to do so—notwithstanding the school's discursive construction of social cohesion as its main institutional feature.

In general, all participants in the schools studied were faced with diverse contradictions of a system combining flexibility and extreme competition (particularly in the two secondary schools). The teachers and heads of schools encountered the challenges of flexible job conditions giving rise to different salaries and degrees of mobility among different schools depending on their outcomes in certain periods of time. These outcomes were strongly related to the number of students passing the standardized tests, which therefore had a severe impact on these teachers and school heads' experiences, of working under very stressful conditions allowing little space for creativity or freedom. As for the students, the right to choose their school spurred competition, given the pyramidal shape and the exam-oriented character of an educational system in which material resources (facilities, teaching aids, staff) and symbolic resources(prestige) are unequally distributed among the schools; hence, the students were pushed to compete against their peers if they wished to access more desirable institutions in subsequent stages of their education.

I, too, was subject to contradictions, in that the collaborations I was asked to engage in during the fieldwork (which were publicly exhibited) were exploited in terms of the social images being discursively constructed at each of the three study sites. In this regard, the emergence of the "Westerner" category discussed in Chapter 1 is not sufficient to account for the institutional transformations taking place at the three schools. This regional identity was localized in different ways according to a logic that required these schools to make different use of it, depending on their local conditions. Therefore, I experienced the difficulty of having to fit into social positions where I did not always feel comfortable, when this involved acting as an expert in linguistics appraising the school's approach, preparing the students for their final examinations, or participating in the evaluation of the teams to represent the school in the collectivist sports competitions at municipal and provincial levels.

In summary, the picture resulting from my experiences in these three experimental schools is indicative of an educational modernization process in which the state retains control over the distribution/allocation of symbolic resources (i.e., deciding which schools, teachers, students, and school heads are considered to be "good", with significant consequences for their access to prestigious institutional categories like "experimental", in the case of the schools, or to prestigious schools and stages of higher education, in the case of teachers, school heads, and students). It does so through extensive monitoring, evaluation, measurement, and standardization, while balancing these measures with economic/bureaucratic deregulation (enabling schools to collect education fees and to take responsibility for managing their own resources), so as to enforce adjustment to local market demands and increasing competition. Such a combination has been regarded by some social scientists as typical of institutional neoliberalization (see, for instance, Harvey, 2005), a major process guiding the restructuring reforms being faced by modern institutions under conditions of late modernity (Appadurai, 1990; Bauman, 1998).

However, neoliberalism is not a completely new process of state/market opposition, nor does it only relate to our contemporary world, as social scientists often remind us; the present strong, and strengthening, interrelation between the state and the liberal market was actually initiated long ago. Neoliberalization does not mean overcoming the state's sway but comprises a specific form of regulation of the market forces within and across the boundaries of the modern state. In this sense, conceptualizations of neoliberalism should go beyond its representation as an abstract entity separated from the state toward considering it as the political economy of the "neoliberal state" (Harvey, 2005: 7). Indeed, a zoom-out view places the features presented in this chapter into a wider historical and institutional context with roots dating back to the beginning of China's 20th century, when the mutually constituted relationship between the modern state and the liberal market was first established.

The story of liberal education in China begins with the publication of the first plan to create a modern educational system, implemented by the Chinese Ministry of Education in 1906 (Peake, 1970: 63). Although still within an imperial regime, this plan introduced several features of a liberal education system, in response to the difficulties experienced by the Chinese elites to ensure the survival of the state as a political entity. After the defeat of the Chinese troops by the European powers in the two Opium Wars, and following the Sino-Japanese war in 1895, in which the "little brother" proved to be much more advanced technologically, the Chinese intellectual reformers looked at the Japanese Meiji Restoration as the socioeconomic model to follow.

Inspired by the Japanese educational model, under the 1906 education plan the former imperial examination system was abolished and progressively replaced by a nationally centralized education system supposedly built upon the basic principles of universality (educational for all instead for just a few) and meritocracy (success by talent and effort instead of by social class). In other words, Chinese education underwent a drastic conceptualization shift away from its traditional role in the education of governors concerning the principles of law and government. It sought to become a modern institution (legitimated by its appeal to fairness/neutrality) aimed at ensuring the continuity of the ideological framework of the nation-state by fostering national identity, official patriotism, military defense knowledge, and adjustment of the whole population to the technical needs of an (increasingly streamed/diversified) industrial economy (Potts, 2003: 11–15).[8]

Nevertheless, this model was to be changed a few years later. Once the Republic of China was officially established in 1912, intellectuals and officials centered their attention on the American version. Although the educational law of 1912 remained based on the Japanese model, it was felt to be inappropriate to the sociopolitical and economic circumstances of the new republic. Moreover, the defeat of Germany in World War I, and the subsequent Treaty of Versailles that ceded to Japan the German concessions in China, caused the German model to lose a great deal of prestige, and also provoked an anti-Japanese sentiment among the Chinese population. Thus, the educational model implemented in the United States came to be generally adopted in Chinese educational guidelines and policies published after

1912 and particularly during the early 1920s (including the new national education law in 1922).

For the purposes of this chapter, the most important consequence of this change in the focus of attention was that the education system was pedagogically, bureaucratically, and financially reorganized in accordance with institutional guidelines promoting decentralization and local autonomy. Thus, the basic principles of universality and meritocracy first implemented at the beginning of the century were thought to be best achieved through an institutional structure in which local administrations and schools, organized within the National Federation of Education Associations since 1915, enjoyed greater responsibility and flexibility in designing, adapting, and implementing their own curriculums, taking into account students' characteristics and requirements in each region of the country.[9] But this model did not last long either. In the context of increasing internal division and of the imperialist external aggressions faced by the Chinese state during the late 1920s (see Chapter 1, Section 1.3), advocates of a more centralized national education system gained support.

In line with the political shift to a centrist nationalism inspired by the European models of the time, the educational reformers of 1925 and later turned their attention to the French and German systems (Hayhoe, 1984: 40), relocating the school as a key modern institution at the service of the state's interests, specifically those concerning the maintenance of a strongly unified national market. As a result, the Chinese education system was again remodeled, this time by combining the properties of the two previous phases to better suit the specific national conditions of modern China. This system, which was to constitute the bedrock of China's contemporary education system, drew together curricular centralization, partial economic/bureaucratic decentralization, academicism, and competition.

The education territorial areas inherited from the early 1920s retained their partial economic decentralization but were nevertheless centralized in many respects concerning bureaucratic management and curriculum reform. With regard to bureaucratic management, the Chinese Ministry of Education assumed control over the design of educational reforms by abolishing the National Federation of Education Associations. Thus, the territorial areas that had previously been managed by diverse associations came to be controlled by government-related cadres, which since then have been responsible for ensuring the effective implementation of the educational guidelines issued by the central government. In addition, key educational positions in schools, like school heads, came under tight state supervision through the implementation of a rotation scheme depending on outcome achievement.

The curriculum was also centralized by the Chinese Ministry of Education, which since then has controlled all processes involved in curriculum design, evaluation, and publication. On the one hand, it maintained the education structure imported from the United States, while recovering the academicist subject orientation introduced at the turn of the 20th century from the Japanese model. On the other hand, it set up a standardized institutional system of tests covering all educational stages, from primary education to university. Legitimized under the modern educational slogans of "meritocracy" and "high standards", the design and evaluation of these tests focused on the assimilation of centralized curricular content and guided the streaming processes of all students through schools, education stages, and academic/vocational branches, which in turn brought about a high degree of competition within the Chinese school system. Finally, the publication of textbooks, which was previously decentralized, also came to be controlled by the Ministry of Education for the whole country.

The changes and reforms carried out in China after the 1930s have been numerous and diverse, but all have ultimately contributed to reinforcing these basic features that were progressively introduced during the first quarter of the 20th century during the construction of modern China. After the establishment of the People's Republic of China in 1949, Mao Zedong oriented all educational reforms to fit the system constructed in preceding decades to the new nationalist program of the Chinese Communist Party.[10] Apart from standardizing Mandarin (普通话) as the official language of compulsory and postcompulsory education across all regions in China,[11] Mao also wished to extend educational institutions throughout China by nationalizing all the private education groups that had previously flourished. This was officially represented as a revolutionary measure to counterbalance the tendency of an inherited education system which was at that time more oriented toward educating social elites than the Chinese population as a whole.[12]

Nonetheless, Mao's reforms of the structural management of the school system ended up favoring a policy of continuity in the development of a modern liberal education in China. As a consequence of the tension of building up a system to ensure the education of the mass population while responding to the socioeconomic demands of an increasingly industrialized economy, Mao's structural reforms combined the expansion of the system nationwide with concentration of available resources within the system. In particular, an officialized "two track" system was built up during the 1960s, in which one of the tracks (the so-called key schools [重点学校]) was centralized (under the direct control/funding of the Ministry of Education) to provide higher education for the new social elites (the Party's military and political members, and civil servants) for the construction of a broad-based communist state bureaucracy, while the other track (the so-called ordinary schools [普通学校]) was financially decentralized, curriculum-streamed,[13] and locally oriented to provide a basic education for the masses in order to facilitate their incorporation into the new modes of agricultural/industrial production that the country needed to achieve economic growth (Lo, 1984: 47–48).

This system was radically dismantled during the first half of the 1970s, in the context of Mao's doctrinal campaigns such as the Cultural Revolution (1966–1976). Drawing on a nativist reforming plan that aimed to eradicate all traces of European, American, and Soviet influence from Chinese education, which were officially represented as sources of capitalist and traditionalist orientations serving the interests of former colonial elites, Mao removed the "two track" policy and implemented a package of educational reforms that transformed the entire education system (Cleverley, 1985: 137; Su, 2002: 13; see also Brugger [1978] for a revision of the nativist contents of these reforms).[14] However, these radical reforms were soon disrupted and the 1960s system was progressively restored between 1974 and 1976, giving way to a period of far-reaching reforms that would facilitate the complete institutionalization of the features described in the previous sections of this chapter.

In the context of the "open door" economic reforms of the 1980s instituted by Deng Xiaoping, the new social conceptualization of education as a key institutional space both for the modernization of all economic sectors and also for the positioning of China as a new international power gave greater prominence to the modern education values of efficiency, quality, meritocracy, selectivity, streaming, and scientificism. These values were definitively institutionalized in 1985, with the "Resolution for the reform of the education system" (教育体制改革的决定), which brought about the conditions for the exponential increase of competition across all sectors of Chinese education, and which were subsequently continued with the "Outline for the reform and development of education in China" (中国教育发展和改革纲要), issued in 1993, and the "Education law of the People's Republic of China" (中华人民共和国教育法), issued in 1995.

Among the structural properties formally regulated by these policy documents, the most important were a specific plan for universalizing nine-year compulsory education,[15] the opening up of criteria for categorizing schools as "key" or "ordinary" (with important funding implications in terms of the resources provided by the Ministry of Education) depending on students' examination results, a minutely detailed economic decentralization setting out the funding responsibilities of local governments and schools,[16] parents' right to choose their children's school at the municipality level, and the administrative deregulation of schools' capacity to hire, fire, or incentivize their teachers (Rosen, 1984: 74–80; Cleverley, 1985: 223–225, 1991: 337; Ding, 2001: 172; Su, 2002: 15–18; Potts, 2003: 244; L. Li, 2004: 236–237, 394).

The previously mentioned principles, thus, accentuated the liberalizing trend in modern Chinese education by establishing a partially deregulated system which pushes schools and their members toward competition in preparing for standardized tests that determine official rankings and access to the resources made available by the state (i.e., institutional categories that guarantee more state funding and more social prestige in the local communities, thus attracting more students).[17] Nevertheless, progressive neoliberalization and its subsequent emphasis on testing was not the only layer involved in the everyday implementation of the modernization reforms in the three experimental schools in Zhejiang. Discourses and practices of educational modernization brought with them supplementary meanings not having to do directly with curricular subjects or national examinations. These other meanings will be carefully examined in the following chapter.

4 Learning to Be a Good Community Member

4.1 BEYOND MERITOCRACY

We saw in Chapter 3 how the diverse social images discursively produced for the social construction of the three schools in Zhejiang as "good experimental schools" reflect an institutional process of increasing neoliberalization. The heightened control of the state over the curriculum, together with progressive economic/bureaucratic deregulation, seems to be strengthening institutional processes of selection, streaming, and competition. This process raises concerns about the consequent stress, pressure, and individual uncertainty provoked among all members of the school community (school heads, teachers, and students). But these were not the only elements to emerge from my examination of how the three schools coped with the reforms aimed at educational modernization.

Besides the discursive orientation of the whole system toward preparation for the national examinations—as the main legitimate indicator guiding selection and streaming, in line with the modern, liberal educational discourse of meritocracy—the participants in the three experimental schools also engaged in a set of social practices that played a significant role even though they were not directly related to curricular subjects. There were certain moments and spaces in which the schools' members gathered to participate in "institutional rituals" (Bernstein, 1971, 1975; Bourdieu, 1991; Bourdieu & Passeron, 1977) in the sense that they were expected to engage in "a mode of delivery that entails a high degree of fluency, without hesitations, in a stylised intonation contour, accompanied by prescribed postures, proxemics, behaviours, attitudes and trappings" (Du Bois, 1986: 317, as cited in Rampton, 2006: 181).

These other symbolic spaces were a key factor in the regulation of social life both inside and outside the classrooms at the three schools studied. This was evident in their importance within the schools' weekly timetables as well as in the existence of organizers specifically responsible for their control, supervision, and evaluation. Regarding their consequence within the schools' weekly routine, these ritualized activities involving the school members played a very important part, as illustrated in Table 4.1, where these activities are highlighted by shading and bold print.

Table 4.1 Schools' weekly timetable

	Monday	Tuesday – Friday	Saturday
7:00	Entrance to the school, greeting, registration, and management of students' flow along the corridors		
7:00-7:15	Collaborative cleaning		
7:15-7:45	Review period (one different subject per day)		
7:45-7:50	Recess: management of students' flow along the corridors		
7:50-8:35	Class period		
8:35-8:40	Recess: management of students' flow along the corridors		
8:40-9:00	Monday meeting	Physical exercises	
9:00-9:05	Recess: management of students' flow along the corridors		
9:05-9:50	Class period		
9:50-10:00	Recess: management of students' flow along the corridors		
10:00-10:45	Class period		
10:45-10:50	Recess: management of students' flow along the corridors		
10:50-11:00	Eyesight exercises		
11:00-11:45	Class period		
11:45-13:30	LUNCH TIME		
13:30-14:15	Class period		No class
14:15-14:20	Eyesight exercises		No class
14:20-15:05	Class period		No class
15:05-15:50	Class period		No class
15:50-16:35	Class period		No class
16:35	Management of students' flow along the corridors and good-bye routine		

As for the control, supervision, and evaluation of these activities, there were distinctive school figures, namely the "class on duty" (班值周) and the "student managers" (管理的学生), who played a very important role in the schools' material and symbolic organization. Firstly, the class on duty was a title distributed by shifts, on a weekly basis, among all the class groups in each school. During the corresponding week, each group was in charge of managing all the ritualized activities as well as of evaluating all students according to their participation in the course of such activities. Secondly, the student managers included two subfigures, the "group leaders" (中队长) and the "school leaders" (大队长), who were annually peer-nominated by vote on the basis of their academic records and of what the teachers and students called "leadership skills". These students, who obtained extra grades in their education records for this role,[1] were supposed to ensure that all students and the class on duty were properly coordinated during the school year.

This hierarchical and rotational organization of the school community around ritualized activities not directly related to the curricular subjects also impacted on the students' evaluation. These practices had consequences on the students' educational records; all of them started the academic year with 100 extra points added to their final scores in the national examinations,[2] which were progressively subtracted whenever their performance in these ritualized practices linked to community organization was judged inappropriate. In other words, these practices were relevant for our understanding of the social construction of what counted institutionally as a "good student" in these schools. In the course of a research interview (Extract 4.1), Miss Laura, an English teacher at Hangzhou Primary School, explains the requirements at her school to be considered a good student:

Extract 4.1   "I Think the Most Important is His Moral Character"

1	Miguel:	一个那个 / 一个。。。 / 特别好的学生 / 为什么是那一个特别好学生？ /
2		那个比如说那个。。。 / 你觉得 – 在你们小学一个那个。。。/ 为了是最
3		最好的学生他应该是怎么样？
4		*one uh / oone / particularly good student / why is this person a particularly
5		good student? / uuh for example uuh / do you think- in your school one uuh /
6		what must a student be like to be the very best student?*
7	Laura:	怎么样的？他 &
8		*how? he &*
9	Miguel:	*& 那个这样的学生为什么是那个最好的？
10		*& why is that type of student the best student?*
11	Laura:	啊为什么是最好的？/ 因为他成绩好
12		*ah! why is he the best? / because he has the best academic results*
13	Miguel:	成绩是？
14		*academic results?*
15	Laura:	上课认真 / 上课时候很认真 / 积极举手发言 / 作业认真完成 / 尊敬老师 / 然
16		后有很好的一个行为习惯 / 不会打架 / 不会去做很坏的一些事情 / 这才是
17		一个优秀的好学生 / 最重要的我觉得是他的品德
18		*very serious in class / very serious during the class / raises hands actively to
19		speak / completes the tasks seriously / respects the teacher / then has good

20		behavior / doesn't fight / doesn't do bad things / this is an exceptional student / I
21		think what is most important is his moral character*
22	Miguel:	品德
23		*moral character*
24	Laura:	就是说 / 他的一个 moral
25		*that is / his moral*
26	Miguel:	嗯
27		*ah!*
28	Laura:	他会尊敬你老师 / 他会很愿意帮助同学 / 然后他很愿意为集体做事情 / 愿
29		意- 很愿意比如说留下来打扫卫生 / 来。。。 / 为班级来做事情 // 他有一
30		颗 为别人服务的一个心 / 他愿意帮助别人 / 他爱国主义 // 另外我觉得一个好
31		的学生就是他能够很自觉地 / 很努力地学习 / working very hard in study
32		*he respects you as a teacher / he wants to help other classmates / then he is
33		willing to do things for the collective / willing- willing to for example to do
34		cleaning tasks / coomes / to do things for the class // he has an obliging heart to
35		help other people / he is patriotic // furthermore I think a good student simply is
36		able to study conscientiously / and very hard*

(Interview with an English teacher. Hangzhou Primary School.
Recording code:19dp_Zh_P24112006E)

When asked about the social characteristics of the good student, Miss Laura first emphasizes good academic results and a focused attitude in class (lines 1–20). However, her definition of a good student then veers toward less academic aspects, such as "moral character" (品德) (line 21). This moral dimension is expanded in her last turn, in reaction to my repetition of the "moral character" label (line 22–23), which seems to be interpreted by her as a lack of understanding on my part. Indeed, this repetition is first followed by her reformulation of the label in English (line 24), and then by a long paraphrase in which she explains the concept of moral character in relation to general values of respect, solidarity, collective collaboration, community services, patriotism, and hard work (lines 28–36).

Therefore, the value of the previously mentioned ritualized practices, going beyond the confines of the curricular subject, was related to these extra values complementing the academic emphasis on examinations. These practices were accounted for by school heads and teachers on the basis of a comprehensive three-dimension educational model in which intellectual, physical, and moral aspects were understood to be equally important in evaluating the "quality" of the students. An example from one of the schools' institutional documents is provided in Extract 4.2, showing how these different educational dimensions are explicitly integrated and quantified for the recommendation of students to the school's senior division, in accordance with the official guidelines for the provision of quality education approved by the municipal government:

Extract 4.2   "Method for Determining the Students' Chronological Order"

市属重点高中保送生推荐办法

根据杭州市教育局的有关文件精神，特制订本推荐办法。

一. 推荐原则

[...]
二) 全面性原则
综合考评学生的全面素质, 鼓励学生在学好文化课的同时, 拓展各项素质。按照学生德, 智, 体方面的表现, 优先推荐品学兼优, 学有特长的学生。

二. 推荐办法

一) 实行文化课成绩与德育及特长加分综合量化评定的办法确定学生的先后排列, 按量化分值从高到底依次填报的方式进行。

Approaches for the Recommendation of Students to the Municipal Key High School

According to the spirit of the Hangzhou City Department of Education.

Recommending Principles

[...]
B. Principle of comprehensiveness
To integrate the overall quality of the comprehensive evaluation of the students while stimulating them to learn the core subjects, and to expand every quality item. In accordance with the students' performance in physical, intellectual, and moral aspects, first priority will be given to high academic achievers, the talented students.

1. Recommending Methods

A. To implement a method for determining the students' chronological order to be recommended, from the first downward, according to a quantitative and comprehensive assessment of talent, moral education, and results in the core subjects.

(Institutional document from Hangzhou
Secondary School, p. 106)

Examples of informal discourses referring to the combination of intellectual, physical, and moral dimensions as constitutive of modernization in Chinese education were analyzed in Chapter 1, Section 1.2. This modernizing project is aimed at counterbalancing the increasing global interconnectedness by emphasizing moral education in order to avoid the moral problems supposedly being faced in contemporary Western education (see Extract 1.4). However, we still need to understand (a) what forms of knowledge emerged from the ritualized practices of community organization linked to physical and moral education in the three schools; (b) what official forms of discursive representation were institutionalized to legitimize this emphasis on academicism combined with community organization; and (c) how these discourses and interactional practices about the community were connected to the construction of a modern education system in China.

Section 4.2 will explore in detail these ritualized practices, examining the institutional and interpersonal meanings that are locally co-constructed and negotiated by their participants. Section 4.3 goes on to analyze the discursive representation of community values in the schools' documents and in other forms of multimodal discourse presented in their physical installations. Finally, Section 4.4 will focus on the historical emergence and development of discourses about the community in the modern Chinese curriculum, which will allow us to identify the ideological function of these discourses in the process of educational modernization in China.

4.2　SOLIDARITY AND AMBIVALENCE IN THE CO-CONSTRUCTION OF COLLECTIVE MEMBERSHIP

In the three schools studied, the ritualized practices discursively linked to a physically and morally based community organization were constructed upon different participation structures, sequential forms of coordinated actions, spatial distributions of the participants on the scene, patterns of body displacement, and objects/artifacts. Yet the corresponding social actions were in all cases built upon a common participation framework involving participant statuses of *animators* (Goffman, 1981: 144) and supervisors of the animating practices, who contributed to legitimate peer evaluation and collective synchronization based on verbal and nonverbal actions.

Such a participation framework was far from being unambiguously reproduced in all practices, and in fact the analysis of the moments in which participants (intentionally or otherwise) failed to perform the activities as required helps us identify both the interactional rules (i.e., the institutional constraints) and the social positioning of the participants in this respect (i.e., interpersonal agency). I will begin by broadly systematizing the recurring participation features of the ritualized practices and then analyze one in depth in order to exemplify the role of ambiguous discontinuity as a constitutive part of these practices.

4.2.1　Multiple Institutional Rituals, One Collectivist Framework of Participation

To understand how the different structures of participation, sequential forms of coordinated actions, spatial distribution of the participants on the scene, patterns of body displacement, and objects/artifacts were articulated under a common participation framework of collectivist synchronization, we must take into consideration the specific goals institutionally assigned to each of the rituals. According to the three schools' institutional documents, these goals varied in great detail, from performing patriotism (i.e., the Monday meeting [周一开会]), to practicing body health care (i.e., physical exercises [锻炼]), to protecting eyesight (i.e., the eyesight exercises [眼操]), to maintaining discipline and order throughout the transitional periods during the school day (i.e., the management of students' flow), to assuming responsibility in services for the community (i.e., collaborative cleaning).

During the patriotic activity carried out during the Monday meeting on the athletics track, the participants' actions were coordinated around the raising of the Chinese national flag (see Table 4.2 for an overview of the participant statuses and of the recurrent sequences of action in the Monday meeting). This activity was sequentially achieved through instruction-response structures of participation between the teacher on duty, who stood in front of the athletics track and spoke through a microphone connected

Table 4.2 Participants, space, and sequences of actions in the Monday meetings

Type of Practice	Participants, proxemia, and statuses	Sequences of coordinated actions
Monday meeting	*Teacher on duty* (standing at the front): requests verbal and non-verbal actions. *Class students* (in rows): animate actions, in collectively synchronized fashion. *Students on duty* (one standing in front of each row): supervise the students in their row, coordinate body actions. *Manager students* (standing as a group behind the students on duty): supervise the actions of all students, including those on duty. *Teacher tutors* (walking in between rows): supervise and correct the students in the rows.	The teacher on duty (TD) announces the event > TD tells all to turn around > students on duty count to two in unison > all students turn around to face the flagpole > TD tells all to salute the flag > all students raise their right arm while the flag is raised and the national anthem is played > TD tells all to end the salute> all students lower their right arm while the national anthem continues > TD tells all to sing the national anthem > all students sing the anthem in unison > TD tells all to turn around > students on duty count to two in unison > all students turn around and applaud.

to loudspeakers located throughout the school, while all students in the school stood in rows, one per class group. This teacher on duty led the saluting of the Chinese national flag and the singing of the national anthem (in line with the official guidelines and with the audio material provided by the Ministry of Education, which acted as the *author* [Goffman, 1981: 144] of the sentiments and semiotic forms expressed during the event).

The students, on the other hand, were expected to act as addressed recipients of the teacher on duty, putting into practice the actions instructed (verbal and nonverbal), in simultaneous synchrony. This also applied to the students on duty and the student managers, who simultaneously carried out the requests made and supervised their peers' performance. The students on duty (marked with letter A in Figure 4.1) stood at the front of the rows, on a one-row-one-student-on-duty basis, which allowed them to view all the students in the rows (except for the moment when all participants turned to face the national flag, as shown in Figure 4.1). Meanwhile, the student managers (marked with letter B in Figure 4.1) stood in a group behind the students on duty, supervising both the students on duty and the class students in the rows (except for the moment when all participants turned to face the national flag, as shown in Figure 4.1).

Apart from the teacher on duty and the students, the teacher tutors (marked with letter C in Figure 4.1) walked up and down the rows, looking left and right at each student in turn to check that an upright body posture was being maintained at all times during the event. In this regard, they

Figure 4.1　Monday meeting on the athletics track

positioned themselves as unaddressed recipients of the teacher on duty; that is to say, they did not carry out the actions requested, but merely engaged in nonverbal forms of supervision.

The body-health-care activity, as part of the physical practice session, was also conducted on the athletics track, with a similar spatial arrangement to that used for the Monday meeting. However, there were significant differences between the two activities (see Table 4.3 for an overview of the participant statuses and of the recurrent sequences of action in the body-health-care activity). In this case, social actions were collectively coordinated in the form of a predefined set of body movements to be performed simultaneously by all the students, lined up in rows, in a collectively synchronized fashion and directly following the instructions emitted by an audio recording provided by the Ministry of Education for this event. In other words, this activity was not led by the teacher on duty but by the instructions and the music provided by the audio recording, which set the pace and form for the correct performance of the body exercises.

In this physical activity, the activities of the unaddressed recipients were distributed in a different way from the Monday meetings; this role was played by three different types of participants: the students on duty, the manager students, and the teacher tutors (marked as A, B, and C, respectively, in Figure 4.2). As unaddressed recipients of the audio instructions, these participants merely engaged in different forms of supervision (i.e., visual scrutiny and body displacement, addressing individual attention to each of the participants in the scene).

Figure 4.2   Physical exercises on the athletics track

Table 4.3 Participants, space, and sequences of actions in the physical exercises

Type of practice	Participants, proxemia, and statuses	Sequences of coordinated actions
Physical exercises	*Audio player*: requests body actions. *Class students* (in rows): animate actions, in collectively synchronized fashion. *Students on duty* (one standing in front of each row): supervise the students in their row. *Manager students* (standing together behind the students on duty): supervise all students. *Teacher tutors* (walking up and down the rows): supervise and correct the students in the rows.	Audio announcement of the event followed by lively music > count from one to eight, while class students raise and lower their left arm > count from one to eight, while class students raise and lower both arms simultaneously > count from one to eight, while class students march on the spot > count from one to eight, while class students raise and lower their arms simultaneously three times in coordination with squatting and taking one step forward/one step backward with the left foot > count from one to eight, while class students do the same as in the previous sequence > count from one to eight, while the class students do the same as in the previous sequence but with the right foot > count from one to eight, while the class students do the same as in the previous sequence but with the left foot > count from one to eight, while the class students raise and lower both arms alternatively in coordination with squatting (two consecutive times) > count from one to eight, while the class students step forward-backward, move their hands in circles, lean forward and raise both hands laterally at 90° from the trunk > count from one to eight, while the class students raise and lower both arms alternatively in coordination with squatting (two consecutive times).

During the classroom activity aimed at protecting the students' eyesight, the participants' collective and simultaneous synchronization did not require them to congregate in the same physical setting, as was the case of the two ritualized practices that took place on the athletics track (see Table 4.4 for an overview of the participant statuses and of the recurrent sequences of action in the eyesight exercises). Twice daily, for 10 minutes between class periods, the beginning of the event was signaled by an official audio recording, broadcast through the loudspeakers located in every classroom.

Table 4.4 Participants, space, and sequences of actions in the eyesight exercises

Type of practice	Participants, proxemia, and statuses	Sequences of coordinated actions
Eye massage	*Audio player:* instructs body actions. *Class students* (seated): animate the actions, in synchronized fashion. *Class monitor* (standing, in front of the students): supervise the students. *Teacher tutors* (standing, beside the class monitor): supervise the students. *Students on duty* (one per class, standing by the door): supervise all participants.	Audio announcement of the event followed by slow music > announcement of the first exercise > students sit facing the windows, putting one finger in front of their face > count of eight series of enumerations, from one to eight, while the students alternate the focus of their visual attention between their finger and the windows > announcement of the second exercise > students turn to face the blackboard, putting their elbows on the desks, and placing the index finger and thumb of one hand on their nasal septum > count of eight series of enumerations, from one to eight, while the students squeeze their nasal septum with their index finger and thumb in circular movements > announcement of the third exercise > the students remain in the same position, close their eyes and put the index finger of each hand on their cheeks > count of eight series of enumerations, from one to eight, while the students press their cheeks with their index fingers in circular movements > announcement of the fourth exercise > students remain in the same position, and raise the palms of their hands in front of their faces > count of eight series of enumerations, from one to eight, while the students massage their faces with their palms, in circular movements.

Prior to these activities, all the students in each class remained in their seats, waiting for their teacher tutors (marked with letter A in Figure 4.3) to enter the classrooms and stand at the front beside the class monitor (marked with letter B in Figure 4.3). Meanwhile, the students on duty (marked with letter C in Figure 4.3) divided up, with each one moving to stand by a classroom door. Once everyone was in position, the actions in all the classrooms were simultaneously focused on the performance (by the students) and supervision (by the teacher tutor, the class monitor, and the student on duty) of a well-defined sequence of exercises requiring coordinated shifts of visual focus, eye massages, and changes in posture.

With regard to the collectivist synchronization of practices concerning discipline and order within transitional periods during the school day, these did not involve the simultaneous participation of all the students. Unlike those conducted on the athletics track and within the classrooms between class periods, these activities were constituted as spaces shaping (and being shaped by) the actions of only a few participants at a time; they applied to different physical locations within the schools, namely the entrances and the corridors, each of which was associated with brief verbal and nonverbal forms of engagement that were enacted and reinitiated every time a student or group of students entered these spaces. The routine at the school entrance involved the coordinated participation of all students entering/leaving the schools at a given moment and of the students/teacher on duty supervising

Figure 4.3   Eyesight exercises in the classrooms

their entry/exit (see Table 4.5 for an overview of the participant statuses and of the recurrent sequences of action in the entrance and exit routines).

Every morning at 7:00am, and every afternoon at 4:35pm, six members of the class on duty took up their position at the schools' main door, standing in two rows of three students, on either side of the entrance (marked with letter A, in Figure 4.4). Then, all the students entering or leaving the school walked in line (each class in turn) between the two rows formed by the students on duty, who initiated a greeting/good-bye ritual as soon as the first student heading each class group approached them. This physical distribution provided the students on duty with a clear sight of each of the students entering or leaving (marked with the letter B in Figure 4.4). The students were required to enter and leave the school buildings in an orderly formation and, most importantly, in an "appropriate appearance", concerning gender-differentiated forms of dress and hairstyle, upright body posture, and the clear display of identification cards on their clothes. The whole ritual was visually supervised by the teacher on duty (marked with letter C in Figure 4.4), who was in charge of ensuring that all participants acted appropriately.

The routine in the school corridors was arranged on the basis of sporadic encounters between the students on duty, who stood individually beside the stairs on each floor in the school, and the students moving along the corridors during the five-minute recess periods (see Table 4.6 for an overview of the participant statuses and of the recurrent sequences of action in the entry and exit routines).

On these occasions, the students on duty were expected to stand in an upright position and make eye contact with any student passing by their

Table 4.5 Participants, space, and sequences of actions at entrances and exits

Type of practice	Participants, proxemia, and statuses	Sequences of coordinated actions
Entrances and exits	*Students on duty* (six of them, standing in two rows of three, on each side of the school entrance): greet and supervise the students on entry. *Class students* (entering between the two rows of students on duty): walk in, in line, by class groups, with ID card correctly visible on clothes, presenting good physical appearance. *Teacher on duty* (behind the two rows): supervise all participants.	The students on duty stand still, upright, with their legs together and arms at their side > the students from one class approach the entrance, in line > one student on duty instructs the other students on duty to greet those entering > all students on duty raise their right arm in synchrony > the class students enter, in an upright body posture, walking in synchrony > the students on duty lower their right arms.

Figure 4.4   Greeting and good-bye routines at the school entrance

Table 4.6 Participants, space, and sequences of actions in the management of flow

Type of practice	Participants, proxemia, and statuses	Sequences of coordinated actions
Management of students' flow	*Students on duty* (one standing by the stairs on each floor): supervise class students' flow. *Class students*: move along the corridors	The students walking along the corridor approach the student on duty > the student on duty scrutinizes the passing students > the students passing by reduce their speed and the volume of their conversation.

position (marked with letter A in Figure 4.5). The students passing by their peers on duty were required to lower their voices and reduce their walking speed (i.e., no shouting or running) (see participants marked with letter B in Figure 4.5, who slowed down and walked in line, as did those marked with letter C, once the student on duty looked at them immediately after this photo was taken). The use of swearwords was particularly frowned upon, and so both the students on duty and the class students were expected to be very careful to prevent this.

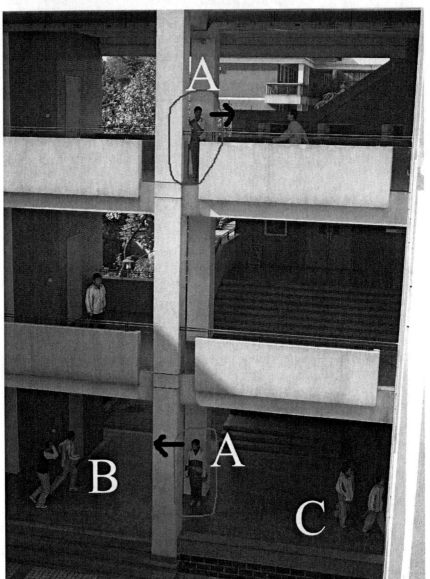

Figure 4.5   Management of student flow along the corridors

Finally, the activity that was institutionally guided to maximize the students' responsibility in collaborative services, for the community was clearly distinguished from the other activities (see Table 4.7 for an overview of the participant statuses and of the recurrent sequences of action in the cleaning practices). This activity did not require the simultaneous synchrony of all students, nor was sporadic coordination expected, on a one-person/

Table 4.7 Participants, space, and sequences of actions in the cleaning practices

Type of practice	Participants, proxemia, and statuses	Sequences of coordinated actions
Cleaning the school	*Class students* (small group): clean their classroom and surrounding corridors/bathrooms. *Class monitor*: coordinate and supervise the cleaning of the classroom. *Students on duty*: coordinate and supervise the cleaning of the corridors. *Student managers*: coordinate and supervise the cleaning of external areas and bathrooms.	Supervisors in the classrooms, corridors/bathrooms, and external areas jointly issue instructions for cleaning their assigned spaces, at the same time > the class students responsible for the cleaning during the week, in pairs, start their preset tasks in each area (floors, windows, desks, blackboards, walls) at the same time, in energetic and coordinated fashion.

group-at-a-time basis. This ritualized practice was implemented under a recurrent participation framework requiring the simultaneous coordination of selected students from each class who, on a weekly rotation basis, were organized in small groups to clean the different parts of school installations at the same time (classrooms, corridors, bathrooms, and external areas) according to a predetermined arrangement of tasks.

This arrangement involved various students organized in pairs, with each pair carrying out the coordinated cleaning of different elements (windows, floors, walls, desks, and blackboards), and one supervising figure standing and giving instructions in each area of the school. The class monitors supervised the classrooms while the students on duty and the student managers supervised the corridors/bathrooms and external areas, respectively (a pair of students cleaning the corridor floors is shown in Figure 4.6).

In sum, the set of ritualized practices just described shows an institutional space in which daily life was very much structured around collectivist frameworks of hierarchical participation, where the periodically shifting distribution of animation/evaluation participant statuses among the school members legitimated coordination, simultaneity, and synchrony, with respect to patriotic, physical, and community-service activities. In fact, these values were not only reconstituted daily in the course of the ritualized practices; they were also present in the rules of conduct displayed in the institutional documents and on the signs and posters throughout the schools' installations. Extract 4.3 corresponds to one of the institutional documents in Wenzhou Secondary School, and it illustrates the central position assigned to these values and activities:

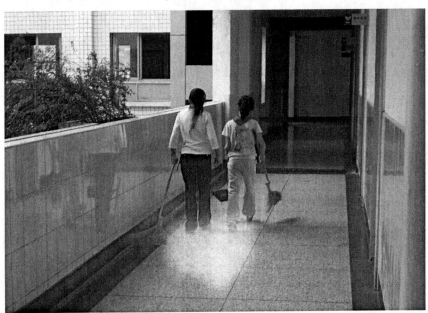

Figure 4.6 Collaborative cleaning in the corridors

Extract 4.3 "Comply with School Rules"

学生守则

1、热爱祖国，热爱人民，热爱中国共产党。
2、遵守法律法规，增强法律意识。遵守校规校纪，遵守社会公德。
3、热爱科学，努力学习，勤思好问，乐于探究，积极参加社会实践和有益的活动。
4、珍爱生命，注意安全，锻炼身体，讲究卫生。
5、自尊自爱，自信自强，生活习惯文明健康。
6、积极参加劳动，勤俭朴素，自己能做的事自己做。
7、孝敬父母，尊敬师长，礼貌待人。
8、热爱集体，团结同学，互相帮助，关心他人。
9、诚实守信，言行一致，知错就改，有责任心。
10、热爱大自然，爱护生活环境。

Rules of Conduct for Students

1. Love the country, the people, and the Chinese Communist Party.
2. Obey laws and rules, uphold the law. Comply with school rules, respect social morality.
3. Love science, study hard, think and ask questions diligently, be willing to explore, participate actively in social practices and beneficial activities.

4. Love life, pay attention to safety, take exercise, pay attention to health.
5. Exercise self-esteem, self-confidence, self-reliance, and civilized and healthy life habits.
6. Participate actively in work obligations and do so with diligence, selflessness, and self-sufficiency.
7. Respect your parents, respect your teacher, treat others politely.
8. Love the collective, join with your peers, help each other, care for others.
9. Be honest and trustworthy, match your words and deeds, acknowledge your mistakes, assume your responsibility.
10. Love nature, care for the living environment.

(Institutional document, Wenzhou Secondary
School, p. 73)

Against this background of apparently continuous/harmonious/stabilized activity, I shall now move on to an unhurried immersion in one specific ritualized activity. The analysis of this will help to exemplify the complex forms of discontinuity that always underpinned these collectively coordinated spaces in the three schools studied, even when all involved seemed, at first sight, to be perfectly orchestrated.

4.2.2 One Collectivist Framework of Participation, Multiple Doubled-Voices

The arrangement of participation frameworks involving the simultaneous coordination of animators and supervisors contributed to ensuring, most of the time, the performance of the expected (verbal and nonverbal) social actions in the course of all the ritualized activities at the three schools. These practices were perceived by external visitors as spectacular moments of collective synchronization, which in some cases involved more than 2,000 participants performing at the same time. Nevertheless, the previously described recurrent actions for each of the ritualized activities were not necessarily reproduced unambiguously in mono-logic discourse. Rather, they were recursively reconstructed in *heteroglossic, double-voiced,* or *discursively dialogic* attitudes (Bakhtin, 1981, 1986, 1994); they were constantly actualized through semiotic forms that allowed the participants, simultaneously, to reconstitute the official voices institutionally inscribed in the activity, on the one hand, and the carnivalesque voices interpersonally produced in the course of playful, irreverent, and/or subversive meaning-making practices, on the other.

As in other contexts where these heteroglossic practices have been widely documented (see Lemke, 2002; Van Lier, 2002; Lin & Luk, 2005; Maybin, 2006; Rampton, 2006; Luk, 2008; Blackledge & Creese, 2010), the activity in the ritualized practices was full of "spontaneous moments when [participants] were artfully reflexive about the dichotomous values that they tacitly reproduced in the variability of their routine speech, moments when they crystallized the high-low structuring principles that were influential but normally much more obscure in their everyday variability" (Rampton, 2006: 364, quoted in Blackledge & Creese, 2010). In other words, for the students and teachers at the three schools studied, the statuses of animation and evaluation were not the only resources on which they could draw to construct meaning and social relations; while acting as animators or supervisors, they were also able to engage creatively in *keying* practices (Goffman, 1974) to signal their attitude toward the interactional norms that they themselves were reproducing.

However, and in general, these signaling cues were not concerned with ironic accents displayed to populate the prescribed forms of verbal interaction, as is the case in most previous analyses of heteroglossic practices in educational settings. Rather, the population of the prescribed forms of participation involved the stylization of certain nonverbal features intimately linked to the actions expected and required in the daily ritualized routines. These recurrently consisted in the performing of body postures and movements that allowed the students to position themselves as participants who, while not being highly disruptive, were not necessarily aligned with the sentiments institutionally associated with each activity (i.e., expressing concern with patriotism, health care, discipline, or community service).

Furthermore, the enactment of these ambivalent forms of participation not only offered a window showing how the students ambiguously positioned themselves with respect to the activities they were engaging in; close analysis of those moments was also very revealing of the forms of solidarity co-constructed by animators and supervisors (including the teachers). To put it another way, the exploration of these moments threw into relief the practices of "collusion" (McDermott & Tylbor, 1986) by which students and teachers coordinated their actions to overcome the constraints of the official policies and discourses that shaped their everyday practices. Extract 4.4 is taken from the physical exercises performed in one of the schools and exemplifies how all these social meanings at institutional and interpersonal levels overlapped and were negotiated by participants, in the course of the ritualized practices.

Extract 4.4   "Yuan Yi Raises Her Arms in Relaxed Fashion and at Low Intensity"

1 {The video pans across to show the students standing in rows, maintaining an upright
2 position with their legs together and arms close to the torso. At the front of each row, the
3 student on duty for this class stands looking at the others in the row. The teacher monitors
4 walk up and down the rows supervising each student in the row that corresponds to their
5 class. In front of all the rows, two student leaders in charge of the physical exercises walk
6 across, supervising all participants in the scene.}
7 **Speakers:** 全国中学生套广播体操

8   *national   program   of   physical   exercises   for   secondary   education
9   students*
10   {just music for 5", after which a voice enumerates a series of numbers
11   accompanied by the music} 一 ↓ 二↓/ 三↓/ 四↓/ 五↓/ 六↓/ 七↓/ 八↓
12   [二↓/二↓/三↓/四↓/五↓/六↓/七↓/八↓]
13   *one↓ / two↓ / three↓ / four↓ / five↓ / six↓ / seven↓ / eight↓ // [two↓ /
14   two↓ / three↓ / four↓ / five↓ / six↓ / seven↓ / eight↓]*
15   [{The students in the rows simultaneously raise their left arms to 90°
16   from their body and then lower it to the initial position. The students at
17   the front of the rows maintain their initial position and make no
18   movements}]
19 Speakers: =[三↓/二↓/三↓/四↓/五↓/六↓/七↓/八↓]
20   *[three↓ / two↓ / three↓ / four↓ / five↓ / six↓ / seven↓ / eight↓]*
21   [{The students in the rows simultaneously raise both arms above their
22   heads and then lower them to the initial position. The students at the
23   front of the rows maintain their initial position and make no
24   movements}]
25 Speakers: = [四↓/二↓/三↓/四↓/五↓/六↓/七↓/八↓]
26   *[four↓ / two↓ / three↓ / four↓ / five↓ / six↓ / seven↓ / eight↓]*
27   [{The students in the rows simultaneously raise their feet, alternately,
28   simulating a march. The students at the front of the rows maintain their
29   initial position and make no movements}]
30 Speakers: = [五↓/ 二↓/ 三↓]
31   *[five↓ / two↓ / three↓]*
32   [{The students in the rows simultaneously raise both arms in front of
33   their torsos and then lower them, and at the same time squat down. The
34   students at the front of the rows maintain their initial position and make
35   no movements}]
36 {The camera gradually pans across all the rows and zooms in on one teacher, Ms. Zhu, who
37 passes the last student of one of the rows, turns and walks back to the first student}
38 Speakers: = [四↓/ 五↓/ 六↓/ 七↓/ 八↓]
39   *[five↓ / two↓ / three↓ / four↓ / five↓ / six↓ / seven↓ / eight↓]*
40   [{When the teacher has turned around, the students in the row in focus
41   are repeating the same sequence of body movements as in the previous
42   count. One student in the middle of the row, Yuan Yi, raises her arms in
43   relaxed fashion and at low intensity, which results in a slight lack of
44   coordination with the other students in the row. The teacher passes this
45   student and looks at her smiling, without stopping. The student smiles at
46   the teacher, and accelerates her body movements to coordinate with her
47   peers. The teacher passes the student, still smiling. Once the teacher has
48   passed, the student returns to her previous relaxed body movements and
49   looks back to the student beside her in the row, Xiaoyun, and they both
50   laugh}]

(Video recording. Physical exercises in Hangzhou Secondary
School. Recording code:3v_Zh_S15112006EC)

As part of the physical practice the participants were expected to reproduce every morning, the activity in Extract 4.4 is carried out following the
sequence of body movements as described in Table 4.2. These participants,
who are physically positioned on the athletics track in accordance with their
participant statuses of animators and supervisors (lines 1–6), coordinate
their actions following various sequences of eight numbers broadcast on

the schools' loudspeakers to implement the "National program of physical exercises for secondary education students" (line 7). These enumerations are grouped in four series, with the position of each one being signaled by the first number of the series (see Table 4.8 for the visual organization of the logic underpinning the series of enumerations).

Following this basic arrangement of the activity, each enumeration functions as a direct instruction for the animators to perform a particular sequence of body movements under the visual attention of the supervisors. These movements range from those for one arm (lines 11–18) to those involving the simultaneous coordination of the two arms (lines 19–24) to those involving the legs (lines 25–29) to those requiring the coordination of both arms and legs (lines 30–50). However, one of the most striking aspects to emerge from the video recording transcribed in Extract 4.3 is how the camera zoom in line 37 provides a completely new representation of the actions. In contrast to a panoramic view of the activity, where small details might be lost in favor of holistic perceptions, a close look at the actions of a small number of participants brings discontinuity to the forefront of the analysis (lines 38–50).

This discontinuity is made particularly explicit by a detailed analysis of the *byplays* (Goffman, 1981: 134) or interactions among participants performing different statuses of participation. Thus, the analyst can empirically identify, on the one hand, what counts as legitimate or illegitimate forms of action, from the perspective of the participants, and on the other, how these participants position themselves and others with respect to such forms of evaluation. In this example, the interaction across the lines of the different statuses of participation occurs between Ms. Zhu, the tutor of a grade eight class, and Yuan Yi and Xiaoyun, two of her female students located in one of the rows on the athletics track. Figure 4.7 shows the photograms extracted from the video recording and captures the highly condensed meaning of the series of nonverbal actions that take place during the five seconds

Table 4.8 Series of enumerations

Series of enumerations							
First number in each series	**Rest of the numbers in each series**						
1	2	3	4	5	6	7	8
2	2	3	4	5	6	7	8
3	2	3	4	5	6	7	8
4	2	3	4	5	6	7	8

of time transcribed in lines 42–50 of Extract 4.4 (Ms. Zhu and Yuan Yi are identified in red in the photograms).

Part I in Figure 4.7 corresponds to the photogram time-stamped 1'15.19" of the recording and illustrates the action described in lines 43–45. Yuan Yi participates by carrying out the required body movements in an exaggerated attitude of boredom, moving her arms at very low intensity and speed. As a result of this pattern of participation she becomes uncoordinated with the rest of the students in her row, drawing the attention of Ms. Zhu, as shown in Part II, corresponding to the photogram time-stamped 1'18.08". The teacher establishes eye contact with Yuan Yi and both laugh, after which the student modulates the intensity/speed of her body movements to coordinate with the student in front of her in the row (lines 46–48). Finally, Part III portrays the photogram time-stamped 1'20.03", when the teacher walks away from Yuan Yi. Once Ms. Zhu is looking away, the student reestablishes the previous pattern of slow and uncoordinated movements, and turns to the girl behind her, Xiaoyun, to laugh with her (lines 49–52).

This sequence of coordinated actions reveals which forms of interaction are co-constructed by the participants as part of the *frontstage/backstage* (Goffman, 1971: 114) of the scene, highlighting which forms of engagement are institutionally exhibited and which are concealed. In the present example, these mainly involve nonverbal features concerning the speed, intensity, and coordination of body movements: high speed/intensity and good coordination are exhibited while low speed/intensity and poor coordination are hidden. But most importantly, this sequence makes explicit how participants collaborate in exhibiting and concealing these forms of participation, beyond the framework of the strict differentiation of statuses where the supervisor acts as the representative of the institution and the animator carries out the actions required.

The participation of the students in the ritualized practices was far from achieving a constant "mode of delivery that entails a high degree of fluency, without hesitations, in a stylised intonation contour, accompanied by prescribed postures, proxemics, behaviours, attitudes and trappings" (Du Bois,

Figure 4.7 Collusion practices across participant statuses

1986:, as cited in Rampton, 2006: 181). Lack of coordination, low intensity suggesting boredom, exaggeration of certain movements in a mocking attitude and other forms of low-level disruptive engagement were also intrinsic to the moment-to-moment of the action taking place during the activities in the three schools. Thus, both students and teachers had learned to build different (and nonnecessarily coherent/stable) kinds of solidarity that allowed them to resolve the tension of having to perform their attributed institutional roles while engaging simultaneously in other practices of disalignment, framed in the construction of interpersonal relations other than institutional roles.

Ms. Zhu, Yuan Yi, and Xiaoyun's actions could be interpreted from this standpoint. Ms. Zhu's eye contact with Yuan Yi occurs immediately after the student loses coordination with the rest of her peers in the row, and in the interaction this is interpreted as a warning cue; her movements, intensity, and speed are synchronized with those of the others as soon as the teacher looks at her. This sequence of oriented actions points to the local emergence of an animator-supervisor public participation framework where the different requirements and obligations faced by each of the statuses are accepted/ratified by the participants (i.e., displaying the expected actions, in the case of the animator, and controlling and enforcing these actions, in the case of the supervisors). However, they do so while simultaneously performing other forms of nonverbal participation, like smiling and laughing, that show the enactment of parallel and private affiliations built upon the pleasure of the short-lived disengagements.[3]

On the one hand, the smile shared by Ms. Zhu and Yuan Yi in line 45, when they establish eye contact, signals an instance of complicity in which Ms. Zhu positions herself merely as an animator of institutional dictates. Although she looks specifically at the student in passing, and this seems to function as a warning cue, the shared smile between these two participants, together with the fact that the teacher does not stop walking along the row when she sees Yuan Yi is not coordinated with her peers, allows Ms. Zhu to distance herself from the authority inscribed in her public status of participation. In other words, she is performing a double-voiced practice that makes room for both her official status as a participant who is institutionally expected to ensure the upholding of the laws and also her individual persona, as someone who enjoys momentary forms of disengagement.

On the other hand, the laughter between Yuan Yi and Xiaoyun in line 50 shows an instance of peer solidarity, locally enacted in the concealed action of an inappropriate form of participation. Immediately following Yuan Yi's modulation of her body movements, and when the teacher walks away from her, the student returns to the uncoordinated actions, turns back to Xiaoyun, and they both laugh. This coordinated action between the two students in the activity sequence again reflects the interpersonal enjoyment of transgressing what is interactionally constructed as the legitimate participation framework. In Extract 4.5, taken from a later interview with

Xiaoyun, the student explains the reason why these kinds of practices take place during the physical exercises:

Extract 4.5 "The Physical Exercises Are Not Interesting at All"

Miguel: 所以。。。/ 还有那个。。。/ 星期一二三四五有那个。。。/那个。。。/ 不知道。。。

soo / there is also uuh / from Monday to Friday there is uuh / uuh / I don't know

Xiaoyun: 体操？

gymnastics?

Miguel: 对/就是那个为什么做那个。。。

right / just uuh why doing uuh

Xiaoyun: 学校那个领导那个想法说是锻炼身体阿/但是。。。/ 我觉得锻炼身体啊还不如平时多给我们一点锻炼身体的机会//早操的话。。。/ 我觉得就是有些/有些同学都已经/都这样子做的话/都已经起步到锻炼的作用了/反而是在那边发呆一会儿然后又回去了/没什么意义 // 而且/广播操也没有什么有趣的//广播操的姿势都太死板了

the idea of the school leaders is physical exercise / buut / I think it is better to give us more time and opportunity to do exercise in general rather than just let us do physical exercise/ regarding the physical exercises / I think there are some / some classmates have already / do this kind of activity / like what they do / is pointless / they are just doing them in a trance and then go back / it's useless // moreover / the physical exercises are not interesting at all // the positions of the exercises are too rigid

(Retrospective interview with Yuan Yi and Xiaoyun. Hangzhou Secondary School. Recording code: 22dp_Zh_S24112006E)

These examples show that interpersonal solidarity based on a mocking disalignment with collectivist frameworks of participation was a constitutive part of the ritualized practices that were institutionally aimed at promoting coordination, simultaneity, synchrony, patriotism, health, and community service. This defiant interpersonal solidarity was constantly enacted across the boundaries of the changing participation statuses (animators and supervisors) and the stable institutional roles (teachers and students) involved in the organization of these practices. Let us now examine the discursive forms mobilized in the three schools to legitimize these community values that have been shown as institutionally promoted and interpersonally shaped in daily interactions at the three schools, as part of the wider model emphasizing both academicism (as linked to intellectual education) and community organization (as linked to physical and moral education).

4.3   COMMUNITY ORGANIZATION: IT'S GOOD, IT'S LEGAL, IT'S SOCIOCULTURALLY ROOTED

Community organization was not only reconstituted in the course of the ritualized practices analyzed previously; it was also discursively institutionalized through semantic strategies of legitimization (van Dijk, 1987; Kress & van Leeuwen, 1990; Kress, 1996, 2001; van Leeuwen, 1995; Martín-Rojo & van Dijk, 1997; Martín-Rojo 2003) that represented the combination of academicism and all the collectivist values associated with the community organization practices analyzed previously, viewed as being (a) essentially good; (b) framed in the political legacy of the Chinese Communist Party (CCP); and (c) socioculturally rooted both in the international standards of science and in Chinese cultural traditions. These forms of representation were built upon the articulation of various discursive forms of grammatical-textual organization (e.g., lexical selection, semantic roles, categorization, predicate strategies, nomination strategies, discursive connectives) and multimodality (e.g., the distribution of para-textual elements and the combination of different semiotic codes) across the material and symbolic spaces of the three schools.

The representation of this combination as essentially good was constantly evidenced in a semantic form of moral evaluation that highlighted the goodness of linking the values of scientism, solidarity, cooperation, discipline, law abidance, social responsibility, and patriotism. Thus, Extracts 4.1 and 4.3 illustrate, through the construction of explicit moral categories (the "good student") and norms of conduct ("rules to be observed by the students"), that all these values were represented as reference points for the social definition of a good member of the school community. However, they were not the only forms of moral evaluation articulated in the schools; Figure 4.8, translated in Table 4.9, illustrates other discursive resources displayed in the panels and government posters displayed in the schools.

The values mentioned in Figure 4.8 are differentiated by text distribution, lexical choice, predication, and use of color. The lexical items referring to

Table 4.9 "Eight honors and eight disgraces"

Establish a socialist concept of honor Eight honors and eight disgraces	
Pride in loving the motherland	The shame of harming the motherland
Pride in serving the People	The shame of deviating from the People
Pride in advocating science	The shame of ignorance
Pride in working hard	The shame of indolence
Pride in solidarity	The shame of selfishness
Pride in honesty and trustworthiness	The shame of dishonesty
Pride in abiding the law	The shame of breaking the law
Pride in diligence	The shame of self-indulgence

Figure 4.8 Good and bad, as officialized on school notice boards

patriotism, scientism, hard work, solidarity, honesty, and lawfulness (and their antonyms) are distributed in two different columns: on the left, in red (traditionally associated with good fortune and happiness in Chinese popular culture), predicating actions referred to loving, serving, advocating, and conforming, while on the right, in blue (traditionally considered as the color of immorality in Chinese popular culture), predicating actions of harming, deviating, ignoring, or transgressing. Thus, the management of these discursive resources reinforced the attribution of positive meanings to the combination of academicism and the values of community organization.

The discourse representing this combination, as framed in the political legacy of the CCP, was based on semantic strategies of authorization that stressed the subordination of all values to institutional processes of bureaucratic objectification or to the government's foundational ideological guidelines. Extract 4.2 is an example of authorization through bureaucratic objectification, consisting in the introduction of a quantitative assessment method to evaluate the academic, physical, and moral aspects of students' behavior, following specific institutional guidelines laid down by the Department of Education. Figure 4.8 also illustrates how this is authorized by focusing more explicitly on the link with the CCP's ideological guidelines.

The two columns predicating the positive and negative meanings are headed by a main title ("Establish a socialist concept of honor") and a subtitle ("Eight honors and eight disgraces") that, juxtaposed with the image of Hu Jintao (the president of the People's Republic of China at the time of the data collection) and with the principles of the CCP just below the image (these principles being shown in yellow, the color traditionally associated with the Chinese empire in Chinese popular culture), represent them as being anchored in the basic principles of Chinese socialism. This discursive anchoring was made even more explicit in the guiding ideology section of the schools' documents, as illustrated in Extract 4.6:

Extract 4.6   "According to the Three Representatives"

指导思想

　　按照邓小平同志提出的"三个面向"及党中央提出的"三个代表"要求，切实贯彻国务院"基础教育改革和发展的规定"精神，围绕"建设设施一流，师资精良，管理规范，质量上乘的(城)市现代化标志性实验学校"的办学生目标，巩固"为了学生的末来，提供最好而可行的教育，让每个学获得成功"的办学理念，确立"目找压力，目我奋进"的办学精神，形成"笃志，博学，多思，豁达"的师生形象，挖掘各种办学资源，加强团结合作，努力拓创新，科学高校管理，面向全体学生，全面提升办学水平。

Guiding ideology

In accordance with the call for the "Three Represents" made by the Party's Central Committee and that for the "Three Faces" made by comrade Deng Xiaoping, to implement conscientiously the spirit of the "Provisions for the development and reform of basic education" by the State Council, to focus on the educational goal of "building experimental schools as reference points for modern standard schools characterized by quality, management criteria, excellent teachers, and first-quality facilities, to consolidate the educational philosophy of "providing the best possible education and enabling all students' success for their own future", to establish the educational spirit of "success involves pressure and personal effort", to encourage students' and teachers' to be "tenacious, knowledgeable, reflexive, and open-minded", to tap a variety of educational resources, to strengthen unity and cooperation, to strive to develop innovation and scientific management, to enhance the overall level of all schools and students.

(Institutional document in Hangzhou Secondary School, p. 3)

Excellence, success, effort, tenacity, knowledgeability, reflexivity, open-mindedness, innovation, scientific management, unity, and cooperation, among others, are represented in Extract 4.6 as principles emanating from an educational law-goal-philosophy-spirit-image that is directly derived from the main ideological guidelines of the CCP. This is discursively constructed on the basis of the syntactic and semantic organization of the text.

On the one hand, the opening of the section with the discursive connective "in accordance with" followed by noun groups referring to the ideological guidelines of the CCP ("Three Represents" and "Three Faces") and by predicative actions emphasizing the agent role of political authorities ("Party Central Committee") and presidents ("Deng Xiaoping") represents the rest of the elements in the text as semantically subordinated (see Chapter 1, Section 1.3, for an overview of the role of political guidelines such as the "Three Represents" in the political strategies of Deng Xiaoping, Jiang Zeming, and Hu Jintao). On the other hand, the organization of the main noun groups in the text according to a holo-meronymic semantic relationship, from wider political theories to national education laws to the emanating principles, strengthens the semantic authorization of these principles by placing them in a top-down hierarchical scheme.

Discourses representing the combination of academicism and community organization as socioculturally rooted, both in the international standards of science and in Chinese cultural traditions, were recurrently circulated in the form of posters and sculptures located in the classrooms and in the schools' main halls and corridors (see Figure 4.9). These other discursive forms contributed to authorizing the combination of scientism, solidarity, cooperation, discipline, law abidance, social responsibility, and patriotism by juxtaposing images/texts of international scientists, Chinese communist leaders, and Confucian philosophers advocating science,[4] love of the CCP's great history in saving the modern Chinese nation,[5] and respect for disciplined diligence and collective cooperation,[6] respectively.

Overall, the analysis of the discursive forms of representation in the official documents and texts at the three experimental schools points to an ongoing educational institutionalization of community organization practices. These practices not only played a significant role in the organization of the schools' everyday routines and in the students' educational records (as we saw in Sections 4.1 and 4.2), but the values associated with them (as emerged

Figure 4.9   International science, Chinese communism, and Confucianism in sculptures

from the interactional analysis of the ritualized practices) were also officially legitimated through semantic strategies of moral evaluation and authorization that linked these values to relevant moral categories in the schools (the "good students"), to the Chinese communist ideological and legal frameworks, and to traditional Chinese canons regarding Confucian culture.

These discourses contributed to naturalize the representation of the three-dimension model (intellectual, physical, and moral education), and the derived formulas of academicism (i.e., emphasis on intellectual knowledge across the curricular subjects) and collectivism (i.e., emphasis on community practices based on ritualized patriotic and physical activities), as resulting from the combination of international scientific excellence, Chinese communism, and Chinese cultural traditions. This combination becomes institutionalized in a moralized definition of the school community in which the construction of the good member relies not only on meritocratic criteria regarding academic results but also on a patriotic-plus-Confucian-based collectivist ethos that requires students to conform to a school-based hierarchical and disciplined social organization. The last section in this chapter will move the focus of attention to this process of institutionalization by tracing the discursive emergence of these moralized discourses about the community in the context of the construction of a modern Chinese national curriculum. This backtracking will enable us to better identify the ideological basis of the links between everyday life in the three schools in Zhejiang, the institutional reforms for educational modernization in China, and the wider politics of national identity (re)produced and constantly challenged in the process of Chinese nation-state building.

4.4   EDUCATIONAL MODERNIZATION AND MORAL EDUCATION IN CONTEMPORARY CHINA

The interplay between curriculum, knowledge, and ideology has been widely documented in relation to different space-time locations, following Apple's pioneering work on this issue (Apple, 1979). In the case of China, studies have historically tended to focus on comparative analyses of educational systems in China and elsewhere, with no clear critical advocacy, although there have been important contributions linking educational reforms, curriculum developments, and China's modern politics of identity (see, for instance, Hu, 1969; Peake, 1970; Cleverley, 1985; Pepper, 1996; Harrison, 2000; Li, Zhong, Lin, & Zhang, 2004; Murphy, 2004; Jones, 2005; Vickers, 2009). The present study provides a basis for identifying the discursive traces between the legitimate knowledge about what counts as "a good student" and "good practice" in the everyday interactions, interviews, and official documents, as analyzed in the previous sections, on the one hand, and the historical developments of the Chinese educational curriculum during the construction of modern China, on the other.

This basis is particularly apparent when we observe the institutional designing of the intellectual-physical-moral axis that has historically underpinned modern Chinese education. Such an axis was first officially established as one of the main pillars for the articulation of curriculum design in the modern education law of 1906, which drastically shifted the conceptualization of education (see Chapter 3, Section 3.3). From its traditional role of grounding future administrators in the principles of law and government, education evolved into a modern institution aimed at ensuring the reproduction of the ideological framework of the nation-state, by fostering national identity, official patriotism, military defense knowledge, and economic development. This plan set out the following goals for the Chinese educational curriculum: to promote a collective identity though public moral education; to instruct in militarism through physical education based on games, rituals, and military training exercises; and to teach academic knowledge through practical textbooks (Peake, 1970: 63).

Since then, intellectual, physical, and moral dimensions have all been officially considered as essential elements of all nationwide curriculum reforms. Nevertheless, important differences have been described in relation to their corresponding contents. Among these differences, those concerning the designing of "moral education" are of special relevance; this concept has been discursively embodied in the form of different labels by successive Chinese governments according to the criteria politically mobilized in each period for defining legitimate membership of the political community of the nation. From Public Morality to Citizenship to Three Principles to Politics to Thought and Values, a brief review of these five official labels reveals the most important discursive shifts in the institutionalization of the moral educational dimension in modern curricula in China, and this in turn allows us to identify the progressive emergence of the discourses and practices of community organization that are analyzed in the previous sections.

The incorporation of a curricular subject for moral education in the 1906 law passed by the Qing court was part of the wider educational reform imported from Japan, which was represented as the most suitable adaptation of modern European sciences and industrial modes of production to a Confucian politico-cultural framework supposedly shared throughout East Asia. Thus, although the subject was oriented to the modern interest of promoting a collective identity, much emphasis was still placed on promoting "an integrative role—bringing rulers and ruled together in pursuit of higher collective goals [which] echoed the old Confucian ideal of 'using morals (*de*, rather than laws—*fa*) to rule the country'" (Vickers, 2009: 59); in other words, moral education was at that time geared toward inculcating membership of a political community that was discursively constructed around the premodern cultural values of loyalty to the throne, law, and government, filial piety, social hierarchy, and social harmony that had been inherited from Chinese traditions.[7]

Nevertheless, these values soon disappeared from the national curriculum, with the overthrow of the Chinese imperial system in 1911. The rise of intellectual and social movements (i.e., the New Cultural movement) seeking a Westernized Chineseness as a way to facilitate China's international acceptance in the modern world and to escape from what was considered as backwardness led to widespread public debate and institutional restructuring. Attempts to establish a constitutional monarchy were aborted and the victory of the Republic Revolution then gave rise to attempts to construct a modern China, impelled by intense antitraditionalism, which was crystalized in the 1912 education law. The collective identity institutionally legitimized in the curriculum in the form of moral education was no longer discursively constructed upon traditional cultural values. Instead, this identity came to be constructed on the basis of a discourse that stressed the need to reject local traditions and to adopt Western values, institutions, and cultures in order to ensure the sovereignty of the Chinese state within a wider international system of sovereign states and nations (Pepper, 1996: 61).

The official shift to a new modern conceptualization of moral education in the Chinese educational system was made explicit in the 1922 national education law, which first embodied moral education with the label of "Citizenship" (Cleverley, 1985: 50–55). In line with Chinese republicans' interest in the U.S. educational system (see Chapter 3, Section 3.3), this new subject was designed according to a liberal conceptualization of the nation. Thus, the collective identity institutionally legitimized through the subject contents paralleled official discourses representing the People as a democratic body of sovereign (self-regulating) citizens who were nationals of the state, regardless of ethnicity, religion, or lineage (see Chapter 1, Section 1.3). But the subject of "Citizenship" experienced another reshaping at the end of the 1920s once antitraditionalist Chinese intellectuals were able to mobilize public support against American republicanism, in favor of the political economy represented by European centrism.

Legitimized by popular and intellectual movements of the time, which demanded a stronger and more centralized government to avoid territorial disintegration, the authoritarian turn taken by the Chinese Nationalist Party (CNP) led to the embodiment of moral education under the label of the "Three Principles". This subject incorporated new national historical narratives, together with the political slogan of the "Three Principles of the People," which became the Party's main ideological foundation in 1927. Thus, moral education was shaped according to a new discursive construction of the legitimate nation in which the People came to be conceived as united around the principles of patriotism, restricted rights under the tutelage of the Party, and economic development (Cleverley, 1985: 55). These new narratives were articulated in the curriculum around self-reinforcing ideas that represented the Party as the only element capable of defending the Chinese state against foreign invaders and of enabling the accumulation of wealth and power among the Chinese nation.

To this aim, episodes of national humiliation at the hands of Western colonial powers were incorporated as part of the official contents in the subjects of History and the Three Principles. The movement for citizenship education became closely identified with the "National Salvation" movement. In other words, the previous republican idea of citizenship was reconstituted under a new moral frame which was officially intended to "show how the interests of the nation and the people were one and the same and thereby cause to flourish the spirit of patriotism; to create in the people a willingness to sacrifice all for the nation and to show them the necessity for supporting the 'National Salvation Movement'" (Peake, 1970: 116). In addition, new collective rituals, like the physical practices and the Monday meetings described in this chapter, were institutionalized as complementary activities to enhance militarist training and patriotic sentiments (see Harrison, 2000). However, this official definition of moral education again collapsed, as soon as the official nationalism underpinning it was destabilized by new forms of popular and intellectual concerns in China that emerged in response to changing local and global conditions.

This latter change in the form and content of moral education was triggered by new antitraditionalist discourses that circulated in China following the public and intellectual discontent with the international decisions taken at the Versailles Peace Conference in 1919 (see also Chapter 3, Section 3.3). Having rejected both Chinese tradition and Western liberalism, new intellectual and popular movements arose in China, like the so-called May Fourth movement, which set the conditions and ideological basis for the advent of the CCP and the subsequent revision and reevaluation of the narrative of national history after 1949. The "Three Principles" curriculum subject was replaced by the one named "Politics," which brought with it the dictates of historical materialism and highlighted the themes of class struggle, revolutionary heroism. and socialist morality (Vickers, 2009: 60).

Following the new Constitution of the People's Republic of China in 1954, with its definition of the People as the political community constituted of peasants, workers, sympathetic bourgeoisies, and the supporting intellectuals of the CCP, the whole education system was restructured on the basis of the educational slogan of "Red and expert" (红而专). This slogan appealed to the maxims of productive labor, applied technical training, and Marxist-Leninist doctrine (in contrast to the humanist, theoretical, and feudalist principles attributed to the educational system ruled by the CNP). Thus, moral education in the curriculum of Politics as well as in other everyday school activities was constrained by these socialist maxims. On the one hand, they were incorporated in the subject of Politics through official organization of its contents around the so-called Five Loves—the love of the motherland, the People, labor, scientific knowledge, and public property. These contents included the Marxist categorization of the stages of societal development (from primitive communism to slave, feudal and bourgeois stages to socialism), historical narratives representing the party as the legitimate heir of the Chinese antitraditionalist, antiliberal, and anti-imperialist revolution, and the reinvention of national heroes and villains that now depended heavily on class identity (Hu, 1969: 2–5; Jones, 2005: 90). On the other hand, the maxims derived from the slogan of "Red and expert" were institutionalized in the form of cross-cutting principles that sought to establish a collectivist organization of the schools as well as of all teaching-learning activity in the classrooms (Cleverley, 1985: 133, 187). Moral education, nevertheless, went through another process of official revision, this time as a consequence of the disconnection between the official communist rhetoric, which remained substantially unaltered until the 1980s, and the economic liberal reforms undertaken by Deng Xiaoping after 1978.

This revision was particularly noticeable from the 1990s, in the framework of the Patriotic Educational Campaign that was first launched immediately following the Tiananmen events in 1989 and that has been continuously developed to the present day (see Chapter 1, Section 1.3). The cultural change accompanying the widespread socioeconomic liberalization reforms, which led to people's everyday lives being increasingly based upon a nonsocialist reality, produced a further historical clash between popular and official forms of nationalism that boosted the contemporary educational design of moral education. In line with the key themes in the Guidelines for Patriotic Education issued by the State Education Commission in 1994 (see Table 4.10, based on Zhao, 1998), which attempted to counterbalance a nonofficial patriotism based on the principles of science, liberal democracy, and nationalism, this educational dimension was officially aimed at promoting love of a culturally distinct ancient community of people (that is, "different from a supposedly Western cultural liberalism") whose modernization is guided and guarded by the CCP (Murphy, 2004).

Such a conceptualization shift in moral education has been particularly reflected in the curriculum through the relabeling of "Politics" as "Thought and Values" (see Li et al., 2004; Hughes, 2006). Under the guidelines of the Program for Improving Civil Morality issued by the Central Committee of the CCP in 2001, as a further development of the Patriotic Education Campaign in education, this subject has recovered the discourse of citizenship in China by dividing morality into the three categories of "public morality", "family virtue", and "professional ethics", whereby the ancient Confucian emphasis on individual, family, and community duties is recovered and balanced with a new discussion on rights (Li et al., 2004: 458). That is, morality has been extended beyond a representation purely in terms of socialist or communist values, even though socialism still retains a status as the "highest stage of morality" (Li et al., 2004: 458).

In fact, Mao Zedong is now barely visible in the editions of the Thought and Values textbooks published after 2003. In contrast to the chairman's former prominence, in textbooks published in the mid-1990s, contemporary editions include instead numerous quotations from Jiang Zemin, Hu Jintao, Deng Xiaoping, and Confucius (Vickers, 2009: 69). These textbooks now feature as exemplars of moral behavior "an eclectic mix of Chinese and

Table 4.10 Key themes in the Guidelines for Patriotic Education

- A focus on Chinese history (especially modern history and the role of the CCP).
- China's special characteristics and realities, highlighting their incompatibility with Western values.
- CCP heroism and the examples of revolutionary martyrs.
- The CCP's fundamental principles and policies.
- The great achievements of modernization under the CCP.
- Socialist conceptions of democracy and the rule of law in contrast to the Western conception of the rule of law
- National security and defense (against "peaceful evolutionism" and hostile forces).
- Peaceful reunification and the principle of "one country, two systems".

foreigners (notably scientists such as Newton and Einstein), but relatively few communists" (Vickers, 2009: 69), which resonates with some of the discursive and multimodal examples found in the three experimental schools analyzed in this chapter.

In particular, and following Vickers's (2009) study, the contents of the new Morality subject have been organized in contemporary China so as to highlight three core aspects: (a) the leading role of the CCP, whether in protecting a glorious Chinese civilization of 5,000 years of history or in pushing it through a scientific modernization; (b) an emphasis on the need for an intercultural consciousness upon which to inculcate students' awareness of cultural differences in the world and the attachment to the Chinese nation; and (c) the advocacy of a collectivist-based school community which blurs the boundaries between civic discourses on rights/duties and ancient cultural codes on social harmony, politeness, collaboration, hard work, discipline, respect for laws, and awareness of every individual's responsibility toward the community.

Li Lanqing, former Chinese vice premier and one of the main political actors in the educational reforms carried out between 1993 and 2003, explicitly stated the extent to which contemporary official discourses on socialism, cultural traditionalism, and modernization had become institutionalized in the new conceptualization of moral education:

Our realistic ideal is to build socialism with Chinese characteristics and to turn our country into a prosperous, democratic and modern socialist country with a high degree of civilization. To be morally sound is to carry forward Chinese moral traditions while fostering elevated sentiments in the spirit of the times and in compliance with modern rules of moral conduct. To be well-educated is to be able to carry forward our cultural traditions while absorbing the achievements of advanced cultures of other nations in the world. Having a sense of discipline means that we understand and observe law and discipline. For this reason, under the guidance of Marxism-Leninism, Mao Zedong Thought, Deng Xiaoping Theory and the Three Represents, moral education should follow the general goals of education and the laws governing student development, set the content and requirements for each stage of education, and formulate a sequence of step-by-step objectives for installing moral values and rules of conduct in students. Education in dialectical materialism and historical materialism must be advanced to help students foster scientific perspectives. It is also necessary to have well-defined targets for education in patriotism, collectivism and socialism in our national culture and revolutionary traditions, and education in ideals, moral principles and conduct, in Chinese history in general, and modern history in particular. (L. Li, 2004: 318)

Thus far, we have explored the situated implications of the modernization reforms carried out in China, analyzing the discursive organization of three experimental schools in Zhejiang. In the last two chapters, we have identified the neoliberal and cultural traditionalist forces that guide these reforms, examining the social construction of what counts as a "good experimental school" or a "good student" in daily life at these schools. A close analysis of their discursive and ritualized interactional organization has shown the local emergence of such forces both from institutional constraints and from the interpersonal spaces for agency that are (re)constituted and negotiated by the school heads, English-language teachers, and students involved. Although in these previous chapters little attention has been paid to the English-language classes attended by these participants, I shall now examine this aspect more closely, to better connect these emerging meaning-making practices with the institutional processes of English-language reform in China that were initially discussed in Chapter 1.

5 Reform and Innovation in China's English-Language Education
Insights from the Classroom

5.1 ENGLISH-LANGUAGE EDUCATION POLICIES AND PEDAGOGY, FROM BELOW

In the previous two chapters, I discussed the molding of China's modern education system within the organizing principles of academicism and moral education, and showed how meaning-making actions in everyday life at three experimental schools shape (and are shaped by) the institutionalization of curricular and complementary activities that emphasize both meritocratic and community organization values. However, I have said very little so far about the classroom activity taking place within the curriculum subjects, and this is another aspect occupying a meaningful social space among China's modernization reforms. One such subject, English-language teaching, has played a crucial role in contemporary educational reforms, in accordance with the discursive equation officially established since the late 1970s between this international language and the Chinese national plan for economic development (Hu, 2002: 37–38; Adamson, 2004: 2–3; Wang, 2007: 96–99; see also Chapter 1, Section 1.1.).

As part of the curriculum innovation reforms developed by the Chinese Ministry of Education since 1978 (see Ministry of Education, 1978), this subject has undergone pedagogical adjustments in line with wider institutional and national economic policies aimed at modernization (Hu, 2005; Feng, 2007; Wang, 2007; Fong, 2009; Lo Bianco, Orton & Gao, 2009). During the 1980s, immediately following the "open door" national policies that put an end to a long period of political and economic isolation from the rest of the world, language education policies in China were based on a cautious social representation of English aimed at introducing the language into the national education system so as to ensure the country's integration within the international scene while protecting the Chinese nation from supposedly threatening cultural influences from the West (see an example of official discourse on this in L. Li [2004: 349]). In these policies, English was conceived of as a necessary set of technical skills for knowledge acquisition, stripped of any association with foreign nations, locations, or traditions.

In line with this representation, the new language policies were accompanied by a pedagogical approach focused on traditional methodologies, and so English-language curricula were structured in accordance with the behaviorist and grammatical interests of audio-lingual and grammar translation methods (Wang, 2007: 89). Classroom contents and activities, thus, were organized on the basis of a normative grammar; that is, they were designed from a teacher-centered perspective to provide students with a set of prescribed and decontextualized lexical and grammatical repertoires which avoided any sociocultural content.

Subsequently, in the 1990s, curriculum innovations were focused toward a new social representation of English, as a resource for international communication (see Ministry of Education, 1993). In line with increasing interest within Chinese political and economic circles in the new service-oriented international market, the country's new language education policies viewed English as a commodity that was indispensable for successful participation in this market. Thus, traditional grammar gave way to the adoption of communicative language teaching methods, and in particular the task-based approach (TBA), in which attention was shifted to a learner-centered approach, focusing on authentic language and communication opportunities. Following the Tiananmen events, these curriculum reforms were also subject to the national policy measures embodied in the Patriotic Education campaign to strengthen intercultural competence and enhance students' awareness of cultural differences in an increasingly internationalized world while reinforcing their sense of belonging to a distinctly Chinese culture (Fong, 2009: 48).

This latter approach has been institutionally emphasized since the 2000s, with much weight being placed on the cultural adaptation of international teaching methodologies to the specifically Chinese educational context (see Ministry of Education, 2000, 2001). This institutional stress on cultural adaptation is derived from various discursive domains, not necessarily aligned, taking into account (a) the CCP's national policies calling for international knowledge to be adapted to Chinese national conditions, in accordance with the political slogan of "Socialism with Chinese characteristics" (具有中国特色的社会主义) (see Chapter 1, Section 1.3); (b) Chinese intellectual criticism of the imposition of Western pedagogical approaches, and their related language teaching industries based on legitimate/profitable publishing companies and textbooks (Ouyang, 2000); and/or (c) the claims made by in-service language teacher educators, who defend bottom-up reforms taking into account local teachers' knowledge on issues of curriculum change (X. Wu, 2005; Z. Wu, 2005).

However, this interconnectivity between economic processes of change, Chinese language education policies, curriculum modernization reforms, and official pedagogical approaches to English-language teaching raises questions about its real applicability to explaining what happens (or has happened) in everyday English-language classes. Do these national, institutional, and pedagogical discourses provide a clear frame for understanding the organization of English classroom activity at any given space-time in the Chinese context? Can it be taken for granted that any English-language classroom in China since the 2000s will be characterized by a more or less pure implementation of TBA? My ethnographic observation at the three experimental schools studied in Zhejiang suggested that this is not necessarily the case.

The sixth- and eighth-grade classes observed at these three schools were all traversed by traditional, communicative, and culturally contrastive principles. The traditional approach was reflected in the overall management of the activity, which contributed no type of interaction other than the teacher-centered approach. The teachers made all decisions about the topics deemed legitimate, the forms of interaction, and the timing, with little or no space left for spontaneous/non–previously prescribed routines. This appeared to be reinforced by aspects such as the high numbers of students—around 50, as described in Chapter 3, Section 3.2, the space arrangement—pupils arranged in rows facing the blackboard, in all classes—and the highly conventionalized organization of activity monitored by the teachers during most of the class-time, as illustrated in Extract 5.2 taken from my own field notes from one of the first English classes I observed in Zhejiang (see also Chapter 1, Section 1.1).

Extract 5.1   "I Could Not Follow the Rhythm of the Interaction"

As in the case of the other classes that I observed today, everything went quite fast once the activity started in grade 6. I could not follow the rhythm of the interaction. I was not even able to write my field notes, as paying attention to how the teacher managed to coordinate her students' actions in the course of the interaction was hard enough. There seemed to be an established routine for all the participants, who seemed capable of following the teacher through different activities and transitions involving the use of the textbook, Power Point presentation, and audio player without any slow down in the pace.

(Notebook 1, p. 11)

The participants' high speed and coordination in class activities were possible because they were already members of a community whose members were all aware of the rules and conventions for participation and task completion. However, this conventionalized organization made it harder for newcomers like me to keep up; furthermore, the fact that classroom activity was based on a predefined arrangement meant that little space was available for improvisation or for real communicative situations, as would be theoretically desirable in a communicative approach to language education.

On the other hand, there were also traces of the communicative teaching philosophy in the English classes observed. The textbooks used in these classes

Figure 5.1   "Who is more popular?"

were all co-published by the People's Education Press and North American companies (Lingo Media for the sixth-grade classes, and Thomson Learning for the eighth-grade classes) and explicitly acknowledged their orientation toward TBA teaching. In most cases, too, classroom activities were organized around the use of new technologies, providing students with audiovisual communicative interactions such as dialogues and e-mails.

Finally, the cultural contrast was present in daily classroom life through varied activities and visual media, stressing the comparison between popular culture, celebrities, monuments, food, and traditional festivals in China, Europe (particularly the UK), and North America (particularly the USA). Figure 5.1 and Extract 5.2, both taken from the course of an activity in an eighth-grade class, illustrate this point.

Extract 5.2   "Guangzhou or New York, Which One Is More Beautiful?"

{The teacher shows a slide with two pictures, of Guangzhou and New York, each identified by name. Under the pictures is the question, "Which one is more beautiful?" Various parallel conversations emerge at this point}.

Some: Guangzhou [laughs]

Zhu: (()) 广州 或者 纽约 / 那个 比较 漂亮? (()) / Shaonan / what's your opinion?
          Guangzhou or New York / which one is more beautiful?

Shaonan: {stands up} aah /那个 . . .[uuh] / Guangzhou is more beautiful than New York {he sits down}
          uuh

{Some students clap loudly. The teacher then presents the next slide, showing a picture of Beckham and Zhao Benzhan accompanied by the question, "Who is more popular?" Again many laughs and parallel conversations among students emerge at this point.}

(Audio recording made at Hangzhou Secondary School.
Recording code: 7dp_Zh_S271020006I)

This local combination of pedagogical traditions, historically linked to the national policies and political and economic questions mentioned previously, raises further questions: how do these traditions shape (and how are they shaped by) the ongoing activity in their English-language classes? What forms of knowledge emerge as appropriate, according to the organization of classroom interactions? How do participants and institutional actors position themselves and others in relation to these forms of knowledge? In an attempt to provide some tentative answers to these questions, this chapter will provide a systematized description of the English classroom practices in the three experimental schools.

I will first explore the recurrent organization of classroom interactions, paying special attention to the recursive *sequential forms of social action* (Seedhouse, 2004) and *participation frameworks* (Goffman, 1981: 137) through which teachers and students collaboratively constructed what was deemed to be the legitimate performance of language (Section 5.2). This investigation of the overall organization of classroom activities leads us to the specific value of choral repetition, which is found to constitute a fundamental, ritualized form of participation involved in the production and contestation of educational and cultural meanings (Section 5.3). By systematizing the collection of all the interactional sequences in which the participants coordinated their actions around forms of choral repetition, across the entire corpus data obtained at the three experimental schools, I will demonstrate their conventional, pedagogical, institutional, and interpersonal relevance to China's reforms and innovations in English-language education.

Both of these dimensions—the general overview of what is considered as legitimate linguistic performance in the organization of activities and the specific socio-institutional meanings rooted in classroom choral repetitions—will provide a more informed base for filling in the currently broad gaps in our knowledge of the links between economic processes of change, language education policies, curriculum reforms, and official pedagogical approaches to English-language teaching in China (Section 5.4).

5.2 THE SEQUENTIAL ORGANIZATION OF THE ENGLISH LESSONS

This study of the interactional organization of classroom activity was focused on the English-language classes in the sixth and eighth grades at the three schools in question. Initially, I observed all sessions of these classes at each school, but after completing one unit lesson I decided to concentrate on a single representative class in each level for further observation and audio-video recording of classroom practice. In particular, the data in this chapter come from the English classes at the two schools in Hangzhou city, Hangzhou Primary School and Hangzhou Secondary School (see Chapter 3 for an in-depth analysis of these two schools), which account for 42 of the 52 observed class periods in the collected data corpus (see Chapter 2, Section 2.2 for an overview of this data corpus).

In exploring the construction of what was viewed as the legitimate performance of language, my analysis in the two focal classrooms was particularly focused on how the participants coordinated their social actions via the management of *conventions of interactional ritualization* (Heller & Martin-Jones, 2001: 13) such as turn-taking and code-switching. The study of this management revealed that what was judged appropriate performance varied according to the position of the interaction in the progressive development of the core educational activities performed in each unit lesson. Thus, any consideration of the definition of legitimate linguistic performance underlying the design of English-language education in these schools requires a detailed interactional description of the recurrent sequential organization of social actions within these core activities (see Table 5.1 for an overview of the recursive activities and sequences of action).

The previously delineated sequence of activities—introducing audio-visual texts, stressing key grammar and pronunciation, performing dialogues, doing written exercises and dictations, and testing—were all part of the unit lessons in the sixth- and eighth-grade classes observed. However, the first three items made up the largest number of sessions per unit in each case, as they constituted a fixed series that was applied to work on all the audiovisual texts in each unit lesson; in the English textbooks studied, the unit lessons were normally divided into four sections, each organized around one main audiovisual text. In other words, most of the interactional work in the classrooms (five of the seven sessions per unit, on average) was based on a cycle of activities beginning with the introduction of a given audiovisual text, continuing with the highlighting of key grammatical/phonetic items, and concluding with its performance in class.

Only when this cycle was completed did the focus of classroom activity shift to written exercises, dictations and tests. I shall begin by focusing on the introductory activities for the work on each unit lesson.

Table 5.1 Recurrent activities and sequences of action in each unit lesson, in sixth and eighth grades

	Unit lesson				
Classroom sessions	1, 2, 3, 4, 5	1, 2, 3, 4, 5	1, 2, 3, 4, 5	5, 6	7
Educational activities	Introducing audiovisual texts	Stressing key grammar and pronunciation	Practicing dialogues	Dictations and exercises	Testing
Sequences of coordinated action	The students listen to audiovisual texts > the teacher elicits the students' comprehension of texts > the teacher and the students repeat the audio-played texts	The students copy down the teacher's grammatical explanation > the teacher and the students engage in repetition exchanges of rules > the teachers and the students engage in repetition exchanges of the syllables > the teacher elicits the students' fill-in-the-blank practice	Collective reading of the dialogues of the audio-played texts > the students perform the dialogues, in private pair work > the students perform the dialogues in public pair work	The teacher and the students repeat, one by one, the vocabulary of the unit > dictation practice of the key vocabulary items > the teacher elicits the students' comprehension of their homework	The students fill in a formal test paper individually during the class while the teacher walks around and supervises

5.2.1 Introducing Audiovisual Texts: Words, Grammatical Contexts and Social Functions

The introduction of audiovisual texts was recurrently carried out as sequences of listening, the elicitation of comprehension and the choral reading of interactional turns based on simulated communicative situations presented in the form of oral dialogues or e-mails/letters in the students' textbooks. These sequences oriented the participants' actions toward (a) the oral identification of certain words in the texts; (b) the oral collocation of these words in given grammatical contexts; and (c) the choral reading of complete interactional turns representing specific social functions in the corresponding audiovisual text. Extract 5.3, taken from the sixth-grade class, illustrates the initial focus on words and grammatical contexts with respect to a text on future actions appearing in section B of Unit 3, "What are you going to do?"

Extract 5.3   "We Listen Once"

1	Laura:	32 页 / let's talk
2		*page 32*
3		{noise of participants turning pages}
4	Laura:	ok // {plays the audio-recorder} 好 / 我们来听一遍
5		*well / we listen once*
6	Player:	{participant A} where are you going this afternoon? {participant B} I'm going to the
7		bookstore // {participant A} what are you going to buy? {participant B} I'm going to
8		buy a comic book // {participant A} when are you going? {participant B} I'm going
9		at 3 o'clock
10		{students remain silent while the dialogue is played}
11	Laura:	{stops the audio-player} ok / so / who can tell me WHO wants to go to the bookstore?
12		/ [Aimee or Chen Jie?]
13	Some:	[Chen Jie]
14	Laura:	Chen Jie // Chen Jie wants to go to the ↑
15	Some:	bookstore
16	Laura:	and WHICH book does Aimee / [(( ))] &
17	Guojie:	[comic book]
18	Laura:	& Chen Jie
19	Some:	comic book
20	Laura:	yes / Chen Jie is going to buy a ↑
21	All:	COMIC BOOK
22	Laura:	and WHEN / when does Chen Jie [going to]
23	Guojie:	[3 o'clock]
24	Laura:	yes / and she is going to at ↑ / [3 o'clock]
25	Some:	[3 o'clock]
26	Laura:	yes / afternoon

(Sixth-grade English-language class. Recording
code: lldp_Zh_P311020006I)

Laura's management of the participation allows her to scaffold her students' identification of the key words in the dialogue and to call their attention to the position of these words in the grammatical context of future actions in the continuous present form. Through an initial focus action (lines 1–3) accompanied by the action of starting the audio player, as well as by an explicit request in Chinese (line 4), the teacher begins the activity by focusing the students' attention on listening to the audio recording of the dialogue shown on page 32 of their books (see Figure 5.2) in which two characters engage in question-answer exchanges about future plan actions (lines 6–10). Once they have listened to three brief exchanges, she stops the player (line 11) and elicits comprehension on the basis of a question-answer turn-taking which follows a recursive *participant structure* (Philips, 1972: 3) of five turns.

In the first turn, Laura posts display questions in general solicit form (i.e., without selecting a particular addressee) focusing on the who, what and when of the actions mentioned by the speakers (lines 11, 16, 22). The questions are answered by some of the students, who self-select to offer the required words, as voiced in the recording (lines 13, 17, 23), after which Laura repeats what has been said by these students or provides an explicit affirmation that seems to function as a positive evaluation. This evaluation is immediately followed by her enunciation of an incomplete linguistic structure of future action in continuous present form, with rising intonation, which the students must complete by using the words elicited in the previous turn (lines 20 and 24; although this sequence does not apply to line 14, as the word previously elicited in line 13, Chen Jie, is the subject of the action, and unsuitable for this form of enunciation). This "completion" form of participation is interactionally constructed by the teacher, who does not initiate a new participant structure until the students have completed the previous one (lines 15, 21, 25). Thus, Laura's last turn functions both as a positive evaluation of the students' previous turn and as the beginning of the new participant structure (although she sometimes provides an explicit evaluation, as in line 26).

Figure 5.2   Primary English students' textbook (sixth grade), Section B, page 32

After having elicited the agents, objects, and temporality of the actions enunciated in the recording, and once all of these have been orally collocated in the appropriate grammatical context provided by the teacher during the knowledge-checking questions, the choral reading of the audiovisual text follows as shown in Extract 5.4. This example corresponds to a later moment in the same activity, in which Laura guides her students' participation toward the choral reading of the turns which, in the previously played dialogue, fulfill the social functions of requesting and providing information about future actions.

Extract 5.4   "Now We Are Going to Read It Once"

1	Laura:	ok / so let's look again // 接下来我们来读一遍 (2") {plays the audio-recorder}
2		*now we are going to read it once*
3	{Player}:	{participant A} where are you going this afternoon? {participant B} I'm going to the
4		bookstore // {participant A} what are you going to buy? {participant B} I'm going to
5		buy a comic book // {participant A} when are you going? {participant B} I'm going at
6		3 o'clock
7	Laura:	AT THREE O'CLOCK// ok / now / first part {plays the audio-recorder}
8	{Player}:	where are you going? {stops the audio-recorder}
9	Laura:	all together / *whēre āre yŏu gōing thĭs ăftērnŏon?*
10	Students:	{in unison} *WHĒRE ĀRĒ YŎU GŌING THĬS ĂFTĒRNŌON?*
11	Laura:	*whēre āre yŏu gōing thĭs ăftērnŏon?*
12	Students:	{in unison} *WHĒRE ĀRE YŎU GŌING THĬS ĂFTĒRNŌON?*
13	Laura:	今天下午你将要去哪儿？
14		*where are you going this afternoon?*

(Sixth-grade English-language class. Recording
code: 11dp_Zh_P311020061)

The transition to the new participation framework is guided here by Laura's demarcating and framing particles ("ok", "now", "first part"), by the direct requests in English ("let's look again", "all together") and in Chinese ("接下来我们来读一遍" [now we are going to read it once]), by the actions of playing and stopping the player, and by the repetition of what has just been played with a strongly marked intonation ("whēre āre yŏu gōing thĭs afternŏon?"). These communicative resources activate a new frame of action which orients the students' forms of participation to a new sequence of choral reading of each of the questions and answers enunciated in the dialogue. This sequence is interactionally played out through a recursive participant structure of six turns which begins with the actions of playing and listening to a segment corresponding to one of the questions/answers posted by the characters (lines 7–8); after this, the audio player is stopped and there are two consecutive exchanges of reading out loud between Laura and the students in unison, who repeat the questions/answers twice (lines 8–12); in the final turn (line 13), the teacher provides the meaning of the repeated words, translating them into Chinese (with no subsequent repetition by the students).

As is apparent in these sequences, the recurrent interactional development of the activities involving the audiovisual texts positioned the students in accordance to the participant status of a collective body of recipients addressed by the teacher, on the one hand, and to the production format of oral animation of the voices provided by the audiovisual recordings, on the other. The teacher's management of turn-taking and language choice contributed to this positioning by coordinating the students' actions via a segmentation of the key words, linguistic structures, and interactional turns heard. The lesson goals were achieved by appropriately playing/stopping the recordings, posting display questions in general solicit form, and scaffolding the students' participation in order to elicit the required responses, as in Extract 5.3, or by attributing different social functions to Chinese and English so as to signal which parts of the teacher's speech corresponded to instances of meaning contextualization and which parts to the repetitions elicited, as in Extract 5.4.

As soon as the audiovisual text had been introduced through these sequences of listening, elicitation of comprehension, and choral reading, the students' attention was directed to the key grammatical and phonetic elements in the text.

5.2.2   Stressing Grammar and Pronunciation: Rules, Syllables, and Fill-in-the-Blank Exercises

These subsequent activities provided a more explicit context for meta-grammatical reflection about the key linguistic structures featured in the audiovisual text, and included recurrent sequences of teacher-monologued explanation of the grammatical rules involved, choral repetition of related linguistic structures and their constituting syllables, and oral performance of filling-in-the-blanks activities in which these structures were put into practice. Figure 5.3 shows what Laura wrote on the blackboard when she was explaining the grammatical form of the continuous present for talking about future plans, immediately following the sequences of choral repetition, in Extract 5.4.

During the monologued explanation of the grammatical rule of the future action in continuous present form, conducted entirely in Chinese except for the labeling of segments written in English on the blackboard, the students were expected to remain silent and to write down her voiced words in their notebooks. At the end of this explanation, the shift to the choral repetition of this linguistic structure took the form shown in Extract 5.5.

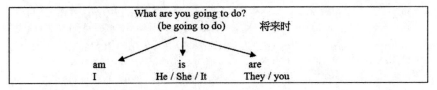

Figure 5.3   Laura's writing on the blackboard

Extract 5.5   "Follow Me"

1	Laura:	follow me / ī ăm gŏing tŏ dŏ
2	Students:	{in unison} Ī Ă M GŎING TŎ DŎ
3	Laura:	hē īs gŏing tŏ dŏ
4	Students:	{in unison} HĒ ĪS GŎING TŎ DŎ
5	Laura:	shē īs gŏing tŏ dŏ
6	Students:	{in unison} SHĒ ĪS GŎING TŎ DŎ

(Sixth-grade English-language class.
Recording code: 11dp_Zh_P311020061)

By means of a direct request followed by reading out loud with strongly marked intonation (line 1), Laura activated the new frame of participation in which she and her students engaged in exchanges of repetition of each of the grammatical options written out on the blackboard (lines 1–6). After completing the different options, the repetitions continued, with the same participant structure, but now the target of the repetitions was each of the syllables constituting the lexical elements in the linguistic structure in question. In particular, Laura and her students engaged in repetition exchanges of syllabification of each of the verbs under the arrows ("/ei/ /em/, /æm/!; / ai/ /es/, /iz/; /ei/ /a:r/, a:r!") which allowed her to focus the repetitions on the changing forms of the verb "to be" in the context of the "be going to do" linguistic structure.

As soon as this linguistic structure had been explained, copied down, repeated, and syllabified, its public elicitation through oral filling-in-the-blanks practice was carried out as shown in Extract 5.6, taken from the work of lesson Unit 6 ("I'm more outgoing than my sister") in the eighth-grade class group, focusing on the grammatical structure of comparisons.

Extract 5.6   "Fill in the Blank"

1	Zhu:	open your book / turn to / section A / section A / section A / quickly
2		{noise of pages being turned (7″)}
3	Zhu:	ah lesson 6 / lesson 6 3-a / dear Isabel / ready? go!
4	Students:	*DEAR ISABEL / THANK YOU FOR YOUR LAST LETTER / HERE ARE PHOTOS*
5		*OF ME AND MY TWIN SISTER LIU YING / AS YOU CAN SEE / IN SOME WAYS*
6		*WE LOOK THE SAME / AND IN SOME WAYS WE LOOK DIFFERENT / WE BOTH*
7		*HAVE BLACK EYES AND BLACK HAIR / ALTHOUGH MY HAIR IS SHORTER*
8		*THAN HERS / WE BOTH LIKE SPORTS / ALTHOUGH LI YING IS MORE*
9		*ATHLETIC THAN ME / SHE IS MORE OUTGOING AND I'M QUIETER / I THINK*
10		*I'M SMARTER THAN HER / MY FAVORITE SUBJECTS ARE PHYSICS AND*
11		*CHEMISTRY AND HER FAVORITE SUBJECT IS P.E. / HOWEVER / WE BOTH*
12		*ENJOY GOING TO PARTIES / PLEASE VISIT US SOON / LOVE / LIU LI*
13	Zhu:	好的 / fill in the blank
14		*good*

15	Peiyuan:	(fill in / the blank)°
16	Zhu:	FILL IN THE BLANK {using a *Power Point* slide, projects a table on the screen} /
17		复习了是不是阿 / 好行 / ((什么地方一样不一样)) / first one
18		*you have reviewed it, haven't you? / all right / ((what similarities and differences))*
19	Some:	(( ))
20	Zhu:	what are the differences between them? (3") differences / first? (3") first? (8") now / I
21		give you an example / example / Liu Li's hair is shorter than Liu Lin's / am I right?
22	Some:	哦
23		*yes*
24	Zhu:	Liu Li's hair is shorter than Liu Lin's / the second one / (( )) difference is ↑
25	Students:	(( )) {uncoordinated talk, barely understandable} &
26	Zhu:	& Liu Ying is ↑ / [more athletic than Liu Lin]
27	Students:	[LIU YING IS MORE ATHLETIC THAN LIU LIN]
28	Zhu:	the third one is who is more outgoing?
29	Students:	LIU LIN IS [MORE OUTGOING]
30	Zhu:	[Liu Lin is more outgoing] / yes good / then?

(Eighth-grade English-language class.
Recording code: 8dp_Zh_S30102006I)

After what is interactionally constructed as an appropriate choral reading of a written text (lines 1–12, see Zhu's positive evaluation in line 13), the activity is oriented according to a sequence of fill-in instruction. The teacher opens up the new sequence by labeling the genre of the activity ("fill in the blank") followed by a contextualization in Chinese in which she establishes the link with previous sessions ("you have reviewed it, haven't you?") and explains the purpose of the task ("what similarities and differences") with the support of a projected table (lines 13–20; see Table 5.2). Once this is done, the students are required to engage publicly in the oral elicitation of grammatical structures of comparison that appeared in the text. This is clearly reflected in the interactional efforts made by Zhu, who uses different strategies to ensure the students' elicitations. Initially, she tries to coordinate her students' forms of participation on the basis of question-answer exchanges.

The teacher initiates these exchanges by posting oral knowledge-checking questions, in general solicit form, about the differences between the characters that appear in the text (line 20). However, the students do not seem to collaborate as expected in the closing of those exchanges. When Zhu asks about the first difference, they do not offer any clear answer, and so the teacher repeats the same question, three times; she even makes long pauses after each question, marking the transition point in the turn-taking, for her students to take the floor and answer the question (line 20). Since the students have yet to take the floor, Zhu decides to offer an example of an appropriate answer and reads out the only blank that is filled in in the table (line 21). However, this arouses only a timid response from a few of the students, who simply affirm what they hear (line 22); the teacher then repeats the text, and asks explicitly for the second difference (line 24).

Table 5.2 Table projected as PowerPoint slide (Field notes, notebook 2, p. 16

The same	Different
We look the same	Liu Li's hair is shorter than Liu Ying's
We both have black eyes	. . .
We both have black hair	. . .
We both like sports	. . .

This new question does achieve a response from the students (line 25), although they still reply inaudibly and in an uncoordinated way, which does not seem to be accepted by Zhu as an appropriate closing of the exchange. Therefore, she takes the floor and scaffolds the expected answer by providing the first part of the structure, expressed with a strongly marked intonation and making a brief pause to signal the preferred point for the students to complete the second difference (line 26). This strategy seems to produce the desired effects; the students take the floor in unison and overlap with her in the completion of the second part (lines 26–27), after which the teacher initiates a further exchange by asking for the third difference (line 28). This question is clearly and completely answered by all the students in unison (line 29), a response that finally receives an explicit positive evaluation by Zhu (line 30). In this way, she sanctions the legitimacy attributed both to this grammatical form and to the required pattern of participation.

Thus, the activities focusing on grammar and pronunciation continued to position the students as a collective body addressed by the teacher, required to produce language and following the same format of animation as was employed in the introductory activities. However, significant differences were apparent in this case, as regards the modalities of the animation employed. In contrast to the previous activities, whereby the students were expected to pronounce the words of the audiovisual recordings, these activities oriented the students' attention toward both the written record of the teachers' grammatical explanations (see Extract 5.5) and the oral performance of the written transcripts of the audiovisual texts that had been played previously, and which could be read in their textbooks (see Extract 5.6). To this end, the teacher's arrangements of turn-taking and language choice involved monologued explanations in Chinese as well as new material supports (technologies) such as the blackboard (see Figure 5.3), while written transcripts were used as the basis for choral repetitions, for displaying questions in general solicit form, and for scaffolding strategies.

When the audiovisual text had been introduced, and the key linguistic structure had been explained, repeated, syllabified, and chorally practiced in the form of fill-in-the-blank activities, the classroom activity then shifted to practicing the related communicative dialogue.

5.2.3   Practicing Dialogues: Public and Private Communicative-like Practice

Communicative-like dialogue practice, carried out through sequences of collective reading and private-public practice in pairs, was justified by one teacher as constituting "the language drills required to promote task-based teaching" (interview with Laura). Extract 5.7 provides an example of the transition to this activity and shows how the participants were coordinated in the course of the two mentioned recurrent interactional sequences.

Extract 5.7   "It Has to Seem as Fluent as a Dialogue"

1	Laura:	I'm going at 3 o'clock // now this time I ask / and all of you answer / ok? I ask you
2		answer / 我问你答 / *where are you going this afternoon?*
3		*I ask you answer*
4	Students:	*I'M GOING TO THE BOOKSTORE*
5	Laura:	*what are you going to buy?*
6	Students:	*I'M GOING TO BUY A COMIC BOOK*
7	Laura:	good / *when are you going?*
8	Students:	*I'M GOING AT 3 O'CLOCK*
9	Laura:	very good / so / let's practice in pairs // 同桌 / 第一个同学先回答 // 开始!
10		*desk-mates / the first mate starts answering // start now!*
11		{the students practice in pairs for 1'15" while the teacher walks around supervising}
12	Laura:	{claps her hands once} ok / stop // (( )) 来 / Liangqi / you two
13		*your turn*
14	Liangqi:	where are you going this afternoon?
15	Qichao:	I'm going to the bookstore
16	Liangqi:	what are you going to buy?
17	Qichao:	I'm going to buy a comic book
18	Liangqi:	when are you going? when are you going?
19	Qichao:	I'm going at 3 o'clock
20	Laura:	very good! 但是 / 说的时候不要背 / 要像聊天那样交流 / 真正交流就好了 //
21		来 / {points to the two students seating behind}
22		*but / you don't have to memorize when practicing it / it has to seem as fluent as a
23		dialogue / a real dialogue is good // your turn*

(Sixth-grade English-language class.
Recording code: 11dp_Zh_P311020006I)

Laura, the teacher who manages the dialogue practice in Extract 5.7, speaks in Chinese when giving instructions and coordinating her students' actions (lines 2, 9, 12, 20–21). The practice is arranged on the basis of an initial performing sequence in which there are two basic types of participants: the teacher, who poses the questions in the dialogue, and the students, who provide the responses in unison (lines 2–9), and Laura's positive evaluations in lines 7 and 9 make explicit the nature of this participation framework. Later, this performing sequence is adapted to a new framework of private practice in pairs, in which each member performs as one of the characters in the same dialogue while the teacher acts as a *bystander* (Goffman, 1981: 132) (lines 9–12); that is, Laura acts as a non-ratified participant of the parallel two-person encounters, whose minimal access to the encounters (temporarily following the dialogue, or catching just fragments of it) is perceptible to the official participants.

Finally, the teacher coordinates her students' participation, through a direct request (line 12), to achieve a sequence of public practice in which each pair performs the dialogue again, but this time in front of the rest of the class, such that the teacher and the other students are fictionally positioned as *bystanders* (lines 13–19). In this last exercise, a particularly important element is the teacher's evaluation (line 20), whereby she occupies the *frontstage* of the scene (Goffman, 1971: 114) and concludes the students' fictitious performance with an explicit statement about the importance of avoiding mechanical repetition and of performing the dialogue in a natural fashion ("but / you don't have to memorize when practicing it / it has to seem as fluent as a dialogue / a real dialogue is good"). In other words, the teacher's management of the students' participation status in the course of dialogue practice activities (as addressee and addressed ratified participants in two-person encounters or as non-ratified participants in other people's fictitious encounters) constructed a legitimate dialogue practice task in which the students were expected to animate the previously reviewed syllables, words, social functions, and linguistic structures in a communicative-like attitude.

All in all, the analysis of the sequential development of this cycle of three activities, recursively applied to the work on the texts constituting each unit lesson, points to an organization of the English classes which begins with an emphasis on reciting (orally and in writing) prescribed repertoires of sounds, words, grammatical rules, and speech acts extracted from language materials emulating communicative situations, and ends with an interest in recreating (artificially) such situations in the situated context of the classroom. Recitation was also the focus of the activity during the last two sessions of each unit, in which the key vocabulary and linguistic structures were individually reviewed and evaluated through dictations, written fill-in-the-blanks exercises and formal tests (see Table 5.1 for details of the interactional sequences through which these other activities were carried out in the classes observed).

Apart from these criteria underlying the organization of the English-language classes, this analysis of the sequential organization of the classroom interaction also highlights the emergence of collective participation as a recursive feature of activities in the English classes. The students' forms of action are mainly framed by the teacher's directives and requests in general solicit form, which reinforces the students' participant status of unaddressed ratified recipients and their production format as an undifferentiated body of *animators* (Goffman, 1981: 144) who merely voice the utterances of others—with these others restricted to the teacher and the teaching materials. Nevertheless, this overview of the recurrent educational activities and sequences of action does not fully capture the significance of this form of participation. I will discuss this aspect further in the following section.

5.3   CHORAL REPETITION: A KEY RITUALIZED PRACTICE

Choral repetitions played a very important position in the English classroom activity observed. Among the interactional sequences that recursively constituted every unit lesson, this form of participation was by far the most prominent. Indeed, these repetitions occupied most of the classroom time, sometimes taking up entire sessions. But not only in quantitative terms did they stand out; as in the case of the out-of-classroom institutional rituals seen in Chapter 4, these interactional spaces were easily distinguishable from other types of classroom sequences in that they involved "a mode of delivery [with] a high degree of fluency, without hesitations, in a stylised intonation contour, accompanied by prescribed postures, proxemics, behaviours, attitudes and trappings" (Du Bois, 1986: 317, as cited in Rampton, 2006: 181).

In particular, these sequences contributed to generating "a mood of collective intensity [. . .] [whereby] the teacher create[s] a state of flow in the classroom" (Rampton, 2006: 197). Extract 5.8 corresponds to the field notes taken after the first day of observation, and shows how some of these characteristics attracted my own attention in the English classes, from the very start.

Extract 5.8   "A Very Peculiar Musicality"

Today, the fact that the activity was mainly built upon choral repetition attracted my attention from the very beginning in the observation of the English classes, both in Primary and Secondary Education. The teachers began these forms of participation by enunciating something and then all the students repeated it in unison. These repetitions struck me very forcefully since they followed a very peculiar musicality and the students engaged in them in a very energetic way to the point that they almost shouted.

(Field notes. Notebook 1, p. 11)

These ethnographic considerations provide an initial basis for arguing that choral repetition played a key ritualized institutional function in the context of the English-language classes examined in this study. But such a claim requires a closer empirical look at the specific contexts of situated emergence of all the sequences of choral repetition, across the entire data corpus. After analysis of the collection of these sequences, the following subsections support this initial assessment, showing that the choral repetitions observed were interactionally conventionalized in varied forms, had a purposely pedagogical motivation, were institutionally showcased, and constituted a space for individual and interpersonal contestation.

5.3.1   A Ritual of Rituals

Far from being a monolithic interactional space rigidly reproduced within a single structure, these repetitions were much more complex than may be inferred from the description in Extract 5.8. The continuation of the fieldwork soon revealed that choral repetition did not necessarily involve a single participation framework in which the teacher spoke first, followed by all the students repeating her words at the same time. The students' reply in chorus (in the peculiar musicality mentioned in Extract 5.8) could be articulated in varied forms, each comprising a single participation framework with a particular constellation of statuses assigned to the students. These forms included all students in unison, all students in a single row (on a one-student-at-a-time basis) and groups of students according to their position in class or their gender. We have already seen examples of the former (see Extracts 5.4 and 5.5), and so the following extracts will focus on repetitions in rows and groups.

To illustrate how these different participation frameworks worked and were articulated one after other in a highly ritualized way, we will return our attention to the point where Laura and her sixth-grade students were working on the unit lesson about future actions, which was initially described in the preceding section. Once these participants had completed the work on the text shown in Figure 5.2, Laura asked her students to look at another text, on a previous page in the book (see Figure 5.4). They then began coordinated actions based on sequences of listening and elicitation of comprehension of the new text; in doing this, they followed the same recursive pattern as shown in Extract 5.3. At one point in the interaction, the activity shifted to choral reading; this was done first within a participation framework in which all the students participated in unison, after which the form described in Extract 5.4 was adopted. After this, they proceeded to choral repetition in rows, as in Extract 5.9.

Extract 5.9   "Good, Next"

1	Laura:	*i'm gŏing tŏ bŭy ā nĕw cd ānd sŏme stŏrybŏoks*
2	Students:	*I'M GŎING TŎ BŬY Ā NĔW CD ĀND SŎME STŎRYBŎOKS*
3	Laura:	*i'm gŏing tŏ bŭy ā nĕw cd ānd sŏme stŏrybŏoks*
4	Students:	*I'M GŎING TŎ BŬY Ā NĔW CD ĀND SŎME STŎRYBŎOKS*
5	Laura:	[pointing to Xianlin, with the palm of her hand open and downward-facing] Xianlin

6   Xianlin: {stands up} (*ī'm gōing tō būy ā nēw cd ānd sōme storybōoks*)°

7   Laura: yes / next {pointing to Yihua}

8   {Xianlin sits down}

9   Yihua: {stands up} (*ī'm gōing tōo*)°

10 Laura: *būy āa* ↑

11 Yihua: (*būy ā / nēw cd ānd sōme storybōoks*)°

12 Laura: yes / next {pointing to Daqiang}

13 {Yihua sits down}

14 Daqiang: {stands up} (*ī'm gōing tō būy ā nēw cd ānd sōme storybōoks*)°

15 Laura: very good {pointing to Weiwei}

16 {Daqiang sits down}

17 Weiwei: {stands up} (*ī'm gōing tō būy ā nēw cd ānd sōme storybōoks*)°

18 Laura: good {pointing to Hongling}

19 {Weiwei sits down}

20 Hongling: {stands up} (*ī'm gōing tō būy ā nēw cd ānd sōme storybōoks*)°

21 Laura: very good {pointing to Weihan}

22 {Hongling sits down}

23 Weihan: {stands up} (*ī'm gōing tō būy - ī'm gōing tō būy ā nēw cd ānd sōme storybōoks*)°

24 Laura: yes // (( )) {pointing to Houli}

25 {Weihan sits down}

26 Houli: {stands up} (*ī'm gōing tō būy ā nēw cd ānd sōme storybōoks*)°

27 Laura: good {Houli sits down} *ī'm gōing tō būy ā nēw cd ānd sōme storybōoks*

28 Students: *Ī'M GŌING TŌ BŪY Ā NĒW CD ĀND SŌME STŌRYBŌOKS*

(Sixth-grade English-language class.

Recording code: lldp_Zh_P311020061)

The initial reading of the text (see Figure 5.4) is carried out through a recursive participant structure of two consecutive exchanges of repetition

---

LET'S READ

Hi, this is Liu Yun. I'm going to have a busy weekend. On Saturday, I'm going to the bookstore by subway. I'm going to buy a new CD and some storybooks. Then, I'm going to go home and read the new books. On Sunday, I'm going to the supermarket with my mother. We're going after lunch. Then, in the evening, I'm going to visit my aunt. We're going to watch TV together. That will be fun! What about you? What are you going to do at the weekend?

Write Liu Yun's weekend plan here.

On Saturday   On Sunday
_____   _____
_____   _____
_____   _____
_____   _____

Figure 5.4   Primary English students' textbook (sixth grade), Section B, page 30

between the teacher and all the students in unison, which is reinitiated for each sentence in the text (lines 1–4 show the point at which they reach the third sentence). Nevertheless, this interactional pattern is not followed uninterruptedly to the end of the text. Before reading the fourth sentence, and once the students have repeated the third sentence twice, Laura signals a change in the frame of the event—a change in footing, in Goffman's term (1981: 128). She prompts this change by means of a set of *contextualization cues*, that is, a set of communicative resources that are used by the participants in the situated action so as to build and negotiate frames of action and interpretation in conventionalized ways (Gumperz, 1992: 231–232).

These communicative resources do not involve explicit explanations letting the students know what they are expected to do—an example of this would be "now you must each, individually and one after the other, stand up to repeat the sentence that we have just seen in the text, using the same marked intonation as in the choral repetitions, and then sit down". Rather, they comprise verbal and nonverbal cues, such as nominating through names ("Xianlin") or adjectives ("next"), pointing, or providing positive evaluations ("yes", "good"), which require specific inferences to be made by the students for the appropriate participation according to this new framework of choral repetition by rows (lines 5–28). To put it another way, the coordination of participants on the basis of these inferential processes reveals the highly ritualized nature of these different participation frameworks of choral repetition.

The shifting back to the initial form of choral participation in lines 27–28 is signaled in a similar way. After the last student of the row has sat down (line 27), the teacher takes the floor and repeats the sentence once again, using the same marked intonation without addressing any individual participant (line 27). From the students' reaction (line 28), this seems to be interpreted as a contextualization cue to change the frame of the event back to choral repetition in unison. On other occasions, more explicit instructions are given, which Laura explained in a retrospective interview as responding to the need to ensure "the students' proper collective practice". This was done later in the activity, when the participants had reached the last sentence of the text, as shown in Extract 5.10.

Extract 5.10   "Now Boys Read on Saturday"

1	Laura:	*whāt āre yōu gōing tō dō ōn thē wēekēnd?*
2	Students:	WHĀT ĀRE YŌU GŌING TŌ DŌ ŌN THĒ WĒEKĒND?
3	Laura:	ok / now boys read on Saturday / and girls read on Sunday // ok?
4	Some:	ok
5	Laura:	来第一个是男孩子的 / 后面是女孩子 // 男孩子准备 // hī / thīs īs līu yūn / ready? go
6		*those who go first are the boys / then the girls // get ready boys*
7	Boys:	HĪ / THĪS ĪS LĪU YŪN / I'M GŌING TŌ HĀVE Ā BŪSY WĒEKĒND // ŌN
8		SĀTURDĀY / I'M GŌING TŌ THĒ BŌOKSTŌRE BY SŪBWĀY // I'M GŌING TŌ

9		*BŪY Ā NĒW CD ĀND SŌME STŌRYBŌOKS // THĒN / I'M GŌING TŌ GŌ HŌME*
10		*ĀND RĒAD THĒ NĒW BŌOKS*
11	Laura:	girls
12	Girls:	*ŌN SŪNDĀY / I'M GŌING TŌ THĒ SŪPĒRMĀRKĒT WĪTH MY MŌTHĒR //*
13		*WĒ'RE GŌING ĀFTĒR LŪNCH // THĒN / ĪN THĒ ĒVĒNĪNG / I'M GŌING TŌ*
14		*VĪSĪT MY ĀUNT // WĒ'RE GŌING TŌ WĀTCH TV TŌGĒTHĒR // THĀT WĪLL BĒ*
15		*FŪN // WHĀT ĀBŌUT YŌU? WHĀT ĀRE YŌU GŌING TŌ DŌ ŌN THĒ*
16		*WĒEKĒND?*
17	Laura:	good

(Sixth-grade English-language class.
Recording code: 11dp_Zh_P311020061)

Although here Laura provides a clear indication for the participants to shift from choral participation to choral repetition in groups (lines 1–4), she still relies on inferential processes to be carried out by the students for this practice to be accorded to a participation framework of choral repetition. These inferential processes are mainly concerned with adhering to the same marked intonation as in the previous sequences of repetition, something that is not made explicit by the teacher. This ritualized character of the choral repetitions and their various conventionalized realizations usually had a clear pedagogical function, and the following subsection addresses this point.

5.3.2   A Pedagogical Resource

Very often, sequences of choral repetition were articulated by teachers and students in actions with pedagogical purposes. That is, this form of participation was not randomly enacted but had a specific function in the context of the ongoing educational activity. In particular, the collection of these sequences, throughout the data corpus, reveals that apart from their function in the recurrent set of activities comprising each unit lesson (see Table 5.1), they also played a predominant role in interactional contexts in which the teachers corrected their students' performance. Thus, these sequences tended to be embedded in the course of other type of interactional sequences, as shown in Extract 5.11, where Zhu and her eighth-grade students continued working on the grammatical structure of comparison introduced in Extract 5.6.

Extract 5.11   "Much Beautiful or Much More Beautiful?"

1	Zhu:	ok / now / how about your friend / (( ))? {she shows another Power Point slide
2		on the screen} / how about your friend with your desk-mate? clear? / now be
3		quick // ask and answer
4	{parallel conversations at a low volume in the background (8")}	
5	Zhu:	{standing next to one student and pointing to her textbook} 性格体形爱好
6		*character and hobbies*
7	{parallel conversations become louder in the background}	

8	**Zhu:**	{pointing to the same textbook} 身材是吧 // 喜好
9		*constitution ok? / preferences*
10	{students carry on working in pairs for 1'40"}	
11	**Zhu:**	OK
12	{parallel conversations continue}	
13	**Zhu:**	hands up
14	{parallel conversations continue; some students raise their hands}	
15	**Zhu:**	{pointing to Shouyi} now first one / ok now good
16	{parallel conversations continue; Shouyi stands up (2")}	
17	**Zhu:**	listen
18	**Shouyi:**	[(Yongyan is my friend / she is much eh / beautiful than me)°]
19	[{various parallel conversations continue}]	
20	**Zhu:**	much beautiful or much more beautiful?
21	**Some:**	[more beautiful]
22	**Zhu:**	[much MOORE beautiful] / yes / mōre beaūtīfūl
23	**Students:**	MŌRE BEAŪTĪFŪL
24	**Zhu:**	mōre beaūtīfūl
25	**Students:**	MŌRE BEAŪTĪFŪL
26	**Zhu:**	mūch mōre beaūtīfūl
27	**Students:**	MŪCH MŌRE BEAŪTĪFŪL
28	**Zhu:**	[yes / good] / next one / let's go on {points to Xiaohua}
29	**Xiaohua:**	Xindan is thinner / than me

(Eighth-grade English-language class.
Recording code: 8dp_Zh_S301020006I)

After practicing the linguistic structure of comparison by means of fill-in-the-blank routines, Zhu shifts the activity to exercises in pairs, by organizing the classroom activity in the same way as previously for dialogue practice (see Section 5.2.3). Thus, once they have collectively read the text containing this structure (see Extract 5.6), the students are expected to apply it through sequences of private-public practice in pairs. To this end, Zhu provides a model, as a table projected on the screen (Table 5.3). This table, following the same pattern as the one used for the fill-in-the-blanks practice (see Table 5.2), gives example sentences to express sameness and difference, as a basis for the students to describe their own differences and similarities.

However, the course of the action does not follow, from start to finish, the recursive form of the sequences of private-public practice in pairs. Zhu starts by giving instructions (lines 1–3) to coordinate her students' actions for private performance (lines 4–10), in which she plays the role of *bystander* and intervenes briefly in parallel two-person encounters to provide support when needed (lines 5–9). As soon as the time for the private practice is over, she signals the change to the sequence of public practice (lines 11–13), during which a breakdown from the expected course of the action takes place. When Shouyi, one of the students in the first public practice pair, speaks, his use of the comparison structure (line 18) is interactionally signaled as an error by Zhu; she repeats his use of the structure and

Table 5.3 PowerPoint slide (Field notes, notebook 2, p. 17)

The same	Different
We're both girls	I'm taller than she is
. . .	My hair is longer than hers
. . .	. . .

contrasts it with an alternative in the form of a disjunction, in an asking intonation (line 20), which prompts some students to offer the proposed alternative (line 21). Zhu then positively evaluates this choice (line 22), and opens up a coordinated exchange of choral repetition between her and all the students in unison, repeating the positively evaluated form (lines 22–27). Once this is done, the teacher shifts the activity back to the previous framework of public practice by means of a positive evaluation (yes / good) and a direct request ("next one / let's go on"), which in the ongoing context functions as a boundary-making action (lines 28–29).

Although semantic understanding is not overtly demonstrated, these repetitions seem to perform an educational purpose, related to the items and contents of the lesson unit in question. To some extent, this pedagogical function reveals the institutional significance attached to this form of participation; nevertheless, we should at this point consider the degree of official "exhibitionism" involved in its achievement.

5.3.3 An Institutional Showcase

Apart from their conventionalized forms and the pedagogical function they played in everyday classroom interaction, an outstanding feature of these choral repetitions was that they were often brought to the front of scenes where participants were observed and/or evaluated by other institutional actors. In other words, these forms of participation were pointedly displayed before non-ratified participants or *bystanders* who, although fictionally constructed by the teacher and students as nonpresent in the event, were part of the scene as observers or potential evaluators of the students' and teacher's performances. This was the case of my own presence as a researcher, in the course of the fieldwork, as well as that of the school's principal and of other English teachers from the same school or from others, in the context of teacher peer-evaluation activities or in the course of institutional competitions among English teachers in different schools at a municipal/provincial level.

Concerning the fieldwork, Extract 5.12 is taken from the field notes and underscores the often highly social relevance of my negotiations with the teachers about the when and where of the classroom observations, since these were always underpinned by different expectations about what was significant for the researcher and what was not.

Extract 5.12 "Oops! I Am Sorry I Forgot to Tell You That Today We Are Going to Review Exercises"

It was 11.05 a.m. when I reached the classroom today. As the English class started at 11.15, I remained outside in the corridor waiting for Laura (. . .) When she arrived, she looked at me in surprise and said "Oops! I am sorry I forgot to tell you that today we are going to review exercises", implying that I would not be interested in observing the class and that therefore I had wasted my time coming to the school today. This issue about what the teachers think is important or not for my research is now attracting my attention, as Zhu told me exactly the same thing yesterday when she sent a text message to my mobile to let me know that I did not have to attend her class the following day because this was the last session of the unit and the students would work independently on several writing exercises; as she put it: "I am afraid this will be boring for you.

(Field notes. Notebook 1, p. 40)

These taken-for-granted ideas about my lack of interest in the last sessions of each unit lesson, where participants worked silently and independently (see Table 5.1), highlight the salience of those in which choral participation played a more prominent position. Indeed, at the beginning of the field-work my classroom observation sessions were deliberately scheduled by the school principals and the focus English teachers to take place in the opening sessions of the unit lessons, in which the participants' forms of coordination were mostly based upon sequential forms of choral repetition. This initial interpretation was supported as the fieldwork developed, when the progressive building up of relations of trust led to the schools' allowing me to freely observe all classes, and thus to identify other forms of participation that had not initially been revealed.

As regards the peer-evaluation activities, Figure 5.5 and Extract 5.13 correspond to the field notes taken in one of the institutional English-language competitions arranged by the local municipality in Hangzhou city; they show the extent to which the chorus repetition sequences were a fundamental part of classroom activity in this type of context in which actions were evaluated by other institutional actors (i.e., other teachers and representatives from the local authorities) who decided which of the English-language teacher competitors (i.e., which English-language teaching styles) were to be considered the "best" in the local area.

Extract 5.13 "Quick Quick, You Have to go Faster!"

The classroom activity in the competitions is similar to that of the ordinary classes in my schools, although in this case more emphasis is made on the repetitions and the high intonation is much more marked

[. . .] The four teachers of today's competition went very quickly in their sessions, going from one activity to another very fast, but the second seemed particularly interesting to me because she was so fast that her students had difficulties in following her during the repetitions. In fact, at one point she stopped the activity and told the students: "quick quick! you have to go faster.

(Field notes. Notebook 1, p. 59)

Therefore, the organization of classroom activity around stylized practices of choral repetition seemed to play an important institutional role in defining what counts as a legitimate teaching-learning practice within the context of the innovation reforms. In fact, these practices were an important part of what I was told in interviews was considered to be a "specifically Chinese way of teaching English language"; they were often referred to by the participants in relation to the enthusiasm of the performance of collectivism and cooperation ("their image / their expression / their temperament / all looks very lively" [他们的这个形象/他们的表情/他们的气质都看上去都是非常活泼的], taken from an interview with a school principal), with these values being discursively tied to traditional Chinese culture. The same was true of

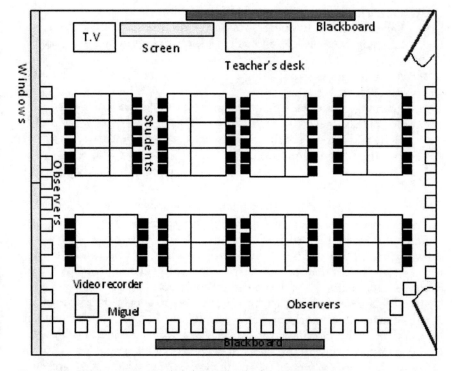

Figure 5.5   Classroom in English-language teacher competitions

relevant institutional documents such as the English-language curriculum designated for experimental schools at the time of my data collection.[1]

This curriculum stated the necessity of complementing English-language teaching with traditional Chinese culture and approved values "in order to filter moral and ideological education and to balance foreign cultural influences on the students' values and life perspectives" (2001 Experimental English Language Curriculum, p. 49); these traditional values were mainly associated with positive attitudes toward patriotism and collectivist cooperation. Thus, official discourses explicitly sanctioned choral repetition as "an assembly animated by passion", one of the features that, according to Durkheim (1912: 128) and Rampton (2006: 197), characterizes institutional rituals.

Figure 5.6, taken from the curriculum and translated in Extract 5.14, shows an instance of how some of these desirable values just mentioned are articulated and combined with others to define the abstract educational category of "comprehensive language use abilities", which has been considered a key concept in the contemporary innovation reforms aiming to establish the basic principle of quality education in China's English-language education (2001 Experimental English Language Curriculum, pp. 1–2).

Extract 5.14 "Comprehensive Language Use Abilities"

Comprehensive language use abilities:
    Language skills: listening, speaking, reading, and writing.
    Language knowledge: phonetics, vocabulary, grammar, pragmatics, themes.
    Attitudes: motivation, confidence, cooperation, patriotism, international perspectives
    Learning strategies: cognitive, organizational, communicative, resource management.
    Cultural awareness: cultural knowledge, cultural understanding, and cross-cultural communication.

(Translation of text in Figure 5.6)

In the official illustration of the different components/layers of the category of "comprehensive language use abilities", cooperation is represented as an attitudinal value that is strongly linked (through the different compartments shown in Figure 5.6) to motivation, patriotism, and internationalism. That is to say, the values that are discursively linked to what is deemed Chinese culture in other parts of the document are constructed in Figure 5.6 as forming part of the core values complementing the international perspectives in the design of innovation reforms in English-language education. This standpoint overlaps with other specific areas concerning linguistic, pedagogical, cognitive, and cultural dimensions, including language skills, grammatical forms of knowledge, learning strategies, and the value of cross-cultural awareness.

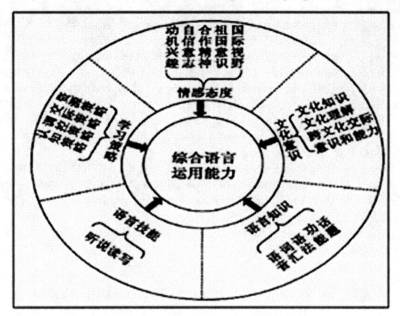

Figure 5.6   Experimental English Language Curriculum, page 6

Therefore, a triangulation of the ethnographic observations of everyday interactional arrangements in the English classroom and the forms of representation mobilized both in the schools and in the official English-language teaching curriculum highlights a stylized choral repetition that is discursively constructed as an inspirational or motivating form of collectivist participation. This attitude is tightly bound to the Chinese national culture and is combined with the perspectives, pedagogical resources, learning strategies, linguistic contents, and skills of advanced international traditions in order to foster the desired language use capabilities in accordance with contemporary China's education reforms aimed at enhancing the quality of English-language learning. Nevertheless, the forms of knowledge officially considered desirable and the performance of institutional manifestations do not necessarily cover all forms of action possible within the social space of the classroom. Students and teachers also managed to display more or less overt individual and interpersonal forms of rejection, as we shall see in the final subsection.

5.3.4   A Space for Rejection

Although choral repetitions played an important pedagogical function and were institutionally legitimized in the three schools studied as forming part of the discourse of educational reform, there were also spaces in which the participants were observed to be reluctant to comply. As in the case of the collective practices analyzed in Chapter 4, ongoing local disorders were part of the apparently orderly choral practices in English-language classrooms. Explicit instances of complicity or collusion between teachers and students were not common, in contrast to the classes analyzed in Chapter 4, as the English teachers were under considerable pressure to keep up the rate of activity with a view to the extensive official monitoring, evaluation, measurement, and standardization on which their own professional careers largely depended (see Chapter 3). However, both teachers and students were able to position themselves as being not necessarily aligned with official expectations regarding choral participation.

In the case of the teachers, these forms of positioning were made apparent only during informal conversations or in the final parts of the interviews, once the audio recorders had been stopped. It was in these moments when they would refer to choral repetitions as forms of participation that they did not like, even though were regarded as providing a showcase for exemplary English-language teaching, in competitions and university performances. Both Laura and Zhu, for example, agreed that such repetitions were types of interaction that, while allowing them to monitor classroom activity in the context of the large groups they were teaching, did not provide their students with opportunities to practice language as in everyday life outside the classroom. In fact, both of these teachers observed that they had received the same style of English-language education and yet, after many years, they were not able to speak English as fluently as they would like.

In the case of the students, these forms of rejection were mainly instantiated through individual and interpersonal forms of interaction displayed during the course of the choral repetitions. In particular, an analysis of the sequences in which choral repetitions were not uniformly reproduced shows three main forms of interactional positioning by which the students signaled rejection: individual acting, parallel conversations, and lack of group engagement. An example of individual acting is shown in Extract 5.15, corresponding to an activity in which the sixth-grade students were supposed to engage in the collective reading of a dialogue in Unit 4, "I have a pen pal".

Extract 5.15   "She Keeps Moving Her Mouth"

1	Laura:	ok / (( )) {going from her desk towards one of the aisles between the students' desks}
2		我们来看第一段啊 / look at- read your books read after me- read after me // dēar
3		Liūyūn {she walks up to where Meiyi is sitting. Meiyi immediately changes her
4		posture, from leaning back and holding a paper under her desk while reading it, to one
5		in which she puts both arms on the desk and looks at her textbook}
6		*let's have a look at the first paragraph*
7	Students:	DĒAR LIŪYŪN
8	Laura:	{turning around and going back towards the blackboard, away from Meiyi} ī ăm
9		hăppy tō hăve ă nēw pĕn păl

10	Students:	Ī ĀM HĂPPY TŌ HĀVE Ā NĒW PĒN PĂL {Meiyi returns to her initial posture,
11		leaning back, hiding her left arm under the desk and paying attention to what she is
12		holding. She moves her mouth during the chorusing practice but without any
13		perceptible voice}
14	Laura:	ī līve īn Āustrāliā
15	Students:	Ī LĪVE ĪN ĀUSTRĀLIĀ

(Sixth-grade English-language class.
Recording code: 7v_Zh_P241120061)

After reading the text twice, with sequences of repetition, Laura establishes the participation framework of collective reading by using a framing turn ("ok") followed by an instruction with language shift to Chinese ("我们来看第一段啊 / look at- read your books read after me") as well as by reading the first sentence of the paragraph with a marked intonation ("dēar Liūyūn"). The most significant aspect of this sequence is that the participants do much more than merely engage in choral repetition, although this fact may be obscured by the temptation to use transcription conventions that tend to focus on collectivist actions rather than on individual ones. In this particular case, it is interesting to examine the local tensions or frictions between, on the one hand, the institutional efforts made by the teacher to maintain the participation framework of choral repetition at the *frontstage* of the activity and, on the other, the local actions of the students who position themselves as participants who act as if they were following the rules (as if they were playing the "official game") while carrying out unofficial/nonlegitimate activities at the *backstage*.

The student Meiyi is not aligned with the required interactional rules (i.e., sitting down with both arms on her desk and looking at the textbook while reading chorally). As can be seen in lines 3–5, this is followed by the teacher's movement across the physical space of the classroom, to approach Meiyi while maintaining verbal engagement with the other students. This movement is understood by the student as a warning cue to reestablish the required verbal/nonverbal pattern of participation, as she immediately changes her posture and engages in the choral repetitions. Nevertheless, she returns to the previous pattern of participation as soon as the teacher turns around and moves away from her, while simulating cooperation by mouthing the text in coordination with the rest of the students, but without vocalizing (lines 10–13).

An example of parallel conversations is shown in Extract 5.16, taken from a later moment of the same classroom interaction.

Extract 5.16   "Jinling and Meiyi Interrupt Their Conversation and Look Back to the Screen"

1	Laura:	ok / so {she walks towards the computer and shows a new slide on the tv screen,
2		which is situated at the front-corner of the class, behind the teacher's desk} / so

3   {parallel conversations}

4   **Laura:**   soo (( )) hŏbby

5   **Students:**   {parallel conversations suddenly stop} HŎBBY

6   **Laura:**   hŏbby

7   **Students:**   HŎBBY

8   **Laura:**   hŏbby

9   **Students:**   HŎBBY

10   **Laura:**   whăt's yŏur hŏbby?

11   **Students:**   WHĂT'S YŎUR HŎBBY?

12   **Laura:**   {looking at and pointing to the screen} ī līke măking kītes

13   **Students:**   [Ī LĪKE MĂKĪNG KĪTES]

14   [{Jinling turns her head and talks to Meiyi, who is sitting in a different row, behind her}]

15   **Laura:**   {looking at and pointing to the screen} ī līke cŏllĕcting stămps {she looks back from

16   the screen to the class, which is followed by changes of posture by Jinling and Meiyi

17   who interrupt their conversation and look back to the screen}

18   **Students:**   [Ī LĪKE CŎLLĔCTING STĂMPS]

19   [{Laura looks back to the screen. Jinling turns her head again to say something to Meiyi, very

20   quickly, and then looks back to the screen}]

21   **Laura:**   ī līke plāyĭng ā vīolīn

22   **Students:**   Ī LĪKE PLĀYĬNG Ā VĪOLĪN

(Sixth-grade English-language class.
Recording code: 7v_Zh_P241120061)

In this case, Laura wishes to focus the students' attention on a new section in the textbook ("Let's talk"), within the same lesson unit of "I have a pen pal". This section shows a dialogue between two characters talking about their hobbies. Before initiating a sequence of listening in which the teacher plays the dialogue on an audio player while the students are supposed to listen to it, the teacher embeds a sequence of choral repetition around the repertoire of actions that are stated in the dialogue. These actions are graphically illustrated on a screen, so that pointing to this screen is a resource used by Laura during the turn-taking between her and the students in chorus (lines 12–13, 15–18, 19–22). Nevertheless, these repetitions are not reproduced without discontinuity, as can be seen by observing the way in which Jinglin and Meiyi participate in the activity, managing their body positions and eye gaze to act as if they were engaging in the repetitions while in fact having a parallel conversation. Thus, they orient their postures and eye gaze to talk to each other when the teacher is looking at the screen (lines 12–14, 19–22) while looking at the screen and repeating in coordination with their peers when the teacher looks at the class (lines 15–18).

Finally, Extract 5.17 offers an example of lack of small group engagement, in the course of an activity in which eighth-grade students were supposed to engage in choral repetitions in groups, according to the gender of the students:

Extract 5.17   "Read Louder"

1	Zhu:	now open your books turn to page // 87 / 87
2		{noise of pages being turned}
3	Zhu:	好了吗? / now I am the interviewer / 采访者哦 / who is Holly? / girls Holly / boys /
4		Maria / (( )) 吗?
5		*finished? / now I am the interviewer / interviewer*
6	Some:	听到了 &
7		*Translation of Chinese: understood*
8	Zhu:	& 听到了吗? / who is your best friend Holly?
9		*understood?*
10	Girls:	PETE
11	Zhu:	why is he a good friend?
12	Girls:	BECAUSE HE LIKES TO DO THE SAME THINGS AS I DO / HE IS POPULAR
13		TOO / AND GOOD AT SPORTS
14	Zhu:	are you good at sport too?
15	Girls:	WELL I LIKE SPORTS / BUT HE IS MORE ATHLETIC THAN ME / I'D SAY
16		WE'RE BOTH PRETTY OUTGOING THOUGH
17	Zhu:	what else do you like about Pete?
18	Girls:	HE IS FUNNIER THAN I AM / AND HE IS WILDER / I'M A LITTLE QUIETER
19	Zhu:	how about you Maria? who is your best friend?
20	Boys:	MY BEST FRIEND IS VERA
21	Zhu:	Vera
22	Boys:	VERA
23	Zhu:	what- what do you like about her?
24	Boys:	(( )) {they do not read in unison. It is difficult to hear clearly what they are reading as
25		they are reading in a low voice}
26	Zhu:	that's important to me / (读好来)° / is she a lot like you?- a lot like you?
27		*read better*
28	Boys:	(( )) {they do not read in unison. It is difficult to hear clearly what they are reading as
29		they are reading softly} &
30	Zhu:	& (( )) 站起来
31		*stand up*
32		{boys stop reading}
33	Zhu:	站起来 // 男生 / 站起来
34		*stand up // boys / stand up*
35		[{boys stand up. Noise of chairs. Parallel conversations}]
36	Zhu:	[ONE TWO / 我数三下] // who is your best friend? / ready? / go
37	Boys:	MY BEST FRIEND IS VERA / WHAT DO YOU LIKE ABOUT HER? / WELL
38		SHE IS A GOOD LISTENER / AND SHE CAN KEEP A SECRET / THAT'S
39		IMPORTANT TO ME / IS SHE A LOT LIKE YOU? / SOME PEOPLE SAY THAT
40		WE LOOK ALIKE / WE'RE BOTH TALL AND WE BOTH HAVE LONG CURLY
41		HAIR / BUT VERA IS MUCH QUIETER THAN ME / AND SHE IS ALSO
42		SMARTER / I'M MORE OUTGOING
43		*I'm going to count down from three*

44	Zhu:	大部分同学都是比较好的哦 / 又不是没吃早饭 / 读大点声音
45		*many of you were better / not as if you had missed lunch / read louder*

(Eighth-grade English-language class.
Recording code: 10dp_Zh_S311020061)

By using a framing turn with instruction, Zhu initiates a sequence that directs the students' attention to the transcript of a dialogue they have been working on previously (lines 1–2). Once the students find the corresponding page in their textbooks, the teacher establishes the choral participation framework, by groups according to the students' gender, doing so by shifting to Chinese language and attributing dialogue roles to each of the two groups (lines 3–4). In this case, she plays the role of the interviewer, reading out the questions, and each group reads out the replies by the corresponding interviewee. Thus, the first half of the sequence is constructed by turn-taking between the teacher and the girls (lines 8–18) while the second half involves turn-taking between the teacher and the boys (lines 19–45).

The second half is particularly interesting in terms of how the participants position themselves with respect to the interactional rules of the required participation framework. During the turn-taking between the teacher and the boys, the students' reading is unsynchronized and almost inaudible, provoking a negative evaluation by the teacher, who exhorts them to read "properly" (lines 24–26). As the boys continue this pattern of participation during two exchanges, the teacher finally stops the sequence without letting the students finish the reading of their text and initiates a new one, requiring the boys to read again from the beginning of their text while standing up (lines 28–36). This achieves the required pattern of participation by the students, who read their texts vigorously and in a synchronized way, which is positively evaluated by Zhu (lines 37–45).

Samples of ongoing local disorders in orderly choral practices were therefore common in the English-language classes studied in the three Chinese experimental schools. The students explained these forms of interactional positioning referring to their boredom or to individual interests that were not necessarily aligned with the official ones. Extract 5.18, for instance, is taken from a questionnaire filled in by Tingting, one of the students who was considered a "good student" by Zhu but who often displayed these "nonofficial" forms of participation in classroom activity:

Extract 5.18 "I Do Not Like Collective Readings"

Miguel: 学习英语什么地方喜欢什么地方不喜欢？为什么？
What do you like and what don't you like about studying English?

Tingting: 学英语,喜欢听 (英文歌 有趣的对话 等) 不喜欢拖拖拉拉的集体朗读.也喜欢写.不喜欢抄

    *I like listening (English songs, interesting dialogues, etc.),
    I do not like collective readings. I also like writing, but I do
    not like copying*

Miguel: 对你来说，为什么中国教育需要英语课？
    Why do you think Chinese education needs English classes?

Tingting: 中国教育需要英语是为了接上世界的轨道.也为中国人铺好
    一条可发展的道路.而对我,则是为了将来的出国等做准备.
    *Chinese education needs English to connect with the world
    track, so that the Chinese can pave a road to development.
    For me, the future is to prepare myself to go abroad*

    (Part of a questionnaire given to eighth-grade students)

As a reaction to my inquiries presented in the questionnaire, focusing on very general topics and national categories, the student constructs a discursive representation of herself as a language learner who is nonunivocally aligned with institutionalized legitimate activities (i.e., collective readings). However, she actually represents herself as a student who wants to learn English for personal goals concerned with travelling or living abroad, goals that are not necessarily framed within the Chinese national interest in preparing citizens to live in China and to contribute to the national economic demands resulting from China's openness to the international market.

5.4 SUMMARY

In the introduction to this chapter, I suggested the existence of links between the emergence of certain pedagogical traditions in China's English-language education reforms, on the one hand, and the implementation of wider Chinese national policies in reaction to the internationalization of China's political economy, on the other. However, pedagogical accounts of methodological and curricular developments often lack rigor, and in many cases are based on overly broad generalizations of what happens in the classrooms. Indeed, a close examination of the local and situated processes by which reforms in English-language education are actually being implemented, focusing on daily life in the English classrooms observed in Zhejiang, produces a rather complex picture, in contrast to the simplified overview we saw in the introductory section.

This complexity involves different aspects of how education methods, institutional processes, and classroom discourses are conceptualized. Regarding methodological issues, the preceding analysis of classroom activity shows how the clear-cut division between the different traditions expected to predominate at different stages within a given context is dissolved in the matrix of social actions and relations upon which classroom activities are always founded. Rather than well-defined and bounded distinctions, my study of these classes suggests there is an overlapping of different views (not necessarily incoherent) based on different assumptions of what a language is comprised of and how it should best be taught/learned.

On the one hand, analysis of the sequential organization of activities in the two focal classrooms reveals the emergence of a recurrent legitimate performance of language that is heavily constrained by the structural linguistics approach and by audio-lingual and grammar translation method views on its teaching and learning. Students in these classes are mainly positioned and position themselves as a collective body of *animators* of repertoires of phonemes, vocabulary items, speech acts, and grammatical structures; that is, they are expected to participate according to the guiding principle of obtaining correct phonetic-lexical-grammatical habits. On the other hand, this form of animation is not only enacted in participation frameworks in which isolated language samples are recited. Such repertoires or linguistic contents, taken from simulated dialogues and other communicative situations, are also expected to be mobilized in recreation activities aimed at displaying communicative-like attitudes. Thus, the construction of the legitimate performance of language is to some extent shaped by the functional linguistics approach to language and by the communicative language teaching method for its teaching/learning.

As regards the conceptualization of institutional processes, the data analyzed in this chapter reveal how the study of language education practices cannot be detached from the specific goals driving the institution in which these practices are inscribed. To some extent, these goals always shape the organization of the classroom activity, in connection with the wider national policies to which the institution is oriented. In the case of the experimental schools I studied, the triangulation of classroom interactions, ethnographic observations of complementary spaces such as the English-language competitions, interviews with all the participants in the classes observed, and official documents like the English-language curriculum for experimental schools reveals how the construction of the previously mentioned legitimate performance of language in these English-language classrooms is linked to sociocultural meanings that have a wider significance, beyond the classroom context.

The production format of collective animation, which is interactionally displayed and showcased through a set of ritualized participation frameworks of stylized choral repetition, is discursively constructed in relation to a passionately Chinese way of teaching English. This discursive construction is authorized in official documents by an abstract educational category ("comprehensive language use abilities") which models China's English-language curriculum on the basis of an approach to education reform combining linguistic skills, attitudinal values referring to motivation, cooperation, patriotism, and internationalism, and cultural forms of knowledge emphasizing cross-cultural awareness. Therefore, in the space of English-language education this category contributes to institutionalizing the same moral values that emerged in my study of ritualized practices in Chapter 4, where the relevant educational category was seen to be the "comprehensiveness principle"; in this case, patriotism and collectivism are naturalized through practices and discourses of innovation that represent Chinese cultural values as a necessary layer to be added to existing scientific international knowledge in language teaching in order to educate students in correct perspectives and values.

Finally, and with regard to the conceptualization of classroom discourse, the interactional analysis of the moment-to-moment of the activity also raises important concerns about the consensual accounts of classroom life often found in the public educational arena. In contrast to the standard view of the classroom as a social space in which the interaction involves the teacher in her or his capacity as instructor, on the one hand, and all students as a whole, on the other, the data analyzed suggest a much less continuous, stable, and predictable setting. Although they perform a strong institutionalized function, choral repetitions do not seem to be reconstituted in constant alignment by their participants. On the contrary, teachers and students manage to construct multiple forms of *backstage* that allow them to fictionally engage in the expected form of choral participation while de-aligning themselves to carry out other types of individual and interpersonal activities at the same time—including the explicit forms of emotional detachment expressed by the participants in the course of interviews.

At this point, I wish to draw together the diverse strands of the analysis conducted here and in previous chapters. Accordingly, in the next (and final) chapter, I shall consider in greater detail some of these processes and their possible consequences, not just for the three experimental schools studied, but overall for contemporary China, in the socioeconomic conditions of late modernity.

6 China, the New Economy, and the Institutionalization of English

6.1 THE THREE EXPERIMENTAL SCHOOLS AND THE DILEMMAS OF LATE MODERN POLITICS OF IDENTITY

A few years after the fieldwork carried out in Zhejiang, I received a copy of a keynote paper delivered by Ruth Hayhoe in 2011, at the International Education Forum and Expo—Learning Journey for the Globalised World. The paper was sent to me by a teacher who was one of the participants in a new research project I was conducting in the educational context of Hong Kong. As a follow-up to one of our lunch-hour conversations in which we informally discussed some of the analyses presented in this book, he asked for my opinion on the perspective offered in Hayhoe's paper, which according to him offered a view that is often considered as "progressivist" in the Hong Kong context. In this keynote paper, Ruth Hayhoe, who headed the Hong Kong Institute of Education from 1997 to 2002 and was a member of the Education Commission in Hong Kong between 1998 and 2001, reflected on the educational reforms carried in Hong Kong during the first decade of the 21st century:

> It is both a great honor and a pleasure to be invited to give this keynote address on Educational Reform and Human Resource Development at an important juncture in Hong Kong's history—just past the fourteenth anniversary of Hong Kong's return to China on July 1 of 1997 and at the culmination of what has probably been the most comprehensive reform of Hong Kong's education system to date. The full implementation of the curricular and structural reforms that have unfolded over these years will probably extend for years to come, and the results will be a richer development of Hong Kong's people—her human resources. This term has broader connotations than human capital, the concept often used by economists concerned with competition in the global knowledge society. It includes moral, aesthetic, emotional and social dimensions, alongside of the cognitive. In reviewing many of the reform documents, I found a recurring concern with the moral aspects of education and the need to strengthen connection to China's classical

heritage, while learning lessons from all that is most advanced in global educational and scientific developments: "It is the society's expectation that education should enrich our moral, emotional, spiritual and cultural life so that we can rise above the material world. . . ." I was touched also by this mention of the spiritual dimension [. . .] We have now just completed the first decade of the 21st century, and China's rise is becoming increasingly clear, as is the recognition that it has been achieved not only by the strategic policies and decisions of its leaders, but by the richness of its educational resources, rooted in a Confucian civilizational heritage that goes back 2500 years. Over its 155 years as a British Colony, Hong Kong had access to educational values that undergirded Britain's remarkable rise and extensive empire, from the 17th century to the mid-20th century. Much has been written about the parallels between the Chinese commitment to nurturing scholar officials and the British concept of the scholar gentleman, but probably only Hong Kong has had such a lengthy experience of the blending of these two traditions. Even though recent reforms have been mainly about fundamental changes in the structures left by British colonialism, positive elements in the values that have made Hong Kong such a dynamic city remain a significant resource for the future.

> ("Education Reform and Human Resource Development:
> A Perspective on Hong Kong", Hong Kong, 14 July 2011,
> pp. 1–4. Retrieved from https://cd.edb.gov.hk/IEFE/4b.asp.
> Accessed 22 September 2012)

Without necessarily intending to, Hayhoe points out the fundamental issue faced by modern (educational) institutions under the conditions of late modernity. These institutions have to adapt to an increasingly international architecture resulting from the managed interaction between the global strategy of a network and the nationally/regionally/locally rooted interests of its components (Castells, 2010). In other words, they have to manage the tensions resulting from the shifting role of the state, from a welfarist orientation (i.e., the creation and protection of nation-state markets with a focus on rights and on the maintenance of language and culture) toward becoming a facilitator of transnational processes of capital mobility in a new scenario where the nation-state is not the only political-economic point of reference.

In Hayhoe's text, this dilemma seems to be approached by advocating the blending of global scientific/educational developments, on the one hand, and China's classical heritage (particularly the Confucian civilizational heritage), on the other. While this may be perceived as a very pragmatic stance to overcome the Han-Chinese ethno-nationalism/global capitalism dualism in the reinvention of the shared cultural values that underpin the imagination of the Chinese nation/people, it still raises concerns about the conceptualization of culture as a naturally given entity disconnected from socioeconomic interests. In fact, we have seen in previous chapters in this book similar ideas emerging from the three experimental schools studied in Zhejiang, whereby discourses on cultural blending are intimately linked to the interests of institutional and national policies of educational modernization.

What is at issue to me, then, is not how to better combine these global and Chinese cultural values, as advocated by Hayhoe, but rather how such an interested discourse of combination is socially constructed, institutionalized, and localized by the social actors involved, in response to changing economic conditions—particularly those brought about by the 1980s "open door" policies in the People's Republic of China. In the case of the three schools studied in Hangzhou and Wenzhou, the institutionalization of such discourses about combining cultural traditions is made evident in the construction of what counts as the "good school", the "good student", and "appropriate knowledge" in day-to-day life, these being very significant social categories upon which the schools organize themselves as social institutions.

Schools, teachers, and students (but also myself as a researcher) are required to adjust their management, teaching, and learning practices (including research practices) in accordance with an educational system driven by the principles of structural neoliberalization and Chinese cultural nativism, whereby the former is discursively linked to values of internationalism, meritocracy, academic excellence, innovation, and competition, while the latter is connected with a patriotic-plus-Confucian-based collectivist ethos framed in the contemporary Chinese state's legal framework and rooted in Chinese cultural traditions. On the one hand, these social actors are expected to conform to centralized policies and standardized practices of institutional evaluation within a deregulated economic system where flexibility and competition for scarce resources at the local order ensure the efficient implementation of the official guidelines. On the other hand, they all have to submit to a school-based hierarchical and disciplined social organization that is institutionalized through a moralized and bureaucratically objectified definition of the school community.

As a result of these two main driving principles, the construction of the good member in the social space of the three experimental schools relies not only on meritocratic criteria regarding academic results (whether those of a single student, of a class, or of the whole school) but also on the participants' engagement with this school-based hierarchical and disciplined social organization. This social construction of what it means to be a good member of the school community is derived from the historical conditions out of which the modern Chinese educational system/curriculum emerged, in line with the specific ways in which the state and the liberal market have become progressively interrelated in modern China. The advent and development of discourses of educational modernization in the Chinese context cannot be detached from the West-global versus China-national cultural polarization on the basis of which the "good national/citizen" outlook has been politically imagined and mobilized by the local elites, at the intersection between the political economies of global capitalism and modern Chinese nationalism.

In particular, the implementation of policies/discourses reinforcing institutional neoliberalization and Chinese cultural nativism in contemporary Chinese education are linked to wider socioeconomic plans of national reform aiming to implement economic liberalization to achieve the successful integration of China's market into the global one—where the nationalization of Asian cultural traditions such as Confucianism into the space-time of traditional China places Chinese cultural industries and related entrepreneurs in a privileged position within the Asian-Pacific market and beyond—while keeping political authoritarianism as the main form of political organization—where the representation of Chinese cultural traditions as rooted in a Confucian-based cultural heritage privileges authoritarian models of organization over the alternatives of individual freedom stemming from liberal democracy.

In the space of the three experimental schools studied in Zhejiang, the combination of these two main driving principles is officially authorized, mainly through discursive forms of educational expertise and social rationalization. With regard to educational expertise, the blending of internationalism, meritocracy, academic excellence, innovation, competition, and patriotic-plus-Confucian-based collectivism is authorized through pedagogical discourses referring to a comprehensive three-dimensional educational model in which intellectual, physical, and moral aspects are understood to be equally important in evaluating the "quality" of education—where the intellectual is constructed in relation to academicism while moral and physical aspects are mainly related to patriotic and collectivist practices aimed at instilling love of the Chinese Communist Party and of Chinese cultural traditions such as Confucianism. As with the discursive forms of social rationalization, the combination is officially justified by representing this comprehensive three-dimensional educational model as a specific Chinese reform in the field of educational modernization aimed at exploiting the economic and technological opportunities provided by the new internationalized market while avoiding the moral contamination and indiscipline that is supposedly rife in the West.

Nevertheless, pressures on school participants to adjust to these driving principles are not free of paradoxes. They are all expected to engage with national guidelines advocating internationalism, excellence, and collectivism; yet, at the same time, they must cope with the need to adapt these values to very local socioeconomic conditions (markets) in order to compete with other school communities in their area for state resources. This adaptation can take the form of symbolic categories such as the "experimental" one, which in turn impacts the schools' capacity to increase student registration numbers and therefore their (partially deregulated) budgets. In a context like this, where much is at stake for all the actors (school heads, teachers, and students), they react by investing in the construction of unique public/frontstage images that allow them to marketize themselves as progressivist institutions actively involved in the latest modernization reforms.

Thus, a public image is constructed in which the emphasis on achieving high student success rates in the standardized national tests is complemented by a unique balance with internationalism and collectivism, depending on the school's population and local socioeconomic circumstances. This, however, brings about subsequent dilemmas, ironies, and paradoxes at the local order, because not all students in a given school will fit into the resulting formula. As the literature on modern nationalism has taught us, bounded communities conformed by a uniform body of people sharing a monolithic cultural background are always part of discursive imagination (Anderson, 1983), and this also applies to the schools studied here. The three school communities in Zhejiang are traversed by differences concerning linguistic repertoires, social class, educational expectations, and individual concerns, goals, and beliefs. Nonetheless, these differences are discursively backstaged in the form of ambiguous social positioning and double-voiced practices through which participants signal their ambivalent attitudes toward the legitimate social categories and forms of knowledge that they are expected to reproduce.

In doing so, these participants find their own ways of coping with the local contradictions arising from the institutional and national policies for modernization that they have to deal with. These contradictions are often explicit in instances of interpersonal collusion among students, or even among students and teachers, which have important consequences for our understanding of the cultural processes of transformation in contemporary institutions, beyond overarching mechanisms of social reproduction. Indeed, instances of interpersonal collusion across the boundaries of different institutional roles show that the framing of teacher-student relationships within a domination axis, in which the former are positioned as representative of an institution whose authority can only be accepted or resisted by the latter, contrasts with the increasing destabilization of these modern institutional positions under conditions of late modernity.

All in all, the case of these three schools reveals an interesting contrast to what has been described in relation to other contexts in Europe or North America (see Heller, 1999, 2002b, 2011; Pujolar, 2007), where sociolinguistic literature points out a transition from the modern politics of identity to the commodification of identity—implying that language and culture are shifting from emblems of nation-states toward valuable capitals in the transnational markets. The institutional and interpersonal processes emerging from the discursive organization of experimental schools in China point to a cultural transformation and to institutional dilemmas that are not necessarily related to a transition from the ideological framework of modern nationalism to that of postnationalism, but instead to the official search for a path to modernization that combines the political and economic agendas of both cultural nationalism and cultural commodification.

This scenario is particularly evident in the terrain of English-language education, where all these social categories, institutional policies, and discursive forms of positioning are articulated at the very intersection between these two socially constructed poles of Chinese modernization.

6.2 FROM "SAFE-TALK" TO "SHOW-TALK": GLOBAL PROGRESSIVISM AND NATIONAL DOMESTICATION IN ENGLISH-LANGUAGE EDUCATION

In the English-language classrooms of the three experimental schools studied in Zhejiang, these links between social categories, institutional policies, and discursive forms of positioning are specifically enacted in relation to choral repetition. As in various educational contexts across the world, this form of participation stands out in that it plays an important function in the organization of the activity and, in turn, in the social construction of what is considered to be good practice and a good participant. Indeed, choral repetition has long been identified in the Chinese context, as testified by Cortazzi and Jin's ethnographic description with reference to the language classrooms they observed in China during the 1980s and early 1990s:

> Children in chorus and individually read the questions aloud and answer them rapidly. The lesson proceeds at a smart pace, with the whole class working on the same material at the same speed. Everything is orchestrated by the teacher, strictly but in a kind manner. Every three or four minutes there is a change of activity without losing the thread of the topic [...] Children are consistently attentive, listening, speaking together in a disciplined chorus [...] The teacher models this extensively with exaggerated gestures and intonation. The children repeat each part in chorus, then individually. The teacher re-enacts the dialogue with individual children and finally children repeat the dialogue in pairs taking roles. The children mimic the pronunciation, intonation and gestures exactly. (1996: 175–176)

Given its historical prominence, choral repetition has always attracted analytical and theoretical attention within classroom discourse studies, particularly in English-language education studies interested in contexts where this language is considered to be a second/foreign language. In fact, this interactional practice has long been regarded as a valuable window for exploring the links between the language classroom and the wider society (see Coleman, 1996). However, interpretations diverge regarding the social and cultural significance of this interactional form of classroom organization, depending on the intellectual traditions within which commentators place themselves. In sociolinguistics, the study of choral repetition has often been trapped between socialization studies and sociolinguistic critique. Thus, choosing chorus repetition as a focus of analysis in classroom discourse studies has always involved some degree of (self- and/or hetero-) positioning between these two main strands.

Those approaching choral repetition from the area of socialization studies have tended to conceptualize it in relation to cultures of learning. In this sense, they search for cultural roots, studying the function and form of this form of participation in a given community. Cortazzi & Jin (1996: 188) and Jin & Cortazzi (2006: 12) offer a good example of this perspective in the Chinese context when they explicitly link the previously described practices with Confucian heritages of learning that are historically tied to a Chinese cultural setting. Although this approach provides a means of describing the processes by which institutions reproduce hegemonic cultural values in situated contexts, its strong emphasis on cultural continuity has often led to culturalist accounts where essentialized, nationally bounded, and consensual understandings of culture are projected into the classroom life.

In reaction to this approach, sociolinguistic critique has investigated the links between this activity arrangement in classrooms and issues of power, social inequality, and domination in the framework of specific sociopolitical and economic conditions (see Arthur, 1996; Bunyi, 2001; Hornberger & Chick, 2001; Ndayipfukamiye, 2001; Annamalai, 2005; Martin, 2005; Rubdy, 2005; Weber, 2008; Ngwaru & Opoku-Amankwa, 2010; for Botswana, Kenya, Peru, Burundi, India, Singapore, Malaysia, Ghana/Zimbabwe, and Luxembourg, respectively). Rather than being just a cultural style of participation transported into the classroom, this form of participation, thus, is tied to social processes and interests.

The pioneer of this line of enquiry was Keith Chick, who referred to choral participation as "safe-talk" (Chick, 1996: 24) to highlight the extent to which this arrangement of activity contributes to reproducing social structures of inequity in contexts where the language of instruction is not the one used in daily life by teachers and students in their local communities. Thus, and following Chick's work, choral repetitions have come to be widely conceptualized in sociolinguistic studies as serving mainly a consensual social function at the expense of an academic one; they are seen as interactional strategies that teachers improvise (with the compliance of their students) in order to solve the immediate tension of having to teach the subject through the medium of a language that neither they nor their students know well. In other words, by engaging in this form of participation, students and teachers are represented as colluding monotonously to preserve their dignity, concealing the fact that no learning is taking place (Chick, 1996: 24).

This is how Chick put it, regarding the context of apartheid in South Africa where all schools had to teach using English as a medium of instruction even though this language was not spoken by the local black communities in their everyday life:

> I see the teacher and [the] students as *colluding* in preserving their dignity by hiding the fact that little or no learning is taking place. While

serving the short-term interests of teachers and students, such strategies, I suggest, contributed to the widely documented high failure rate
in black education in apartheid South Africa, and made teachers and
students resistant to educational innovation [...] The social function of
chorusing became even more clearly evident when I examined the lesson
as a whole. I discovered that the students are required, in response to
both kinds of cues, to provide mainly confirmative one- or two-word
responses, or responses which repeat information on the board or information which has been recycled again and again by [the teacher]. This
suggests that chorusing gives the students opportunities to participate
in ways that reduce the possibility of the loss of face associated with
providing incorrect responses to teacher elicitations, or not being able
to provide responses at all. (Chick, 1996: 24–29)

While providing a more critical stance on how the culture of learning
in a given institutional setting is tied to social order in the wider society,
this other analytical perspective is not yet sufficient to make sense of the
ideological, institutional, and interpersonal dimensions emerging from the
three experimental schools in Zhejiang. In the Chinese context, English is
certainly considered a second/foreign language, and it has been historically
embedded in colonial and postcolonial discourses about modernization,
progress, Westernization, and globalization (see Lo Bianco et al., 2009).
Nevertheless, choral repetition in the studied English-language classrooms
does not seem to fit particularly well into the description provided by Chick.
On the one hand, these choral practices are constructed as institutionalized
rituals and not just as interactional strategies that teachers and students
come up with in order to solve the tension of having to learn/teach through
English as the medium of instruction, in disconnection from discourses and
practices of educational innovation.

Choral repetitions are discursively and interactionally displayed in the
three experimental schools as a form of "show-talk", that is, as education-
ally oriented institutional shows driven by structuralist, functionalist, and
collectivist principles that are grounded on policies of educational reform
and methodological innovation. In particular, the combination of these
principles is represented as a specifically Chinese way of teaching English,
resulting from the combination of Chinese traditional culture and foreign
progressivism. Thus, this ritualized form of participation is linked to an
innovative and passionately Chinese way of teaching/learning English in institutional contexts where the construction of what counts as "good practice", "good teacher", and "good participant" is explicitly at stake (i.e.,
peer evaluation, research observation, and teachers' competitions).

Indeed, the interactional enactment of this institutionally embraced
socio-emotional framework is discursively justified in the official curriculum through the pedagogical principle of "comprehensive language use
abilities", which institutionalizes the previously mentioned combination

by embodying this principle in the juxtaposition of discourses associated with both cultural nationalism (i.e., attitudes and motivation toward cross-cultural awareness, patriotism, and cooperation, which promote a sense of belonging to a supposedly Chinese collectivist culture, contrasting it with foreign cultures) and English-language commodification (i.e., linguistic skills and international perspectives that convey a representation of English as an international skill detached from foreign cultural identity and which needs to be mastered by Chinese citizens to ensure China's successful participation in the new internationalized economy).

On the other hand, a close look at the ongoing local activity within the course of these choral repetitions shows there is an interactional space in which the students and teachers do much more than engage unambiguously with official practices. And this is an important dimension to bear in mind when dealing with ritualization: "there is room for manoeuvre in even the most rigid of rituals [...] and in plural stratified societies, people respond to rituals in different ways, some of them quite at odds with the original design" (Rampton, 2006: 189). In the English classrooms of the three experimental schools, the zoom view of these practices reveals interesting social spaces in which the students engage in interpersonal and agent activities not necessarily aligned with the institutionally legitimated ones.

This is done through different ways of managing the front- and back-stage of the activity, which are employed to overcome the contradictions faced by all in dealing with the institutional guidelines for domesticating the commodification of English language within the ideological framework of Chinese cultural traditionalism, in an educational context strongly traversed by streaming and testing practices. All of the actors are interested in the capitals provided by the schooling system, which for many represent a means of entry to the job market and related social rewards (including teachers, for whom schools are their workplace). Accordingly, they contribute to constructing the fiction of a uniform institutional ritual that is performed unambiguously by all participants (as shown in the description provided previously by Cortazzi and Jin) even though many of them do not actually align themselves emotionally with the form of participation officially constructed as the legitimate/innovative/modern way of teaching/learning English.

These two aspects highlight the need to reconceptualize former ways of describing choral repetition in classroom discourse studies, in order to capture processes of social and cultural change with regard to the institutional context of contemporary China. In contrast to the previously mentioned approaches, in order to understand the organization of daily life in the three Chinese experimental schools we must make an interpretative move away from modernist perspectives in the study of English-language education in order to account for cultural processes of change under conditions of late modernity. This move entails a transition in the focus of attention, from holistic, culturally bounded, socially consensual, and institutionally uninvolved representations of the classroom space (either for reporting cultural continuity, as in Cortazzi and Jin's analysis, or for denouncing an overarching sociocultural reproduction involving the domination by one community of others, as in the use of the "safe-talk" label) toward an account of how discontinuity, heterogeneous perspectives, and institutionalization intersect in language education practice through the implementation of national policies in response to wider socioeconomic processes of change.

In other words, this move involves a reconceptualization of choral practices as a discursive space in which certain social categories are produced, attributed value, circulated, and transformed according to institutional logic and in view of the different interests at stake involved in local, national, and even global cultural politics. Such a reconceptualization puts us in a better position to identify the complex ways by which the modern politics of identity are destabilized (and reshaped) in interaction with the logic of commodification introduced by the new globalized economy.

Certainly, we have seen here some important ways by which all involved in the three experimental schools studied in Zhejiang navigate this complex discursive space in order to manage local, institutional, national, and international interests while positioning themselves with respect to what modernization should mean. My account of these circumstances is an attempt to make sense of the discourses and forms of positioning observed at a particular moment in time and space in urban China, where ideology and practice take the shape described in this book. In exploring how this path of institutional and cultural change, in the context of China's late modernity, might unfold in coming years, we must continue to observe these and other schools, both at this space-time location and at others.

Appendix: Symbols Used in the Transcripts

Laura:	participant
CR	(capital letters) loud talking
( )°	low talking / murmuring
cr	(italics letters) reading
ee	vowel lengthening
ss	consonant lengthening
/	short pause (0.5 seconds)
//	long pause (0.5—1.5 seconds)
(*n*")	*n* seconds pause
[]	turn overlapping with similarly marked turn
=	continuation of utterance after overlapping
(( ))	nonunderstandable fragment
{ }	researcher's comments
↑	rising intonation
↓	falling intonation
-	self interruption
&	latched utterances
Ā	stylized high intonation
**	English translation of words uttered in Chinese
° ° °	vowel lengthening in Chinese
或	(character in frame) loud talking in Chinese

Notes

NOTES TO CHAPTER 1

1. All participants' names in this book are pseudonymous so as to protect their anonymity.
2. This education system was the result of complex interactions among various models imported from different contexts, in line with changing economic and sociopolitical conditions at national and international levels. In particular, the construction of an education model based on academicism emerged in China from the progressive development of a modern national system in the first half of the 20th century, during which Japan, the United States, and Europe (mainly Germany and France) were points of reference, in accordance with their success in the constitution of modern nation-states (see Peake [1970] for a detailed and well-documented historical analysis of the early construction of a modern educational system in China).
3. The main educational policies, directly derived from the "Patriotic Education" campaign, are: "Outline for the reform and development of education in China" (中国教育发展和改革纲要), issued in 1993; "Outline for the implementation of patriotic education" (爱国主义教育实施纲要), issued in 1994; and "Education law of the People's Republic of China" (中华人民共和国教育法), issued in 1995. All the educational guidelines implemented since then explicitly take these three policy documents and their patriotic guiding principles as the starting point from which to continue developing the structure and organization of educational institutions in China. Among these developments, two of the most important are: "21st Century Action Plan for Invigorating Education" (面向21世纪教育振兴行动计划), issued in 1999; and "Decision of the CPC Central Committee and the State Council on the deepening of educational reform and the full promotion of quality education" (中共中央国务院关于深化教育改革全面推进素质教育的决定), issued in 1999.
4. It probably never was, but the pace, intensity, frequency, and degree of the conditions under which the state's political supremacy is being currently challenged are greater (see also Harvey, 1989).
5. These campaigns for the eradication of English from Chinese education took place not only during the Cultural Revolution but also at different and intermittent moments in the 20th century, in line with the close interrelation between colonialism and modern state construction in China's history (see Lam, 2005: 71–83).
6. I wish to acknowledge the support from Luisa Martín-Rojo and the Spanish Ministry of Science and Technology through the project "Socio-pragmatic Analysis of Intercultural Communication in Educational Practices: Toward

Integration in the Classroom" (BFF 2003–04830). This project provided me with the institutional support but most importantly with the theoretical and methodological pillars upon which the research in China was based.

7. This research fellowship was funded by the "Plan Nacional de I+D+I (2000–2003)" of the Spanish Ministry of Science and Technology (BFF 2003–04830).

8. I would like to thank Professor Shi-xu, the director of the Institute of Discourse and Cultural Studies, for his personal and institutional support. He opened his research space in Zhejiang University to me, and this was crucial for me to be able to carry out the fieldwork from which this book is derived.

9. The Nanjing Treaty forced the Chinese Court to cede Victoria Island (Hong Kong) to Great Britain, which remained a British colony until 1997. Both treaties resulted from the two Opium Wars (1839–1842 and 1856–1860) and obliged the Qing court (a) to cede key territories to Great Britain, (b) to open China's main ports to international commerce, and (c) to establish diplomatic relationships with the European powers.

10. This war concluded by the Shimonoseki Treaty (1895), under which China was forced to cede more territories and to open up more ports to the Japanese economy.

11. These intellectuals had begun importing European theories of modern nationalism at the end of the 19th century, through the Hundred Days Reform in 1898, when they tried to convince the imperial court of the need to make changes so as to avoid imperialist aggressions. However, they were soon reprimanded by the conservative elements behind the imperial throne, who considered these reforms dangerous to the maintenance of the imperial political order.

12. Such a multiethnic national community was initially constructed by Sun Yat-sen in a way that concerned only the five nationalities that had been most hostile to the new Chinese nation-state (Manchu, Han, Mongol, Hui, and Tibetan). In fact, these five nationalities were represented in the national flag of the Republic of China in the form of five stripes symbolizing the official doctrine of a republic of five nationalities, although more ethnic groups would be incorporated later, to create the current list of 56 officially recognized ethnic groups in China (Zhao, 2004).

13. Liang Qichao was one of the most important reformist leaders in the implementation of the liberal democracy. He had previously played a very important role at the end of the Qing dynasty, acting as a political advisor for the implementation of modernization reforms.

14. A well-established internal movement demanding the constitution of a federal national system in China gained ground during the 1920s (Chesneaux, 1969). Although provincial networks had historically existed in China since the premodern imperial system, the politicization of provincial consciousness developed throughout the 19th century, when well-integrated provincial elites began to articulate a political role for themselves as the true defenders of the nation against foreign aggressors (Duara, 1993). These regional networks and interests intersected with the foundation of the Republic of China, providing strong support for a federal state, on the basis of discourses appealing for provincial self-governance compatible with the ideological agenda of a liberal state. Nonetheless, these federal movements quickly degenerated into a space in which warlords fought each other.

15. This representation of the political community in relation to the party's tutelage was firstly institutionalized during the 1920s as the ideological foundation of the CNP under the Three Principles of the People, which were defined as follows: nationalism as loving the government and protecting sovereignty against invaders; democracy as restricted political rights; and social welfare as economic development through agricultural productivity, trade, and

modern industry (Esteban, 2007: 27). These principles were later framed within other official slogans and political discourses under the regime of the CCP, although they have remained throughout the 20th century as basic elements of modern Chinese nationalism (Hughes, 2006).

16. In June 1919, after Germany's defeat by the Allies in the First World War, the Treaty of Versailles assigned to Japan the territories that China had previously been obliged to cede to Germany. This caused generalized disappointment among urban sectors in China with respect to the international community's values of freedom and democracy proclaimed as underpinning modernity. Social mobilizations and protests took place in urban areas including Beijing, as part of what became known as the May Fourth Movement (Spence, 1981).

17. As an example of what Fanon (1952) and Chen (2010) have labeled a "hierarchical structure of sentiment", by which the colonized feel inferior to the colonizer as a result of the deep psychological impact of colonial sociopolitical structures on subjectivities, these social actors refused to blame coloniality as the main cause of China's economic problems, considering Chinese traditions to be at the root of the Western powers' ability to exploit China so easily (Teng & Fairbank, 1954: 240).

18. Inspired by the New Cultural movement, which included famous figures such as Chen Duxiu (who later became a Marxist) and Hu Shi (Zhao, 2004: 57).

19. Inspired by the anti-imperialist themes of the May Fourth movement.

20. Since Marxism-Leninism was a universalist critique of the power relationships established by the nation-state's capitalist regime—oriented toward building an international proletarian community ruled by the working class—Mao overcame the contradiction of structuring a universalist framework around the principle of national salvation by representing such a principle as a necessary intermediate goal for the emancipation of the Chinese nation. That is, he represented communism as the ultimate goal of the revolution, and Chinese national prosperity as a necessary prerequisite for this purpose. This particular adaptation of Marxism-Leninism for the purposes of a Chinese nation-building process has been labeled in China as "Mao Zedong's Thought", and it has been part of the CCP's official ideological guidelines since 1949.

21. In particular, Mao took advantage of national and international conditions during World War II to represent the CNP and Chiang Kai-shek as the "puppets" of both the Japanese army during their occupation of Nanjing between 1940 and 1944, and of the U.S. government as the new international power in the post-war period (Mao, 1965: 307).

22. The specific contents and socioeconomic reforms implemented in accordance with these modernizing discourses varied greatly during the almost 30 years of Mao's regime. These differences included periods of a certain degree of openness to ideas and discourses of reform coming from outside China, but also periods of being totally closed to the rest of the world, combined with devastating campaigns of collectivization and ideological indoctrination that caused millions of deaths across the country (see Fairbank [1976], Harding [1997], Zheng [1997], and Brugger [1978] for a detailed analysis of these radicalizing policies and campaigns in their political and economic context).

23. These reforms also had a parallel intellectual development, the New Enlightenment movement, which was based on the principles of critiquing Mao Zedong, importing the theories of individual liberation, supporting economic openness, and endorsing pro-Western socioeconomic programs (Wang & Karl, 1998: 17).

24. This theory was formulated by Jiang Zemin and included officially as part of the CCP's guiding ideology during the 16th National Party Congress in 2000. It was also ratified by Hu Jintao at the 17th edition of the National Party

Congress in 2007. According to this theory, the CCP came to represent the following social actors in China: (a) advanced productive forces, (b) China's advanced culture, and (c) the fundamental interests of the majority of the Chinese people.

25. While being explicitly detached from the discourse of class struggle, socialism began to be officially represented as a means for the liberation of China's productive forces—among which science, technology, and commerce occupy a key position—within a communist project for national building in stages in which the end of rapid national economic growth justified almost any means (including huge social inequalities among different regions; this came to be represented as a necessary step before distributing welfare across the country). Thus, the new professional classes of scientists, engineers, and managers came to be officially considered as representatives of the working class because of their role as advanced productive elements for the nation's economic development (see Deng, 1993).

26. The collapse of the USSR and the end of the Cold War led to the United States implementing economic policies in East Asia to prevent the expansion of communism, immediately after many countries in the region had been politically and militarily decolonized. This produced strong economic growth in the area, headed by the "four Asian dragons" (South Korea, Singapore, Hong Kong, and Taiwan), but also created conditions favorable to the absence of a cultural and psychological decolonization of the region, with subjectivities and cultural imaginaries remaining trapped in a Cold War outlook, suffering an overarching polarization between "the democratic West" and "the rest" without having the opportunity to critically reflect on the previous colonial experience and on new neocolonization knowledge conditions. It is in this context that the previously mentioned countercultural postcolonial and postmodern intellectual movements emerged in East Asia. These movements attempted to deconstruct the former identification with the colonizer (viewed as the embodiment of modernity), but in doing so they leant on nativist nationalisms in which the Other (the opponent of the self-recovery movement) is still the ex-colonizer (thereby reproducing colonization's cultural and psychological structures of reference) (Chen, 2010; see also Lin, 2012).

27. See Tatsuo (1999), Dallmayr (2002), Langguth (2003), and Nieto-Martínez (2007) for a critical review of the consequences of this discourse in reproducing an internal sociopolitical order characterized by huge social inequalities in terms of region, social class, and gender.

28. Indeed, at the 16th Party National Congress, "social harmony" was considered by Hu Jintao as a key attribute for the construction of socialism with Chinese characteristics (Hu, 2007).

NOTES TO CHAPTER 2

1. The anthropologist Franz Boas, in his early work, and the linguists Sapir and Whorf were examples of those who followed these Darwinist ideas (see Briggs, 2005).

2. This structuralist representation was also projected onto writing, giving rise to an autonomous model of writing known as "the literacy thesis" (Halverson, 1992). Under the guiding principle of universality, oral and written language were dichotomized such that the latter was represented as a discrete and context-free system linked to rationality, formality, and cognitive development, while the former was considered as chaotic, context-dependent, and

illogical (Goody & Watt, 1963: 339; Goody, 1977: 37; Olson, 1977: 262; see also Poveda, 2001: chap. 3; Collins & Plot, 2003: 9–34).

3. These poststructuralist ideas also had an impact on the historically constructed division between oral and written language. Thus, they are both now represented as part of multimodal communicative practices in which participants draw on different symbolic and material resources (i.e., artifacts) to build common understandings. This new conceptualization draws greatly from the work done in New Literacy Studies (Street, 1993, 1995; Gee, 1996; Barton & Hamilton, 1998; Barton, Hamilton, & Ivanic, 2000; Martin-Jones & Jones, 2000). This research tradition has contributed to deconstruct the autonomous representation of writing in favor of a sociocultural approach in which reading and writing cannot be detached from the situated practices by which certain people and communities construct and make sense of meaning in social context.

4. In fact, this approach has given rise to a vast amount of research which has explored the communicative differences in socialization practices between the school and the homes of students in minority sociocultural groups, in the context of different nation-states (see Philips, 1972; Au, 1980; Michaels, 1981; Heath, 1983, as canonical examples of studies carried out in the United States, within American, Hawaiian, African American, and Appalachian native communities, respectively).

5. Educational research carried out from within ethno-national communities struggling to participate in the new globalized economy (see Heller 1999 or Jaffe 1999, in relation to ethnolinguistic minorities in Canada and Italy, respectively) or in those postcolonial contexts undergoing profound processes of socioeconomic and political reorganization (see Lin & Martin, 2005; Heller & Martin-Jones, 2001, for research into postcolonial contexts in Africa and Asia) provide us with examples of the very considerable discursive efforts involved in the constitution and reproduction of a given (nonnaturalized) internal social order in contemporary life.

NOTES TO CHAPTER 3

1. See China Education and Research Network (中国教育和研究计算机网), hosted by the Chinese Ministry of Education, www.edu.cn.
2. Schools' names provided are pseudonymous.
3. There is even a saying referring to this city and to Suzhou, another small city close to Hangzhou, which goes like this: "Up there is heaven, down there is Hangzhou and Shuzhou" ("上有天堂，下有苏杭").
4. Source: website of Zhejiang provincial government (www.zei.gov.cn).
5. The Nanxia Party was an army composed of members of the Northeast and Northwest factions, which went south to help organize the Communist Party; the Clandestine Party was based in the south of the country and also played an important role in supporting the Communist Party during the civil war between communists and nationalists; Yan'an was the revolutionary base of the Communist Party (see Pepper, 1999).
6. According to local official statistics, differences in the socioeconomic welfare of Hangzhou and Longgang are enormous: the former has a total population of 6 million people, its economy is based on the tertiary sector (mainly tourism), and it had a GDP of 238.2 billion RMB in 2007; the latter has 200,000 inhabitants, industry is its main economic activity, and it had a GDP of 7.03 billion RMB in the same year. Source: Zhejiang provincial

government (www.zei.gov.cn), Hangzhou city government (www.hangzhou.gov.cn), and Cangnan Governmental Agency (www.cncn.gov.cn).

7. Unlike Hangzhou, the Wenzhou region has always been described as a complex area where many different local language varieties apart from Mandarin are spoken, some of them largely unintelligible to each other (Ramsey, 1989). However, during the fieldwork I hardly registered any instances in which students used languages other than Mandarin in the school's daily life, which was explained by my participants on the basis of an appeal to the emblematic role of Mandarin as the language of cohesion within a school traversed by a linguistically highly diversified student population. In particular, some of the students explained the lack of presence of languages other than Mandarin in their school by reference to values of respect and shared understanding, in the framework of a Chinese diglossic context where Mandarin holds the official status as the legitimate language of the state's institutional spaces while other languages are pushed to the familiar/private domain. That is, they made sense of the monolingual-like organization of everyday life by building up a portrait in which interpersonal and institutional concerns about linguistic diversity, standardization, and social cohesion were made discursively relevant. See Chen (1999) for an in-depth exploration of the historical, sociopolitical and economic conditions of sociolinguistic diglossia in modern China; see also Dong (2009) for an analysis of the everyday practices and ideologies on which such a diglossic distribution is (re)constituted in contemporary China.

8. The public educational structure for China was defined as follows: 5 years of basic primary education circumscribed to the local administrative level; 4 years of higher primary education within the county administrative level; 5 years of secondary education at the prefecture level; 3 years of high school at the provincial level; and 4 years of university education at a national level (Peake, 1970: 67; Hayhoe, 1984: 35–36).

9. Under the new educational law of 1922, the education structure was organized as 6 years of primary education, followed by 3 years of junior secondary education, 3 years of senior secondary education and finally by 4 years of university studies. Furthermore, the curriculum changed its previous emphasis on academic subjects and was set up according to the pragmatic guidelines of "Education for life" or "Learning by doing" endorsed by North American educators such as John Dewey (Peake, 1970: 86; Hayhoe, 1984: 38–39).

10. The main educational guidelines, reports, and laws published during Mao's regime were the following: "Decisions on the reform of the education system", in 1951; "First 1953–1957 quinquennial plan", in 1952; "Guideline on the reorganization and improvement of primary education", in 1953; "Report on the third educational management national conference", in 1956; "Guideline on the management of the rural schools", in 1957; "Guideline on education work", in 1958 (extracted from Cleverley, 1985: 115–116).

11. See Cheng 1999, for a historical review of these language policies of standardization, which had been initiated in 1920 but without much success; see also Postiglione (1999), Newby (2000), and Mackerras (2006) for a review of the intersection of these language standardization policies and the management of ethnic minority languages in China, which were marginally allowed only in the compulsory education of certain regions in line with the development of wider policies of classification and regimentation of ethnic minority groups in modern China.

12. This social representation was authorized by a report published by the League of Nations on the Chinese education system of the 1940s, which was requested by the Chinese government for guiding subsequent education

reforms. This report stated that only a minority of the Chinese population of school age was registered in basic education. According to the report, Chinese education at the end of the civil war constituted a private-urban system oriented to the higher education of the social elites (Hayhoe, 1984: 42; Cleverley, 1985: 58).

13. Curriculum-streaming is particularly present in secondary education, given its intermediate position between primary education and university. Thus, there are mainstream schools preparing students to access university, specialist schools training professionals such as nurses, technical schools training semiskilled technicians (e.g., carpenters), vocational schools for specialist technicians (e.g., photographers), and agricultural schools to train farmers. Streaming even traverses the internal organization of these schools in that each one is differentiated by full/part-time schedules or by its reputation (first- and second-order schools) (see Henze, 1984; Lo, 1984; Rosen, 1984).

14. Among other things, this nativist plan of reform shortened the schooling period and reduced the curriculum by combining the existing subjects and substituting their theoretical contents for longer periods of time dedicated to productive tasks in farms and factories. Standardized tests were also substituted as a meritocratic filter in favor of well-defined social class criteria so that the children of workers and peasants should have priority over the rest in their progress through the different educational stages.

15. However, the goal of universal nine-year compulsory education was adapted to the levels of development of each region in China. Thus, different schedules to reach this goal were set in the 1985 resolution. On the one hand, the rich eastern part of the country, representing a quarter of the population at the time of the resolution, was expected to fulfill the goal by 1990. On the other hand, the regions in inner China, which account for 50% of the population, were allowed to extend the deadline until 1995. Finally, the poorest regions in western China, which represent the remaining 25% of the population, were not obliged to any specific date for complying with the Resolution in this respect (Rong & Shi, 2001).

16. These policies, which focused all state endeavors on the "key" schools and charged local governments and communities with responsibility for the remaining schools, led to a system in which the resources and opportunities to access higher education were unequally distributed by region, ethnicity, social class, and gender in China (Epstein, 1991, 1992; Rosen, 1992; Lan, Zhu, & Lan, 1996; Christensen & Dorn, 1997; Lo, 1999; Postiglione, 1999; Rong & Shi, 2001; X. Li, 2004); it was also widely criticized as it opened the door to the corruption of local authorities, who managed the funding of their assigned schools (Potts, 2003: 11–28), as well as to an increasing difference in the school fees charged in different localities—allowing some wealthy students to be accepted by prestigious urban schools through the payment of large sums of money, used by these schools to hire the most prestigious teachers and to afford cutting-edge technological facilities (Lo, 1999: 46; Potts, 2003: 14; L. Li, 2004: 279). Thus, institutional developments of these reforms during the 1990s and 2000s sought to overcome these criticisms by addressing structural inequalities (see "On the suggestions that promote a balanced development of the compulsory education" [关于进一步推进义务教育均衡发展的若干意见] and "Report on the Chinese national education" [中国全民教育国家报告], both published in 2005). As a result of these efforts, provincial governments have been given a more active role in the financial support of the schools in their regions so as to reduce economic differences among schools, which had depended on the strength of their local districts or municipalities. The "two-track" system was definitively

abolished for compulsory education, although new institutional categories like the "experimental" (实验学校) one analyzed in this book came to covertly assume almost the same symbolic role as the previous "key" (重点) category (see L. Li [2004] for an official perspective on these categorization practices and other related institutional changes). In addition, school fees were officially abolished in Chinese compulsory education just after my data compilation in Zhejiang concluded (see http://news.bbc.co.uk/2/hi/asia-pacific/6174847.stm, accessed 5 April 2012), although practices remain unchanged, as is constantly denounced in the media and by social groups inside and outside China (see http://www.youtube.com/watch?v=yFPORjjLHao, accessed 5 April 2012).

17. Indeed, the national examinations have since been progressively graded into a highly intricate system of standardized tests administered by the district, municipality, province, and state, to which all schools and local authorities must pay close attention, because they define the rankings achieved and the future institutional goals for all school heads and teachers (Lo, 1984: 52–56).

NOTES TO CHAPTER 4

1. These students are awarded an extra 8 points, added to their scores in the final examinations.
2. These national examinations include tests in six curricular subjects, each of which is evaluated up to 100 points.
3. Due to insufficient quality of the photograms, this cannot be shown in Figure 4.7, although smiling expressions are clear in the video recording from which these photograms have been extracted.
4. "Let's give wings of hope to the motherland's scientific cause and make it proudly fly over the world's sky!" (让我们为祖国的科学事业插上希望的翅膀，让它在世界的上空骄傲地腾飞吧!)
5. "The Long March deepened the Chinese Communist Party's knowledge of the national conditions of China, and promoted changes in its political line. At the same time, the Chinese political situation experienced rapid change" (长征加深了中国共产党对中国国情的认识，推动了党的政治路线的转变。与此同时，中国政治形势发生了急剧变化).
6. "Disciplined diligence makes health improve" (勤学守纪健康向上); "solidarity, cooperation, and lively civilization" (团结合作文明活泼).
7. See Lee (2000) for an in-depth historical review of the gradual institutionalization of these premodern values.

NOTES TO CHAPTER 5

1. As in all experimental schools in the country, the English language curriculum used by the schools in question was a specially adapted version, for experimental schools, of the official one published in 2001 (see Ministry of Education, 2001). Although this is still the official curriculum at the time in which the present book is being finalized, a new edition is expected to be published in late 2012.

References

Adamson, B. (2004). *China's English: A history of English in Chinese education.* Hong Kong, China: Hong Kong University Press.

Adamson, B. (2007). Depoliticisation in the English curriculum. In A. Feng (Ed.), *Bilingual Education in China-Practices, Policies and Concepts* (pp. 34–48). Clevedon, UK: Multilingual Matters.

Annamalai, E. (2005). Nation building in a globalized world: Language choice and education in India. In A. Lin & P. Martin (Eds.), *Decolonisation, Globalisation: Language-in-Education Policy and Practice* (pp. 21–38). Clevedon, England: Multilingual Matters.

Anderson, B. (1983). *Imagined communities.* London, England: Verso.

Anderson, G. (1989). Critical ethnography in education: Origins, current status and new directions. *Review of Educational Research, 59,* 249–270.

Angus, L. (1986). Developments in ethnographic research in education: From interpretive to critical ethnography. *Journal of Research and Development in Education, 20*(1), 59–67.

Appadurai, A. (1990). Disjuncture and difference in the global cultural economy. In M. Featherstone (Ed.), *Global Culture* (pp. 295–310). London, England: Sage.

Appadurai, A. (1996). *Modernity at large: Cultural dimensions of globalization.* Minneapolis, MN: University of Minnesota Press.

Apple, M. (1979). *Ideology and curriculum.* Boston, MA: Routledge & Kegan Paul.

Apple, M. (1986). *Teachers and texts: A political economy of class and gender relations in education.* New York: Routledge & Kegan Paul.

Arthur, J. (1996). Code switching and collusion: Classroom interaction in Botswana primary schools. *Linguistics and Education, 8,* 17–33.

Atkinson, J., & Heritage, J. (Eds.). (1984). *Structures of social action: Studies in conversation analysis.* Cambridge, England: Cambridge University Press.

Au, K. H. (1980). Participant structure in a reading lesson with Hawaiian children: Analysis of a culturally appropriate instructional event. *Anthropology and Educational Quarterly, 11,* 91–115.

Austin, J. (1962). *How to do things with words.* Oxford, England: Oxford University Press.

Bakhtin, M. (1981). Discourse in the novel. In C. Emerson & M. Holquist (Eds.), *The dialogic imagination: Four essays* (pp. 259–422). Austin, TX: University of Texas Press.

Bakhtin, M. (1986). *Speech genres and other late essays.* Austin, TX: University of Texas Press.

Bakhtin, M. (1994). Problems of Dostoevsky's poetics. In P. Morris (Ed.), *The Bakhtin reader. Selected writings of Bakhtin, Medvedev, Voloshinov* (pp. 110–113). London, England: Arnold.

Barton, D., & M. Hamilton (1998). Understanding literacy as social practice. In D. Barton & M. Hamilton (Eds.), *Local literacies: Reading and writing in one community* (pp. 3–22). London, England: Routledge.

Barton, D., Hamilton, M., & Ivanic, R. (Eds.). (2000). *Situated literacies: Reading and writing in context*. London, England: Routledge.

Bauman, R., & Briggs, C. (2003). *Voices of modernity: Language ideologies and the politics of inequality*. Cambridge, England: Cambridge University Press.

Bauman, Z. (1998). *Work, consumerism and the new poor*. Cambridge, England: Polity Press.

Bernstein, B. (1964). Elaborated and restricted codes: Their social origins and some consequences. *American Anthropologist, 66*(6), 55–69.

Bernstein, B. (1971). *Class, codes and control* (Vol. 1). London: Routledge & Kegan Paul.

Bernstein, B. (1975). Ritual in education. In B. Bernstein (Ed.), *Class, codes, and control: Towards a theory of educational transmissions* (Vol. 3, pp. 54–66). London: Routledge & Kegan Paul.

Billig, M. (1995). *Banal Nationalism*. London: Sage.

Blackledge, A. (2005). *Discourse and power in a multilingual world*. Amsterdam: John Benjamins.

Blackledge, A., & Creese, A. (2010). *Multilingualism*. London: Continuum.

Block, D., & Cameron, D. (2002). Introduction. In D. Block & D. Cameron (Eds.), *Globalization and language teaching* (pp. 1–10). London: Routledge.

Blommaert, J. (1999). *State ideology and language in Tanzania*. Cologne, Germany: Köppe.

Blommaert, J. (2010). *The Sociolinguistics of Globalization*. Cambridge: Cambridge University Press.

Blommaert, J., & Bulcaen, C. (2000). Critical discourse analysis. *Annual Review of Anthropology, 29*, 447–66.

Bourdieu, P. (1972). *Esquisse d'une théorie de la pratique*. Genève, Switzerland: Droz.

Bourdieu, P. (1977). *Outline of a theory of practice*. Cambridge: Cambridge University Press.

Bourdieu, P. (1982). *Ce que parler veut dire. L'économie des échanges linguistiques*. Paris: Fayard.

Bourdieu, P. (1991). *Language and symbolic power*. Cambridge: Polity Press.

Bourdieu, P., & Passeron, J.C. (1977). *Reproduction in education, society and culture*. London: Sage.

Brace, L., Gamble, G., & Bond, J. (Eds.). (1971). *Race and intelligence*. Washington, DC: American Anthropological Association.

Briggs, Charles L. (2005). Genealogies of race and culture and the failure of vernacular cosmopolitanisms: Rereading Franz Boas and W.E.B. Du Bois. *Public Culture, 17*(1), 75–100.

Brugger, B. (1978). Introduction: The historical perspective. In B. Brugger (Ed.), *China: The impact of the cultural revolution* (pp. 15–34). London: Croom Helm.

Bucholtz, M., & Skapoulli, E. (Eds.). (2009). Youth language at the intersection: From migration to globalization [Special issue]. *Pragmatics, 19*(1), 1–16.

Bunyi, G. (2001). Language and educational inequality in primary schools in Kenya. In M. Heller & M. Martin-Jones (Eds.), *Voices of authority: Education and linguistic difference* (pp. 77–100). Westport, CT: Ablex.

Cameron, D. (1995). *Verbal hygiene*. London: Routledge.

Castells, M. (2010). *The information age: Economy, society and culture: The rise of the network society* (2nd ed., Vol. 1). Oxford: Wiley Blackwell.

Cazden, C.B. (1988). *Classroom discourse: The language of teaching and learning*. Portsmouth, NH: Heinemann.

Cazden, C. B., & Mehan, H. (1989). Principles from sociology and anthropology: Context, code, classroom, and culture. In M. C. Reynolds (Ed.), *Knowledge base for the beginning teacher* (pp. 47–57). Elmsford, NY: Pergamon Press.

Chesneaux, J. (1969). The federalist movement in China. In J. Gray (Ed.), *Modern China's search for a political form* (pp. 96–137). Oxford: Oxford University Press.

Chen, P. (1999). *Modern Chinese. History and sociolinguistics.* Cambridge: Cambridge University Press.

Chen, Y. (2008). *Muslim Uyghur students in a Chinese boarding school: Social re-capitalization as a response to ethnic integration.* Lanham, MD: Lexington Books.

Chen, K. H. (2010). *Asia as method: Toward deimperialization.* Durham, NC: Duke University Press.

Cherryholmes, C. (1988). Construct validity and the discourses of research. *American Journal of Education, 96,* 421–457.

Chick, K. (1996). Safe-talk: Collusion in Apartheid education. In H. Coleman (Ed.), *Society and the language classroom* (pp. 21–39). Cambridge: Cambridge University Press.

Christensen, C., & Dorn, S. (1997). Competing notions of social justice and contradictions in special education reform. *Journal of Special Education, 31,* 181–198.

Chu S. (1999). Lengzhan Hou Zhongguo Anquan Zhanlue Sixiang De Fazhan [The development of China's post-Cold War thinking of security strategy]. *Shijie Jingji Yu Zhengzhi [World Economics and Politics], 5,* 26–30.

Chun, E. (2009). Speaking like Asian immigrants: Intersections of accommodation and mocking at a U.S. high school. In M. Bucholtz & E. Skapoulli (Eds.), *Youth language at the intersection: From migration to globalization* [Special issue]. *Pragmatics, 19*(1), 17–38.

Cicourel, A. (1978). Language and society: Cultural, cognitive and linguistic aspects of language use. *Sozialwissenschaftliche Annalen, 2,* 25–58.

Cicourel, A. (1980). Three models of discourse analysis: The role of social structure. *Discourse Processes, 33,* 101–132.

Cicourel, A. (1992). The interpenetration of communicative contexts: Examples from medical encounters. In C. Goodwin & A. Duranti (Eds.), *Rethinking context: Language as an interactive phenomenon* (pp. 291–310). Cambridge: Cambridge University Press.

Cleverley, J. (1985). *The schooling of China. Tradition and modernity in Chinese education.* Sydney, Australia: George Allen & Unwin.

Cleverley, J. (1991). *The schooling of China. Tradition and modernity in Chinese education* (2nd ed.). Sydney, Australia: George Allen & Unwin.

Codó, E. (2008). *Immigration and bureaucratic control. Language practices in the public administration.* Berlin: Mouton de Gruyter.

Coleman, H. (1996). Autonomy and ideology in the English language classroom. In H. Coleman (Ed.), *Society and the Language Classroom* (pp. 1–15). Cambridge: Cambridge University Press.

Collins, J., & Plot, R. (2003). *Literacy and literacies: Texts, power, and identity.* Cambridge: Cambridge University Press.

Cortazzi, M., & Jin, L. (1996). Cultures of learning: Language classrooms in China. In H. Coleman (Ed.), *Society and the language classroom* (pp. 169–206). Cambridge: Cambridge University Press.

Connors, M. K. (2004). Culture and politics in the Asia-Pacific: Asian values and human rights. In M. K. Connors, R. Davison, & J. Doscho (Eds.), *The new global politics of the Asia-Pacific* (pp. 199–215). London: Routledge.

Dallmayr, F. (2002). Asian values and global human rights. *Philosophy East and West, 52*(2), 173–189.

Davison, R. (2004). China in the Asia-Pacific. In M. K. Connors, R. Davison & J. Doscho (Eds.), *The new global politics of the Asia-Pacific* (pp. 51–71). London: Routledge.

Dendrinos, B. (1992). *The EFL textbook and ideology*. Athens, Greece: Grivas Publications.

Deng, X. (1978). Speech at the National Educational Work Conference [22nd April 1978]. *Beijing Review, 18*.

Deng, X. (1993). *Deng Xiaoping wenxuan* [selected works by Deng Xiaoping] (Vol. 3). Beijing, China: People's Publishing House.

Dikotter, F. (1992). *The discourse of race in Modern China*. Stanford, CA: Stanford University Press.

Ding, G. (2001). Nationalization and internationalization: Two turning points in China's education in the twentieth century. In G. Peterson, R. Hayhoe & L. Yonglin (Eds.), *Education, culture and identity in twentieth century China* (pp. 161–186). Ann Arbor: University of Michigan Press.

Dong, J. (2009). The enregisterment of Putonghua in practice. *Working Papers in Urban Language & Literacies, 56*. Retrieved from http://www.kcl.ac.uk/projects/ldc/LDCPublications/workingpapers/56.pdf

Duara, P. (1993). De-constructing the Chinese Nation, *The Australian Journal of Chinese Affairs, 30*, 1–26.

Duara, P. (1999). La deconstrucción de la nación china. In Jonathan Unger (Ed.), *Nacionalismo chino* (pp. 63–94). Barcelona, Spain: Bellaterra.

Du Bois, J. (1986). Self-evidence and ritual speech. In W. Chafe & J. Nichols (Eds.), *Evidentiality* (pp. 313–333). Norwood, NJ: Ablex.

Durkheim E. (1912). The elementary forms of religious life. In W. Pickering (Ed.), *Durkheim on religion*. London: Routledge and Kegan Paul.

Epstein, I. (1991). Educating China's disadvantaged youth: A case of modernization and its discontents. In I. Epstein (Ed.), *Chinese education: Problems, policies, and prospects* (pp. 196–216). New York: Garland Publishing.

Epstein, I. (1992). Special educational provision in People's Republic of China. In R. Hayhoe (Ed.), *Education and modernization: The Chinese experience* (pp. 285–305). Oxford: Pergamon Press.

Erickson, F. (1992). Ethnographic microanalysis of interaction. In M. LeCompte, W. Millroy & J. Preissle (Eds.), *The handbook of qualitative research in education* (pp. 201–225). New York: Academic Press.

Erickson, F. (1993). Transformation and school success: The politics and culture of educational achievement. In E. Jacob & C. Jordan (Eds.), *Minority education: Anthropological perspectives* (pp. 27–52). New York: Ablex.

Esteban, M. (2007). *China después de Tiananmen. Nacionalismo y cambio político*. Barcelona, Spain: Edicions Bellaterra.

Fairbank, J.K. (1976). *The United States and China*. Cambridge: Cambridge University Press.

Fairclough, N. (1992). *Discourse and social change*. Cambridge: Polity Press.

Fanon, F. (1952). *Peau noire, masques blancs*. Paris: Editions du Seuil.

Feng, A. (2007). *Bilingual education in China. Practices, policies and concepts*. Clevedon, UK: Multilingual Matters.

Ferrero, M. (1995). The economics of socialist nationalism: Evidence and theory. In A. Breton, G. Galeotti, P. Salmon, & R. Wintrobe (Eds.), *Nationalism and rationality* (pp. 204–244). Cambridge: Cambridge University Press.

Fisac, T., & Tsang, S. (Eds.) (2000). *China en transición. Sociedad cultura, política y economía*. Barcelona, Spain: Bellaterra.

Fitzgerald, J. (1995). The nationless state: The search for a nation in modern Chinese nationalism. *The Australian Journal of Chinese Affairs, 33*, 75–107.

Fitzgerarld, J. (1999). El estado sin nación. La búsqueda de la nación en el nacionalismo chino moderno. In J. Unger (Ed.), *Nacionalismo chino* (pp. 95–132). Barcelona: Bellaterra.

Friedman, J. (1994). *Cultural identity and global process*. London: Sage.

Fong, E. T. Y. (2009). Institutional and learner's discourses about English and the implications for 'China English'. *English Today, 97*(25:1), 44–49.

Foucault, M. (1970). *The order of things: An archaeology of the human sciences*. London: Tavistock.

Foucault, M. (1975). *Surveiller et punir: Naissance de la prison*. Paris: Gallimard.

Foucault, M. (1984). Truth and power. In P. Rabinow (Ed.), *The Foucault reader* (pp. 51–75). New York: Pantheon.

Gal, S. (1989). Language and political economy. *Annual Review of Anthropology, 18*, 345–367.

Gal, S. (1995). Lost in a Slavic sea: Linguistic theories and expert knowledge in 19th century Hungary. *Language in Society, 22*(3), 337–360.

Gao, Y. (2009). Sociocultural contexts and English in China: Retaining and reforming the cultural habitus. In J. Lo Bianco, J. Orton, & Y. Gao (Eds.), *China and English. Globalisation and the dilemmas of identity* (pp. 56–78). Bristol, England: Multilingual Matters.

Garfinkel, H. (1967). *Studies in ethnomethodology*. Englewood Cliffs, NJ: Prentice-Hall.

Gee, P. (1996). *Social linguistics and literacies: Ideology in discourses*. London: Falmer.

Giddens, A. (1984). *The constitution of society*. Berkeley: University of California Press.

Giddens, A. (1991). *Modernity and self-identity: Self and Society in the Late Modern Age*. Stanford, CA: Stanford University Press.

Giroux, H. (1988). *Schooling and the struggle for public life*. Minneapolis: University of Minnesota Press.

Giroux, H., & McLaren, P. (1989). Introduction: Schooling, cultural politics, and the struggle for democracy. In H. Giroux & P. McLaren (Eds.), *Critical pedagogy, the state, and cultural struggle* (pp. xi–xxxv). Albany: State University of New York Press.

Gladney, D. C. (1996). *Muslim Chinese: Ethnic nationalism in the People's Republic*. Cambridge, MA: Harvard University, Asia Center.

Goffman, E. (1967). *Interaction ritual. Essays on face-to-face behaviour*. New York: Pantheon Books.

Goffman, E. (1971). *Relations in public: Micro studies of the public order*. New York: Basic Books.

Goffman, E. (1974). *Frame analysis: An essay in the organization of experience*. New York: Harper & Row.

Goffman, E. (1981). *Forms of talk*. Philadelphia: University of Pennsylvania Press.

Golden, S. (2004). Valores asiáticos y multilateralismo. In S. Golden (Ed.), *Multilateralismo versus unilateralismo en Asia: el peso internacional de los 'valores asiáticos'* (pp. 103–132). Barcelona, Spain: Bellaterra.

Goodwin, C. (2000). Action and embodiment within situated human interaction. *Journal of Pragmatics, 32*, 1489–1522.

Goody, J. (1977). *The domestication of the savage mind*. Cambridge: Cambridge University Press.

Goody, J., & Watt, I. (1963). The consequences of literacy. *Comparative Studies in Society and History, 5*, 304–345.

Grillo, R.D. (1989). *Dominant languages: Language and hierarchy in Britain and France*. Cambridge: Cambridge University Press.

Guo, Y. (2004). *Cultural nationalism in contemporary China. The search for national identity under reform*. London: Routledge.

Guo, Y. (2007). "Pacific Rim", "Pacific Era", and interdependence: China's Nationalist Rimspeak. In L. Stephanie & W. Peake (Eds.), *Globalization and regionalization:*

Views from the Pacific Rim (pp. 113–146). Guadalajara, Mexico: Editorial Centro Universitario de Ciencias Sociales y Humanidades.

Gumperz, J. (1982). *Discourse strategies*. Cambridge: Cambridge University Press.

Gumperz, J. (1986). Interactional sociolinguistics in the study of schooling. In J. Cook-Gumperz (Ed.), *The social construction of literacy* (pp. 45–68). Cambridge: Cambridge University Press.

Gumperz, J. (1992): Contextualization and understanding. In A. Duranti & C. Goodwin (Eds.), *Rethinking context: Language as an interactive phenomenon* (pp. 229–52). Cambridge: Cambridge University Press.

Gumperz, J., & Hymes, D. (Eds.). (1972). *Directions in sociolinguistics: The ethnography of communication*. New York: Holt, Rhinehart & Winston.

Halverson, J. (1992). Goody and the implosion of the literacy thesis. *Man, 27*, 301–317.

Harding, H. (1997). The Chinese state in crisis, 1966–9. In M. Macfarquhar (Ed.), *The politics of China. The eras of Mao and Deng* (2nd ed., pp. 148–248). Cambridge: Cambridge University Press.

Harrell, S. (1996). Civilizing projects and the reaction to them. In Stevan Harrell (Ed.), *Cultural encounters on China's ethnic frontiers* (pp. 3–36). Seattle, WA: University of Washington Press.

Harris, K. (1979). *Education and knowledge*. London: Routledge & Kegan Paul.

Harris, R., & Rampton, B. (2009). Ethnicities without guarantees: An empirical approach. In M. Wetherell (Ed.), *Identity in the 21st century: New trends in changing times*. Basingstoke, England: Palgrave.

Harrison, H. (2000). *The making of the republican citizen: Political ceremonies and symbols in China, 1911–1929*. Oxford: Oxford University Press.

Harrison, J. (1969). *Modern Chinese nationalism*. New York: Research Institute on Modern Asia.

Harvey, D. (1989). *The condition of postmodernity*. Oxford: Blackwell.

Harvey, D. (2005). *A brief history of neoliberalism*. Oxford: Oxford University Press.

Hayhoe, R. (1984). The evolution of modern Chinese educational institutions. In R. Hayhoe (Ed.), *Contemporary Chinese education* (pp. 26–476). London: Croom Helm.

Heath, S. B. (1983). *Ways with words*. New York: Cambridge University.

Heller, M. (1999). *Linguistic minorities and modernity. A sociolinguistic ethnography*. London: Longman.

Heller, M. (2001). Discourse and Interaction. In D. Schiffrin, D. Tannen & H.E Hamilton (Eds.), *Handbook of Discourse and Analysis* (pp. 251–264). Oxford: Blackwell.

Heller, M. (2002a). *Éléments d'une sociolinguistique critique*. Paris: Hatier.

Heller, M. (2002b). Language, education and citizenship in the post-national era: notes from the front. *The School Field: International Journal of Theory and Research in Education, 13*(7), 15–31.

Heller, M. (2007a). Bourdieu and "literacy education". In A. Luke & J. Albright (Eds.), *Bourdieu and literacy education* (pp. 50–67). Mahweh, NJ: Lawrence Erlbaum.

Heller, M. (2007b). Bilingualism as ideology and practice. In Monica Heller (Eds.), *Bilingualism: A social approach* (pp. 1–22). London: Palgrave.

Heller, M. (2011). *Paths to post-nationalism: A critical ethnography of language and identity*. Oxford: Oxford University Press.

Heller, M., & Martin-Jones, M. (Eds.). (2001). *Voices of authority. Education and linguistic difference*. Westport, CT: Ablex.

Henze, J. (1984). Higher education: The tension between quality and equity. In R. Hayhoe (Ed.), *Contemporary Chinese education* (pp. 93–153). London: Croom Helm.

Heritage, J. (1984). *Garfinkel and ethnomethodology*. Cambridge: Polity.

Higonnet E. (1980). The politics of linguistic terrorism and grammatical hegemony during the French revolution. *Social History, 5*(1), 41–59.

Hobsbawm, E. (1990). *Nations and nationalism since 1760*. Cambridge: Cambridge University Press.

Hornberger, N. (1995). Ethnography in linguistic perspective: Understanding school processes. *Language and Education, 9*(4), 233–247.

Hornberger, N., & Chick, K. (2001). Co-constructing School Safetime: Safetalk Practices in Peruvian and South African Classrooms. In M. Heller & M. Martin-Jones (Eds.), *Voices of authority: Education and linguistic difference* (pp. 31–56). Westport, CT: Ablex.

Hu, C. (1969). Orthodoxy over historicity: The teaching of history in Communist China. *Comparative Education Review, 13*(1), 2–19.

Hu, G. (2002). Recent important developments in secondary English-language teaching in the People's Republic of China. *Language, Culture and Curriculum, 15*(1), 30–49.

Hu, G. (2005). English language education in China: Policies, progress and problems. *Language Policy, 4*, 5–24.

Hu, J. (2007). Report to the Seventeenth National Congress of the Communist Party of China on Oct. 15, 2007. *Xinhua*, October 24. Retrieved from: http://news.xinhuanet.com/english/2007–10/24/content_6938749.htm

Hughes, C.R. (2006). *Chinese nationalism in the global era*. London: Routledge.

Hunt, M.H. (1993). Chinese national identity and the strong state: The Late Qing-republican crisis. In L. Dittmer & S.S. Kim (Eds.), *China's quest for national identity* (pp. 62–79). Ithaca, NY: Cornell University Press.

Hunt, M.H. (1996). *The genesis of Chinese communist foreign policy*. New York: Columbia University Press.

Hymes, D.H. (1964). Introduction: Toward ethnographies of communication. In J. Gumperz & D.H. Hymes (Eds.), *The ethnography of communication* (pp. 1–34). Washington, DC: American Anthropological Association.

Irvine, J.T., & Gal, S. (2000). Language ideology and linguistic differentiation. In P.V. Kroskrity (Ed.), *Regimes of language* (pp. 35–83). Santa Fe, NM: School of American Research Press.

Jacob, E., & Jordan, C. (1993). Understanding minority education: Framing the issues. In E. Jacob & C. Jordan (Eds), *Minority education: Anthropological perspectives* (pp. 3–14). New York: Ablex.

Jaffe, A. (1999). *Ideologies in action: Language politics on Corsica*. Berlin: Mouton, Walter de Gruyter.

Jaspers, J. (2005). Linguistic sabotage in a context of monolingualism and standardization. *Language and Communication, 25*(3), 279–297.

Jenkins, R. (1982). Pierre Bourdieu and the reproduction of determinism. *Sociology, 20*(1): 270–81.

Jick, T. (1979). Mixing Qualitative and Quantitative Methods: Triangulation in Action. *Administrative Science Quarterly, 24*, 602–611.

Jin, L., & Cortazzi, M. (2006). Changing practices in Chinese cultures of learning. *Language, Culture and Curriculum, 19*(1), 5–20.

Johnson, C.A. (1962). *Peasant nationalism and communist power: The emergence of revolutionary China 1937–1945*. Stanford, CA: Stanford University Press.

Jones, A. (2005). *Changing the past to serve the present: History education in mainland China*. In E. Vickers & A. Jones (Eds.), *History education and national identity in East Asia* (pp. 65–100). London: Routledge.

Kandiah, T. (1991). Extenuatory sociolinguistics: Diverting attention from issues to symptoms in cross-cultural communication studies. *Multilingua, 10*(4), 345–80.

Karmel, S. (2000). *China and the People's Liberation Army*. New York: St. Martin's Press.

Kress, G., & van Leeuwen, T. (1990). *Reading images*. Geelong, Australia: Deakin University Press.

Kress, G. (1996). *Reading images: The grammar of visual design*. London: Routledge.

Kress, G. (2001). *Multimodal discourse—The modes and media of contemporary communication*. London: Arnold.

Kroskrity, P. (2000). Regimenting languages: Language ideological perspectves. In P. Kroskrity (Ed.), *Regimes of language: Ideologies, polities, and identities* (pp 1–34). Sante Fe, NM: School of American Research Press.

Kubota, R., & Lin, A. (Eds.). (2009). *Race, culture, and identity in second language education: Exploring critically engaged practice*. New York: Routledge.

Labov, W. (1969). Contraction, deletion, and inherent variability of the English copula. *Language, 45*, 715–762.

Labov, W. (1972). *Sociolinguistic patterns*. Philadelphia: University of Pennsylvania Press.

Laitinen, K. (1990). *Chinese nationalism in the late Qing dynasty: Zhang Binglin as an anti-Manchu propagandist*. London: Curzon Press.

Lam, A. S. L. (2005). *Language education in China*. Hong Kong, China: Hong Kong University Press.

Lam, A. S. L. (2007). Bilingual or multilingual education in China: Policy and learner experience. In A. S. L. Lam (Ed.), *Bilingual education in China* (pp. 13–33). Clevedon, England: Multilingual Matters.

Lan, W., Zhu, Y., & Lan, J. (1996). Education reform in China since 1978. In J. Hu, Z. Hong, & E. Stavrou (Eds.), *Search of a Chinese road towards modernization: Economic and educational issues in China's reform process* (pp. 225–244). New York: The Edwin Mellen Press.

Langguth, G. (2003). Asian values revisited. *Asia Europe Journal, 1*, 25–42.

Lee, T. H. C. (2000). *Education in traditional China, a history*. Leiden, the Netherlands: Brill.

Lemke, J.L. (2002). Language development and identity: Multiple timescales in the social ecology of learning. In C. Kramsch (Ed.), *Language acquisition and language socialization* (pp. 68–87). London: Continuum.

Li, L. (2004). *Education for 1.3 billion. Former Chinese Vicepremier Li Lanqing on 10 years of education reform and development*. Beijing, China: Foreign Education and Research Press, Pearson Education.

Li, P., Zhong, M., Lin, B., & Zhang, H. (2004). *Deyu* as moral education in modern China: Ideological functions and transformations. *Journal of Moral Education, 33*(4), 449–464.

Li, X. (2004). Economic reform and the awakening of Chinese women's collective consciousness. In C. Gilmartin, L. Rofel, & T. White (Eds.), *Engendering China: Women, culture and the state* (pp. 360–382). Cambridge, MA: Harvard University Press.

Lin, A.M.Y (2012). Towards transformation of knowledge and subjectivity in curriculum inquiry: Insights from Chen Kuan-Hsing's "Asia as method". *Curriculum Enquiry, 42*(1), 153–178.

Lin, A. M. Y, & Luk, J.C.M. (2005). Local creativity in the face of global domination: Insights of Bakhtin for teaching english for dialogic communication. In J.K. Hall, G. Vitanova, & L. Marchenkova (Eds.), *Dialogue with Bakhtin on second and foreign language learning: New perspectives* (pp. 77–98). Mahwah, NJ: Lawrence Erlbaum.

Lin, A., & Martin, P. (Eds.). (2005). *Decolonisation, globalisation. Language-in-education policy and practice*. Clevedon, England: Multilingual Matters.

Lo, B. (1984). Primary education: A two-track system for dual tasks. In R. Hayhoe (Ed.), *Contemporary Chinese education* (pp. 47–65). London: Croom Helm.

Lo, L. (1999). Raising funds and raising quality for schools in China. *School Effectiveness and School Improvement, 10*(1), 31–54.

Lo Bianco, Orton, J., & Gao, Y. (Eds.). (2009). *China and English. Globalisation and the dilemmas of identity.* Bristol, England: Multilingual Matters.

Luk, J. (2008). Classroom discourse and the construction of learner and teacher identities. In M. Martin-Jones, A.M. de Mejia, & N.H. Hornberger (Eds.), *Encyclopedia of language and education: Discourse and education* (Vol. 3, pp. 121–134). New York: Springer.

Mackerras, C. (2006). Ethnic minorities. In C. Tubilewicz (Ed.), *Critical issues in contemporary China* (pp. 167–192). New York: Routledge.

Mao, Z. (1965). *Mao Zedong zhu zuo xuan du: Yi zhong ben.* Beijing, China: Zhongguo qing nian chu ban she.

Márquez-Réiter, R., & Martín-Rojo L. (Eds.). (2010). Sociolinguistic and pragmatic aspects of institutional discourse: Service encounters in multilingual and multicultural contexts [Special issue]. *Sociolinguistic Studies, 4*(2), 297–332.

Martin, P. (2005). "Safe" language practices in two rural schools in Malaysia: Tensions between policy and practice. In A. Lin & P. Martin (Eds.), *Decolonisation, globalisation: Language-in-education policy and practice* (pp. 73–97). Clevedon, England: Multilingual Matters.

Martin-Jones, M. (2007). Bilingualism, education and the regulation of access to language resources. In M. Heller (Ed.), *Bilingualism: A social approach* (pp. 161–182). London: Palgrave.

Martin-Jones, M., & Jones, K. (Eds.). (2000). *Multilingual literacies: Reading and writing different worlds.* Amsterdam, the Netherlands: John Benjamins.

Martín-Rojo L. (1997). El orden social de los discursos. *Discurso* (spring), 1–37.

Martín-Rojo L. (2003). El análisis crítico del discurso: una mirada indisciplinada. In L. Iñiguez Rueda (Ed.), *Análisis del discurso. Manual para las ciencias sociales* (pp. 157–191). Barcelona, Spain: Ediciones de la Universidad Oberta de Catalunya.

Martín-Rojo L. (2010). *Constructing inequality in multilingual classrooms.* Berlin: Mouton de Gruyter.

Martín-Rojo L., & van Dijk, T. (1997). "There was a problem and it was solved": Legitimating the expulsion of "illegal" migrants in Spanish parliamentary discourse. *Discourse & Society, 8*(4), 523–566.

Mason, J. (2002). *Qualitative researching.* London: Sage.

Mathur, N. (2007). *Educational reform in post-Mao China.* Delhi, India: APH Publishing Corporation.

Maybin, J. (2006). *Children's voices. Talk, knowledge and identity.* Basingstoke, England: Palgrave.

McDermott, R., & Tylbor, H. (1986). On the necessity of collusion in conversation. In S. Fisher & A. Dundas-Todd (Eds.), *Discourse and institutional authority: Medicine, education and law* (pp. 123–139). New York: Ablex.

Meeuwis, M., & Sarangi, S. (1994). Perspectives on intercultural communication: A critical reading. *Pragmatics, 4*(3), 309–313.

Mehan, H. (1979). *Learning lessons: Social organization in the classroom.* Cambridge, MA: Harvard University Press.

Michaels, S. (1981). "Sharing time": Children's narrative styles and differential access to literacy. *Language in Society, 10*(3), 423–442.

Ministry of Education. (1978). *Ten-year system school English syllabus (Revised).* Beijing, China: People's Education Press (中华人民共和国教育部。1978。全日制中学英语教学大纲 (修订本) 。北京:人民教育出版社).

Ministry of Education. (1993). *Ten-year system school English syllabus (Revised).* Beijing, China: People's Education Press (中华人民共和国教育部。1993。全日制中学英语教学大纲 (修订本) 。北京:人民教育出版社).

Ministry of Education. (2000). *Ten-year system school English syllabus (Revised).* Beijing, China: People's Education Press (中华人民共和国教育部。2000。全日制中学英语教学大纲 (修订本) 。北京:人民教育出版社).

Ministry of Education. (2001). Action plan for vitalizing education in the twenty-first century. *Chinese Education and Society, 34*(49), 18–28.

Mok, K. H. (2006). *Education reform and education policy in East Asia.* London: Routledge.

Moyer, M., & Martín-Rojo L. (2007). Language, migration and citizenship: New challenges in the regulation of bilingualism. In M. Heller (Ed.), *Bilingualism: A social approach* (pp. 137–160). Houndsmills, England: Palgrave Macmillan.

Murphy, R. (2004). Turning Chinese peasants into modern citizens: Population quality, demographic transition, and primary schools. *China Quarterly, 177*, 1–20.

Ndayipfukamiye, L. (2001). The contradictions of teaching bilingually in postcolonial Burundi: From Nyakatsi to Maisons en Etages. In M. Heller & M. Martin-Jones (Eds.), *Voices of authority: Education and linguistic difference* (pp. 101–116). Westport, CT: Ablex.

Newby, L. (2000). Las minorías étnicas. In T. Fisac & S. Tsang (Eds.), *China en transición* (pp. 189–214). Barcelona, Spain: Ediciones Bellaterra.

Ngwaru, J. M., & Opoku-Amankwa, K. (2010). Home and school literacy practices in Africa: Listening to inner voices. *Language and Education, 24*(4), 295–307.

Nieto-Martínez, G. (2007). Los límites a los valores asiáticos: derechos humanos y equidad de género en China. In V. Maquieira (Ed.), *Mujeres, globalización y derechos humanos* (pp. 293–344). Valencia, Spain: Cátedra.

Ogbu, J. (1992). Les frontières culturelles et les enfants des minorités. *Revue française de pédagogie, 101*, 9–26.

Olson, D. R. (1977). From utterance to text: The bias of language in speech and writing. *Harvard Educational Review, 47*(3), 257–281.

Orton, J. (2009). "Just a tool": The role of English in the curriculum. In J. Lo Bianco, J. Orton, & Y. Gao (Eds.), *China and English. Globalisation and the dilemmas of identity* (pp. 137–154). Bristol, England: Multilingual Matters.

Ouyang, H. (2000). One-way ticket: A Story of an innovative teacher in mainland China. *Anthropology and Education Quarterly, 31*(4), 397–425.

Peake, C. H. (1970). *Nationalism and education in Modern China.* New York: Howard Fertig.

Pennycook, A. (1989). The concept of method, interested knowledge, and the politics of language teaching. *TESOL Quarterly, 23*(4), 589–618.

Pepper, S. (1999). *Civil war in China. The political struggle, 1945–1949.* Lanham, MD: Rowman Littlefield Publishers.

Pepper, S. (1996). *Radicalism and Education Reform in 20th-Century China: The Search for an Ideal Development Model.* Cambridge: Cambridge University Press.

Pérez-Milans, M. (2006). Spanish education and Chinese immigrants in a new multicultural context: Cross-cultural and interactive perspectives in the study of language teaching methods. *Journal of Multicultural Discourses* (Multilingual Matters), *1*(1), 60–85.

Pérez-Milans, M. (2007). Las aulas de enlace: un islote de bienvenida. In Martín-Rojo Luisa, Mijares, Laura (Eds.), *Voces del Aula. Etnografías de la Escuela Multicultural* (pp. 113–146). Madrid, Spain: CREADE.

Pérez-Milans, M. (2011). Being a Chinese Newcomer in Madrid Compulsory Education: Ideological Constructions in Language Education Practice. *Journal of Pragmatics, 43*(4), 1005–1022.

Philips, S. (1972). Participant structures and communicative competence: Warm spring children in community and classroom. In C. B. Cazden, V. P. John, & D. Hymes (Eds.), *Functions of language in the classroom* (pp. 370–394). New York: Teachers College Press.

Phillipson, R. (1988). Linguisticism: Structures and ideologies in linguistic imperialism. In J. Cummins & T. Skuttnab-Kangas (Eds.), *Minority education: From shame to struggle* (pp. 339–358). Clevedon, England: Multilingual Matters.

Popkewitz, T. (1984). *Paradigm and ideology in educational research: The social functions of the intellectual.* London: Falmar Press.

Postiglione, G. (1999). Introduction: State schooling and ethnicity in China. In G. Postiglione (Ed.), *China's national minority education. Culture, schooling and development* (pp. 3–20). New York: Falmer Press.

Postiglione, G. (2008). Making Tibetans in China: The educational challenges of harmonious multiculturalism. *Educational Review, 60*(1): 1–20.

Potts, P. (2003). *Modernising education in Britain and China. Comparative perspectives on excellence and social inclusion.* London: Routledge.

Poveda, D. (2001). *Un análisis etnográfico de la interacción en el aula en relación con la alfabetización.* Unpublished thesis. Madrid, Spain: Universidad Autónoma de Madrid.

Pratt, M.L. (1987). Linguistic utopias. In N. Fabb, D. Attridge, A. Durant, & C. MacCabe (Eds.), *The linguistics of writing: Arguments between language and literature* (pp. 48–66). Manchester, England: Manchester University Press.

Price, R.F. (1970). *Education in communist China.* London: Routledge.

Pujolar, J. (2006). *Language, culture and tourism: Perspectives in barcelona and catalonia.* Barcelona, Spain: Turisme de Barcelona.

Pujolar, J. (2007). Bilingualism and the nation-state in the post-national era. In M. Heller (Ed.), *Bilingualism: A social approach* (pp. 71–95). London: Palgrave.

Pye, L. (1999). Civility, social capital and civil society: Three powerful concepts for explaining Asia. *Journal of Interdisciplinary History, 29,* 763–82.

Ramsey, S.R. (1989). *The languages of China.* Princeton, NJ: Princeton University Press.

Rampton, B. (1995). *Crossing: Language and ethnicity among adolescents.* London: Longman.

Rampton, B. (2001). Critique in interaction. *Critique of Anthropology, 21*(1), 83–107.

Rampton, B. (2006). *Language in late modernity. Interaction in an urban school.* Cambridge: Cambridge University Press.

Rhoads, E. (2000). *Manchu & Han: Ethnic relations and political power in late Qing and early republican China, 1861–1928.* Seattle: University of Washington Press.

Rong, X., & Shi, T. (2001). Inequality in Chinese education. *Journal of Contemporary China, 10*(26), 107–124.

Rosen, S. (1984). New directions in secondary education. In R. Hayhoe (Ed.), *Contemporary Chinese education* (pp. 65–92). London: Croom Helm.

Rosen, S. (1992). Women, Education and Modernization. In R. Hayhoe (Ed.), *Education and Modernization in Chinese Experience* (pp. 255–284). New York: Pergamon.

Rubdy, R. (2005). Remaking Singapore for the new age: Official ideology and the realities of practice in language-in-education. In A. Lin & P. Martin (Eds.), *Decolonisation, globalisation: Language-in-education policy and practice* (pp. 55–75). Clevedon, England: Multilingual Matters.

Sacks, H., Schegloff, E., & Jerfferson, G. (1974). A simplest systematics for the organization of turn-taking for conversation. *Language, 50,* 696–735.

Scalapino, R.A. (1999). China: Between tradition and modernity. In E. Sandschneider (Ed.), *The study of modern China.* New York: St. Martin's Press.

Schieffelin, B., Woolard, K., & Kroskrity, P. (1998). *Language ideologies: Practice and theory.* New York: Oxford University Press.

Schensul, S., Schensul, J., & LeCompte, M. (Eds.). (1999). *Ethnographer's toolkit.* Walnut Creek, CA: Sage.

Schram, S. R. (1969). *The political thought of Mao Tse-tung.* New York: Praeger.

Schwartz, B. (1951). *Chinese communism and the rise of Mao.* Cambridge, MA: Harvard University Press.

Searle, J. (1969). *Speech acts.* Cambridge: Cambridge University Press.

Seedhouse, P. (2004). *The interactional architecture of the language classroom: A conversation analysis perspective.* Oxford, England: Blackwell.

Silverstein, M. (1976). Shifters, linguistic categories, and cultural description. In K. H. Basso & H. A. Selby (Eds.), *Meaning in anthropology* (pp. 11–56). Albuquerque: University of New Mexico Press.

Simon, R. (1987). Empowerment as a pedagogy of possibility. *Language Arts, 64,* 370–383.

Sinclair, J., & Coulthard, M. (1975). *Towards an analysis of discourse.* Oxford: Oxford University Press.

Spence, J. D. (1981). *The gate of heavenly peace: The Chinese and their revolution, 1895–1980.* New York: Viking Press

Street, B. (Ed.). (1993). *Cross-cultural approaches to literacy.* Cambridge: Cambridge University Press.

Street, B. (1995). *Social literacies: Critical Approaches to literacy in development, ethnography and education.* London: Longman.

Su, X. (2002). *Education in China. Reforms and innovations.* Beijing, China: China Intercontinental Press.

Tatsuo, I. (1999). Liberal democracy and asian orientalism. In J. R. Bauer & D. A. Bell (Eds.), *The East Asian challenge for human rights* (pp. 27–59). New York: Cambridge University Press.

Teng, S., & Fairbank, J. K. (Eds.). (1954). *China's response to the West: A documentary survey, 1839–1923.* Cambridge, MA: Harvard University Press.

Townsend, J. (1999). Nacionalismo chino. In J. Unger (Ed.), *Nacionalismo chino* (pp. 23–62). Barcelona: Bellaterra.

Tsui, A. B. M. (1995). *Introducing classroom interaction.* London: Penguin.

van Dijk, T. (1987). *Communicating racism: Ethnic prejudice in thought and talk.* Newbury Park, CA: Sage Publications.

van Leeuwen, T. (1995). *The grammar of legitimation.* London: Routledge, Wetherell.

Van Lier, L. (2002). An ecological-semiotic perspective on language and linguistics. In C. Kramsch (Ed.), *Language acquisition and language socialization: Ecological perspectives.* London: Continuum.

Verschueren, J. (1999). *Understanding pragmatics.* London: Edward Arnold.

Vertovec, S. (2009). *Transnationalism.* New York: Routledge.

Vickers, E. (2009). The opportunity of China. Education, patriotic values and the Chinese state. In M. Lall & E. Vickers (Eds.), *Education as a political tool in Asia* (pp. 53–101). London: Routledge.

Wang, Q. (2007). The national curriculum changes and their effects on English language teaching in the People's Republic of China. In J. Cummins & C. Davison (Eds.), *International handbook on English language teaching* (pp. 87–105). New York: Springer.

Wang, H., & Karl, R. (1998). Contemporary Chinese thought and the question of modernity. In X. Zhang (Ed.), *Intellectual politics in post-Tiananmen China* [Special Issue] *Social Text, 55*(16.2), 9–44.

Wang, H., & Hale, M. (2007). The politics of imagining Asia: A genealogical analysis. *Inter-Asia Cultural Studies, 8*(1), 1–33.

Weber, J. J. (2008). Safe-talk revisited, or: Language and ideology in Luxembourgish Educational policy. *Language and Education, 22*(2), 155–169.

Wodak, R. (2000). ¿La sociolingüística necesita una teoría social? Nuevas perspectivas en el Análisis Crítico del Discurso. *Discurso y Sociedad, 3*(2), 123–147.

Wolfram, W. (1969). *A sociolinguistic description of Detroit negro speech*. Washington, DC: Center for Applied Linguistics.

Wu, X. (2005). *Teacher change. Issues in in-service EFL teacher education*. Beijing, China: Foreign Language Teaching and Research Press.

Wu, Z. (2005). *Teachers' knowledge in curriculum change. A critical discourse study of language teaching*. Beijing, China: Foreign Language Teaching and Research Press.

Zheng, S. (1997). *Party vs. state in post-1949 China. The institutional dilemma*. Cambridge: Cambridge University Press.

Zhao, S. (1998). A State-led nationalism: The patriotic educational campaign in post-Tiananmen China. *Communist and Post-Communist Studies, 31*(3), 287–302.

Zhao, S. (2004). *A nation-state by construction. Dynamics of modern Chinese nationalism*. Stanford, CA: Stanford University Press.

Index